Reading
the Malay World

'They knew the white people ... and called them Balanda, which is nothing more than 'Hollanders'; a name used by the Malays, from whom they received it'.

Ludwig Leichhardt,
Journal of an Overland Expedition in Australia (1845)

Flinders University in South Australia is named after the explorer and cartographer Matthew Flinders, commander of the *Investigator*, the first vessel to circumnavigate Australia; he was the first person to use the name the island continent now carries. In 1802, while on his voyage of circumnavigation, Flinders found to his considerable surprise that was he not the first visitor to the north coast of Australia; he found Malays from Makassar, Sulawesi and Timor—or their camp sites—on many of the islands of the north—the Wellesley Islands, Pellew Islands, and the English Company Islands—and in Arnhem Land. These Malay fishermen and small businessmen came to the north coast, set up seasonal camps and searched for local products such as trepang (sea cucumber), sandalwood, and pearl shell for the Chinese market.

Malay visitors to Australia have left some fascinating traces of their many hundreds of years of summer camping along the coast: their camp sites are still marked by tamarind trees, and in some of the Indigenous languages of northern Australia, the word *balanda* is used for 'whitefella'; it is a Makassar word, from the Malay *belanda*, meaning Hollander.

Such historical connections between Australia and the Malay world to our north mark the beginning of long-term relationships of the kind suggested by the production of this volume. The book is published by the Centre for Research in the New Literatures in English (CRNLE), founded in 1977 by Syd Harrex and now part of the Humanities Research Institute of the School of Humanities at Flinders University. The editors wish to thank Nena Bierbaum for her work in helping prepare this volume.

Reading the Malay World

edited by

Rick Hosking, Susan Hosking,
Noritah Omar and Washima Che Dan

CRNLE JOURNAL SPECIAL ISSUE

Wakefield Press

Wakefield Press
1 The Parade West
Kent Town
South Australia 5067
www.wakefieldpress.com.au

First published 2010

Designed and typeset by Michael Deves, Wakefield Press
Printed in Australia by Griffin Digital, Adelaide

National Library of Australia
Cataloguing-in-Publication entry

Title:	Reading the Malay world / edited by Rick Hosking … [et al.].
ISBN:	978 1 86254 894 7 (pbk.).
Notes:	Includes bibliographical references.
Subjects:	Malay literature – History and criticism.
	Malaysian literature (English) – History and criticism.
	Singaporean literature (English) – History and criticism.
Other Authors/ Contributors:	Hosking, Rick.
Dewey Number:	820.99595

Front cover image

Minimini MAMARIKA
Australia, 1904–1972
Anindilyakwa people, Northern Territory
The Malay prau
1948, Umbakumba, Groote Eylandt, Northern Territory
natual pigments on eucalyptus bark, 43.7 x 86.0 cm (irreg)
Gift of Mr Charles P. Mountford 1960
Art Gallery of South Australia, Adelaide

Contents

Preface

The collection of essays in this special issue journal is the culmination of a symposium on the representation of Malays and Malay culture in Singaporean and Malaysian literature in English held in 2004 in Universiti Putra Malaysia (UPM). The symposium, with the theme 'Reading the Malay World through Singaporean and Malaysian Texts in English' was organised as one of the research activities of a nationally funded project under the funding of the Malaysian Ministry of Science, Technology and Innovation. The symposium brought together experts from the fields of literature, language and linguistics to problematise, theorise and spotlight the ways in which Malays and Malay culture are captured in the literary imagination of Singaporean and Malaysian writers writing in English. The symposium highlighted how Malays and Malay culture are imagined and promoted through literature and also explored Malayness from linguistic and cultural perspectives.

Issues of concern addressed in the symposium and the research in general included the construction of the Malays in Singaporean and Malaysian literature in English within orientalist or colonialist discourses of the East, the influence of English on the ways that Malays and Malay culture are represented, how Malayness or Malay identity are defined, and the positioning of the Malays in literary imaginations and social realities.

It has been a pleasant surprise for us to discover that works from this region (including Malaysia and Singapore) have a supportive and interested audience in Australia. This collection has been made possible due to support from our Australian colleagues, particularly out of the initiative of Emeritus Professor John McLaren of Victoria University, who connected us to Associate Professor Dr Rick Hosking of Flinders University and Dr Susan Hosking of the University of Adelaide. Rick and Sue Hosking have enduringly worked with us (assisted most ably by Ms Nena Bierbaum) to ensure the work's completion. The publication is also made possible through the financial support of the Faculty of Modern Languages and Communication of UPM. We hope that this collection will add to critical works in the study of Malay language, literature and culture, and also to the body of works on Malaysian and Singaporean literature in English.

Noritah Omar
Washima Che Dan
Universiti Putra Malaysia

Images of Malays in Malaysian and Singapore Writing in English

JOHN McLAREN
VICTORIA UNIVERSITY, AUSTRALIA

For the reader who has no Malay, the depiction of Malays in literature presents particular problems. First, most Malay writers have chosen to write in Malay, while Chinese and Tamil writers to a great extent ignore the Malay communities. Secondly, there is a difficulty of definition. Historically, the Malay peoples and Malay rule extended over a great part of Southeast Asia, although there was no single Malay authority. The advent of imperialism divided these peoples into new political units, each of which now has its own literature, both in the indigenous languages and in English. In all of these states the earlier religions have been supplanted, if not entirely extinguished. The successive influences of Hinduism and Buddhism have left cultural traces, but, except in the central and northern Philippines, the majority of Malays subscribe to Islam. Their portrayal by Chinese or Tamil writers presents them from an external perspective, recognising them as the first people of the land but seeing their problems as integral to the wider community rather than peculiar to their own situation. In contrast, Malay writers portray a people caught in a dilemma between modernity and tradition.

For writers from the immigrant communities, or in the Philippines, the mixed race *ilustrados*, the Malay was the uncivilised other. The Chinese and Tamil immigrants to Singapore and the British Malay states themselves came mainly from the uneducated coolie classes and, as Edwin Thumboo explains, lacked the Pandits and Mandarins who had preserved cultural traditions in the lands they came from. Their first generation was preoccupied with the mundane, and the writers who came later have had to establish for themselves the rhythms of life in a new environment.[1] For these writers, the Malays belonged in a past that was fading, although they maintained civilities that were absent from a modern, globalised world. Leena, the Tamil woman at the centre of Claire

Tham's story, 'Sundrift', horrifies her Tamil parents by marrying an American, an 'Oriental cowboy', who seems to inhabit 'a permanent American homeland frozen circa 1975'. He has no clear source of income and no wish to settle down. Leena drifts with him and their child around the Malay peninsula, where she finds herself left alone in a series of cheap hotels while he goes about his mysterious business. She finds her solace by walking around the townships with her baby propped in a sling about her shoulders. The Malay people she meets represent fixedness and humanity. They are friendly, responding to the baby, and becoming 'even friendlier when she practised her kindergarten Malay on them, making them laugh'.[2] In the increasingly nightmarish world she wanders through, they become her one link to sanity.

In his own poetry, Thumboo sees the Malay as sharing his alienation from the world of power that encompasses them both, but sees how he himself is one of the agents of this alienation. 'And there is an anger / in that bronze patience', he tells us in the opening lines of the poem which? he addresses to 'Ahmad'. Ahmad is both 'a son of the soil who roves / The outskirts of our jungle' and 'our brother who moves / With the sun so easily'. Yet even as a brother, his eyes still 'have strange fires'.[3] The following poem, 'Ibrahim bin Ahmed', opens with the line, 'We sit in quiet communion',[4] and places its emphasis on the commonality of people. The poem continues with Ibrahim's address to his Singapore brother, the Chinese Indian poet. Ibrahim praises the heroic past of the Malays, symbolised by the warrior who fought against his own Sultan in the name of justice. He worries however that the modern world, with its faith in economic progress, is losing sight of the courtesies and friendliness that bound different people in brotherhood. As Thumboo says in a later poem to a friend in Malacca, neither politics nor administration will restore this spirit, but poets whose duty to the world is not to allow their poems to remain unwritten.[5]

One of the major themes of Thumboo's poetry is the conflict between the individuals realising themselves in their environment and the imposition of economic, administrative and political constraints to this freedom. This conflict acts itself out in words, the words that constrain fighting against the words of the poet, that ultimately arise from the highly personal experiences of love and friendship and the cultural immersion in nature:

Only bring these words of office,
Cool executive, speech and text,
Into the sun, the wind's wide leap
Across the sudden moonbeam. [6]

The natural environments which bring these words into the sun, the wind and the moon range from Malaysia to Africa to Australia, but the figure at their centre is Ahmad, the Malay farmer or fisherman who is a product of the environment that he works to make, and that he listens to in silence.

A quite different portrayal of the Malay appears in the poetry of Muhammad Haji Salleh, who writes in Malay and translates his own poetry into English. Muhammed Haji Salleh is a cosmopolitan, but his work is firmly grounded in Malay history and the Malay poetic tradition. More sharply anti-colonial, or rather anti-imperialist, than Thumboo, his poem 'Standing in Oxford Street' wonders how to pass sentence on 'the nation of shop-keepers'

> that has sold the land and lodge
> of a part of humanity
> for these grand buildings here
> ...
> its riches
> built from the blood
> of the black, brown and yellow peoples
> and on the deception of innocent races and their countries ...[7]

He does not present himself as victim, but as citizen of the world. This poem is one of a section 'This Too Is my World', which sets out in its poems to reclaim the world, and particularly the Malay countryside, from the forces of colonial and capitalist exploitation.

In the next section of the collection, 'The Other Side of Self', individual poems claim for the poet the legacy of Europe in the form of his laboriously re-created Portuguese countryside and the urban splendour of Rome and Florence. In the poet's own words, these legacies are added to the 'leaves, flowers and branches' of the 'enormous, old tree' that is Malay literature.[8] This tree is grounded in Malay history, and its trunk is the epic, particularly *Sejarah Melayu*. Muhammad Haji Salleh's critical study analyses this work and its grounding first in submission to the will of God and then in the order of Malay society. Yet he concludes that, after the defeat of the Malay kingdoms and the later inauguration of a modern state, the appropriate Malay hero is not the loyal Hang Tuah but the rebel Hang Jebat.[9] His own poetic retelling of episodes from the epic is designed to recall for the children of today the glory and wealth of the Malay kingdom, but also the treachery that brought it down. The final poem asks the question, 'the king has flown / where shall the people go?'[10] The answer is implicit in the later poems in the collection: back to the villages, but also out to the world. In the villages he finds people like the faith healer, who brings people together, or the boat-builder, whose labour turns nature into value. Here is the earth 'whose soul and ways / must be rendered tender'. But to restore it, he must also learn from the wider world, bringing its tested knowledge back to his source. As the traveller of legend, Si Tegang, remarks in 'Si Tenggang's Homecoming':

> travel makes me
> a seeker …
> the years at sea and in coastal states
> have taught me to choose,
> to accept only those tested by comparison,
> or that which matches the words of my ancestors,
> which returns me to my village
> and its completeness. [11]

Only the village has completeness, but it has it only when the traveller, the poet, returns to it with his hard-won knowledge. This is utterly different from Salleh ben Joned's telling of the story, where the poet identifies himself with the traveller of legend. In Salleh ben Joned's telling, 'The Salacious Rhymes of a Self-taut [sic] Prodigal' or Si Tegang's 'Homecoming' the journey is an escape into a freedom and self-knowledge that the traditional society denies.[12] As Ruzy Suliza Hashim shows in her chapter in this collection, the traveller returns to the kampong and disillusion. The poem ends with a call for *jihad* or struggle against shallow modernism.

The experience of a divided society fragments individuals, preventing them achieving their fullness. KS Maniam has written that his whole writing career has been devoted to 'pushing the frontiers of consciousness away from a purely social, political and cultural centre … to heal the fragmented self of man … to see man whole …'[13] His earliest short story, 'The Eagles', is about the way poverty divides a Tamil Indian community, preventing any of its members finding wholeness. Their moral condition is summed up in the words of the grocer when he tells the *dhobi* boy, 'Throw the poetry away. Tell me where they buy their provisions.'[14] Yet, in 'Haunting the Tiger', the title story of the collection where 'Eagles' appears, the central character, Muthu, abandons the material to go in search of the poetry of the land, embodied in the mythical figure of the tiger, a figure with particular significance in Malay culture.

Like much of Maniam's work, the apparently simple narrative of this tale moves through time and is entwined in allusion that forces the readers on their own quest for its significance. Ostensibly, it tells of Muthu as an old man remembering going into the jungle to hunt the wild boar. In the jungle, however, he senses the presence of another beast, the tiger, and goes in quest of it. He is encouraged, possibly helped, in this quest by the old villager, Zulkifli, whom he passes on his way to the jungle. Zulkifli advises Muthu that the villagers do not hunt the boar unless it destroys their crops, but he also enigmatically tells him that he won't see anything in the jungle while he looks 'with eyes like that'. Although Zulkifli takes him deep into the jungle, he warns him that the tiger they are going to see is one that no man can possess.

This reading of the story is complicated from the first by the title, which refers not to the hunting but to the 'haunting' of the two men by the tiger. The memory of the tiger, Zulkifli tells us, haunted his forebears as well, going back for centuries. He invites Muthu to his house one evening and their conversation wanders over all things until Zulkifli asks about the hunt.

> 'You've found the thing you want to hunt?' …
> 'You know?'
> 'My forefathers had the same look in their eyes,' Zulkifli says. 'My father told me.'
> 'But you?' Muthu says.
> 'Deep inside. No need to show it so loudly to the world,' Zukifli says. 'And you've lost the way.'
> 'You know so much,' Muthu says.
> 'Centuries of living here,' Zukifli says. 'We'll go together one day?' [15]

Muthu has hitherto dared to enter only the edges of the jungle, fearing he will become lost if he goes further. The tiger, creature at the heart of the jungle, is also the spirit of the land that Muthu fears to penetrate, and which he enters only at night. The tiger belongs to the time when repressed fears emerge, and by seeking it Muthu attempts to allay the fears he has of a land where he cannot feel at home. Zulkifli represents the Malays, the people who have gained the wisdom of the land through centuries of living on it. His promise to go with Muthu is both a promise that the two people can become one, and an offer to Muthu of a harmony denied to him in the city, where he lives, with a job and a discontented family.

The story begins with a cryptic pair of sentences that introduces Muthu as an old man who is having trouble dying. 'The peace he had hoped for was disturbed by dreams.'[16] These dreams tell of the old man's expeditions in his youth in search of the tiger. But these memories are preceded by his thought that 'You have to be landless to be landfull'. The old man is a landowner, but ownership of the land precludes entering into the land, being possessed by it. The condition of possession can be achieved only by first losing the self, as he had done when his mother died, and then by learning, as he does through his marriage, that the only way to fit into the life of another is to 'actually jump out of his skin and be refashioned'. The old villager, Zulkifli, does not have possessions, but he is possessed in this way. Muthu is not prepared to give himself to the land to see the tiger, and so the land remains alien to him. As Maniam explains in his Preface to this collection, the migrant consciousness registers only loss in the face of the native culture's assurance. Yet, as he further comments, the migrant reaches this realisation only 'through the journey of recollection and evaluation;' the indigenous consciousness rests in the false assurance given by ritual. Neither achieves the full awareness brought about through 'a passive but perceptive approach to living and the space that makes possible the living'. Both migrant and native remain actors, refusing to allow themselves to be acted upon.[17]

The tiger that Zulkifli and Muthu go in search of may be a real creature, but it is also the spirit of the jungle. Zulkifli explains that it is not to be shot, but the jungle resists both of them until he gives away his *parang* and Muthu his gun. Then at last the tiger comes to them as a 'booming growl' that 'almost immediately dissipates into innumerable animal and insect cries', and then Muthu 'sees the jungle close in on him in orange bands and black stripes'. But he does not see the tiger, for at this moment, 'with a cry of anguish, he wills his own conscious ness into action'.[18] By running away from the moment of acceptance he destroys his hope of understanding, of becoming fulfilled in the land. Like the present speaker, he remains an outsider, aware of the importance of the tiger in the landscape, but unable to enter into it. He has taken from Zulkifli only his smile, the offer of friendship, not his understanding. So he has remained trapped in his own skin, unable to enter even into his wife's dark knowledge, and approaches death with an empty mind.

It is instructive to compare the tiger in Maniam's story with the one in Shahnon bin Ahmad's Malay-language novel, *Rope of Ash (Rentong).* Maniam's tiger is symbolic, representing the villagers' knowledge of and affinity with the jungle. Ahmad's is strictly realistic, a revered 'Father Stripes' certainly, but a real threat to the security of the village, and accordingly it must be destroyed, even if it is honoured in its death. Yet it also serves a poetic or symbolic function in the novel, as the instrument that resolves the warring factions in the village and restores justice.

The distinction between knowledge and understanding is at the heart of Maniam's latest novel, *Between Lives* (2003).[19] The action of this novel pits an old woman, Sellama, against the state bureaucracy that wants to develop her land for economic gain. The woman is Tamil, and the farm she defends was originally developed before the Second World War by Tamil plantation workers seeking to escape the order imposed on them by white owners and develop a place of their own. But although they were Indian labourers, led by a Tamil manager, their inspiration came from Malay villagers, and particularly from Pak Mat, a Malaikaran, or Malay, elder who was brought to the plantation to deal with wild animals, and then with weeds and jungle clearing. His knowledge and inspiration enable the new settlement to prosper. By the time of the novel, all this effort has been laid waste, and the old woman is the sole survivor of the enterprise.

The place where Sellama lives is planted with mango, jackfruit, chempedak, rambutan, mangosteen, langsat and durian trees, still giving of their plenty although they are now neglected, looking hard and dry. This dusun leads to a natural landscape, where 'age-old trees send down low branches, their trunks networked with all kinds of thick-foliaged creepers, and beneath them, leafy bushes'. This in turn leads to the river, where the old woman still does the washing she had learned to do as a girl. For the developers the beauty of the place makes it ideal for a residential area, a shopping centre, and a theme park. Opposed to them is the spirit of the jungle, symbolised by the cobra that the old woman had seen. With its open hood and gold-dusted body, the cobra lives at the centre of this novel, just as the tiger haunts the earlier short story.[20] The cobra is a symbol of Sellama's unity with the land, which she achieves both through the journeys she takes into the jungle and through the Rama-Sita garden, first created by her father, that she remakes in her old age.

The story is told by Sumitra, the official of the Social Reconstruction Department, who is put in charge of removing the old woman from her land. She is known in the Department as Blue Ice, the uninvolved observer who is able to use all the resources of technology and her professional training in case management to get inside the minds of her clients until she detaches them from their memories and installs them in the mental framework of the Department's plans. In the course of the novel, however, her methods twice fail disastrously. First, Hisham, her Malay subject, turns on his father, stabbing him viciously to death. Hisham has been educated and travelled widely in the west, and Sumitra uses western technologies to persuade him to accept his family and professional obligations, without realising how deeply alienated his Western experience has alienated him from his distant but indulgent father. Before his death, the Department substituted an Indian case-worker, Aisha, as Hisham's case-worker, but she too has failed. Their joint failure begins the steady collapse of the Department's morale.

Aisha's greatest failure is with her central task, removing Sellama from the land. Her relationship with Sellama gradually reverses, as her attempts to get inside the old woman's mind bring Sellama instead into her mind. Instead of trying to dislodge Sellama from her memories, she enters into those memories, and eventually brings her own family into them also to take the place of Sellamas's family. This process not only restores the fullness of Sellama's life, but, just as Sellama has restored 'magical plentifulness' to the land,[21] she heals Sumitra's family of the wounds that have divided her parents, grandmother, and children. Her task is, in her own words, to 'bring back into life what was not living properly'.[22] In her own history, life came first from Appa and Amma, who represented Rama and Sita, who gave life to the Rama-Sita garden they made together.[23] Behind this Hindu mythology, however, lies the Malay kampong, which represents contentedness, the place where the tiger and the deer dwell together. Maniam insists that the kampong and its surrounding jungle are the source of the dreams that give prosperity.[24] This land is not for trading. When Sellama performs the Hindu rituals that restore Sumitra and her family to their health,[25] she is also making her source culture at home in the new land, in distinction from her parents who eventually returned to India, or to the British who never belonged. The legend of Rama and Sita is itself part of a culture that belongs to all of South Asia, and so the ritual is an act of reconciling the Hindu presence both with its Indian past and with its Malay present. At the close of the novel, after Sellama's death, Sumitra is joined by Aisha and their Chinese colleague, Christina, in bathing and sporting in the magical pool in the midst of the jungle. Christina rejects a modernised identity by reverting to her Chinese name, Mei. The pool brings together their three different traditions in a single element that unites them without denying difference.

If, however, we again compare Maniam's work with Ahmad's novel, we can see the distance between their perspectives. Sellama and her father have sought to restore an ideal village that will combine Indian and Malay traditions. Ahmad's village exists in a real life, which is not only torn by conflicts between the modernisers and those who believe that intensive agriculture is a torture for the land that they owe a duty of care for 'as carefully as they cared for their children'.[26] Like villages in all cultures through history, it is torn also by the greed, prejudice and hatreds of its members, but it is subject to the will of God, who desires that his people should not hurt one another. The eventual killing of Dogol by the tiger is a direct result of his own pride and greed, but it is explicitly motivated by God. With the subsequent shooting of the tiger, the balance of tradition is restored to the village as it faces the challenge of modernisation. In Sellama's settlement, by contrast, Maniam shows an attempt to transplant and adapt a foreign tradition within a Malay context.

At its conclusion, the characters in Maniam's novel are faced by a newspaper advertisement placed by the developers, who represent greed coming from outside the village. The advertisement offers starkly contrasting visions of the future. The images in the advertisement contrast a city marked by poverty and violence with a city of peace, order and prosperity. The first picture recalls the racial riots of 1969, the one deviation recognised from Malaysia's continuing progress. The Social Reconstruction Department has been set up to bring about the modernisation that will ensure that this deviation never happens again. Against this, Sumitra and her friends propose the vision in the painting they discover by Sellama's lost brother, Chinnathambi. This suggests a different history of Malaysia:

> The jungle in its mystifying glory: trees, creepers, bushes, insect- and wild-life, all intertwined and inter-dependent. The young boy's face ... trying to merge, like them, into the environment. Men behind him ... offering prayers to the guardians of the jungle ... Then those benevolent faces of the tigers turning savage, the deer nervous with intrusions ... bushes falling to intruding hands ... The fugitives. Other men in brutal chase ... Small gaps, here and there, of the destruction wrought by fights and battles ... most telling of all: a leap into a new-world paradise, the faces of all men, all kinds of men (...Pak Mat, the drifters, the Chinese traders ...) blended into the trunk and branches of a tall, age-old tree.[27]

This tree is a symbol of the universal implanted in Malaysia. But the truth symbolised by this tree is brought by Sellama and, earlier, her father through ritual and cleansing. In Ahmad's novel, God remains apart, but everything in both the village and the surrounding jungle is already subject to His will.

The action of the novel that leads to this choice is left unresolved. The developers continue with their task of clearance and destruction beyond the frail fences Sumitra's father has erected around the land Sellama has left her. Maniam leaves it to his Malaysian readers to decide the outcome, not in fiction but in history. But it is clear that the only satisfactory outcome will be one that reconciles the cultures of the newcomers with the land and the ancient wisdom of the Malays that understands it.

Maniam's work is open to the criticism that he offers an Orientalised view of the Malays, casting them as an ancient race that has only a romantic claim on the present. The values he prizes are cultural, pre-Koranic, and he thus appears to ignore a central part of Malay life. Yet, as he has written of his earlier novel, *The Return*, his fiction 'refers the reader to Malaysian problems and concerns through omission rather than exclusion'.[28] His Tamil characters deliberately adapt their rituals and customs to their new homeland. In doing this, they place Malay traditions at the centre of the present, insisting that the modern nation needs the later comers to establish the link between the land and their own distinctive histories that the Malays have maintained through the years of colonialism, the Japanese occupation, and the modernising forces of independence. Just as Sellama's father learned from the kampong, so her remaking of the settlement gives strength as much to Aisha, the Malay case-worker, as to her Chinese and Tamil colleagues. By contrast, the Hisham and his Malay family are destroyed by their embrace of a modernism that denies their roots.

While Maniam's novel pits the forces of modernism against tradition, Suchen Christine Lim's *Fistful of Colours* takes us into the heart of a Singapore where the forces of modernism are building a new world from the shards of a colonialism that tore people away from their traditional roots and pitted them against each other in a grim struggle to survive in a hierarchy of power grounded in money. The novel deals with the fortunes of 'a group of like-minded English educated malcontents who got together every weekend to grouse about the sanitised politics of Singapore, and dissect the plays they had attended and the paintings they had seen'. Thus far they could be contemporary intellectuals in almost any city in the world, but the present they confront and the pasts that have shaped them belong generally to south-east Asia and specifically to Singapore:

> Theirs was a disparate group of artists, writers, people in the media, a couple of lawyers, doctors and college teachers who drifted in and out. The regulars were Nica [Sivalingam], her live-in boy-friend, Robert Lim who worked in an American bank; Zul Hussein, writing for the *Straits Times* and who had just returned from the states; Janice Wong, his fiancée, who was Suwen's colleague; and Mark Campbell who was teaching English in the same College as Jan and Suwen.[29]

The Singapore they inhabit is an exciting, cosmopolitan city where

> a multitude and diversity of strands from different histories and cultures [are] woven into this modern fabric of many hues and textures by a loom which was moving too quickly for anyone to have more than a glimpse of its emerging shifting patterns, Chinese and not Chinese; Indian and not Indian. . . yet here they were, the new Asians ...[30]

Their immediate forebears were coolies, slaves, peasants, gangsters and businessmen. In this society, only the Malays can look back to a settled past. Yet this past is not romanticised. Zul's grandfather had been forced by poverty to leave his ancestral village for Singapore, where he lived in a kampong:

> Within a maze of thatched huts, attap houses on stilts, and muddy lanes criss-crossed with rotting plans and coconut tree trunks. Straggly bushes and creepers hugged the shallow ditches of frothy stagnant pools. Scrawny chickens scratched among the rubbish heaps of discarded boxes, cartons and rusty tin cans, and ducks with bristly tails poked their heads into the grey pools for slimy scraps of food. Dirty little urchins, brown with the sun, crouched near the ditches, oblivious of the flies and filth, giggling and pointing to the thin curls of turd oozing out of their little brown bottoms.[31]

Whatever Malay society may have been, colonialism and urbanism have transformed it irrevocably. The book's narrative, although set in the present, is a constant reminder of how its families of Malays, Chinese and Tamils have all raised themselves from this kind of poverty.

Class, race and religion are issues in the book. Nica's grandmother forbad her to play with lower-class Tamils, and allowed her to speak only English and 'pure' Tamil. Nica had to abort the child of her first love because its father was 'too cowardly' to acknowledge a mixed-race offspring. Suwen's attachment to Mark Campbell fails because she is unable to overlook his Britishness. When Zul and Jan marry, her parents reject them both because he is a Malay and because she has converted to his religion.

The language that holds this diverse group together is English, which they use proficiently in both formal and colloquial, 'Singlish', modes. Yet paradoxically this is also the language that has oppressed their forebears. Men like Ong Ah Buck, father of Suwen's stepfather, illiterate in their native language, have been oppressed by coteries of English speaking Asians who have gained positions of power in the administration, but exercise it only as delegates of the English themselves. Their English education has freed Suwen and her contemporaries from this oppression, but at the cost of their links to a wider community. They see themselves as the first generation to try to be Asians, rather than members of separate communities, but their English marks them out, and the suspicions of their colleagues stigmatise them. When she starts keeping company with Mark, Suwen detects sidelong glances and hears whispers, 'Not the same colour, man.'[32] Ironically, Mark has himself been cut off from his cultural forbears by the suppression of the Gaelic past he should have inherited from them.

Zul's case is distinct in both class and language terms. Although Jan's parents despise him as a Malay, and believe she is marrying beneath her as well as outside her community and religion, she recognises that he comes from the Malay nobility, the descendant of a village elite. His grandfather had been forced by poverty to leave home and work as a *syce* for the English, but his befriending by a colonial clerk had enabled him to have his son educated at Raffles Institution.

The son in turn had become a journalist on a Malay-language newspaper, because it would have been unthinkable for a Malay to write in English:

> To understand the language was all right, but to use it ... would be looked on as a betrayal of one's roots and nature. We Malays ... felt like the pelandok, an endangered species of mousedeer, surrounded by crocodiles. We had to rally round the community ...[33]

The father is upset when his son chooses to work for an English language paper, and explodes when Zul suggests that the Malay paper had been a 'chauvinist venture'. The venture had been necessary to restore the Malay community, which had been reduced to 'a poor and downtrodden people'. It is through his work that his sons now live better, and are able to write for a better educated community. But his father warns Zul, 'do not forget this. Our roots are as deep and as long as those trees in the jungles! We have our own traditions going back to the shadows of time!'[34] This is the only misgiving he has about his son's marriage to a Chinese, that his grandchildren will belong neither to this tradition nor to any other, and that, if communal conflict returns, his grandchildren will be torn apart by both sides.[35] Yet, although not even the love between Zul and Jan can prevent them quarrelling about race, it does enable them to keep on seeking to overcome the division. Suwen overcomes it only through her art, which brings the human and the natural together in a riot of colour that symbolises the possibilities of a Singapore reconciled to its various pasts. The jungle imagery of her painting however suggests that among these pasts the Malay legacy is the one that provides the vitality. With only English, the language that subordinates and controls, as a common language between the various groups, art alone can maintain this vitality. While literature is necessarily grounded in the specific, art can transcend this. Both are needed for the constitution of a healthy community.

Notes

1 Edwin Thumboo, ed., 'General Introduction', *The Fiction of Singapore* (Singapore: Unipress, 1990) vi.
2 Claire Tham, ed., 'General Introduction', *The Fiction of Singapore* (Singapore: Unipress, 1990) 46.
3 E. Thumboo, *A Third Map: New and Selected Poems* (Singapore: Unipress, 1993) 26.
4 Thumboo, *A Third Map* 27.
5 Thumboo, *A Third Map* 34–5.
6 Thumboo, *A Third Map* 100.
7 Muhammad Haji Salleh, *Beyond The Archipelago: Selected Poems* (Athens: Centre for International Studies, Ohio University, 1995) 153.
8 Muhammad Haji Salleh, *The Mind of the Author* (Kuala Lumpur: Dewan Bahasa & Pustaka, 1991) vii.
9 Muhammad Haji Salleh, *The Mind* 147.
10 Muhammad Haji Salleh, *The Mind* 143.
11 Muhammad Haji Salleh, *Rowing Down Two Rivers* (Bangi, Malaysia: Penerbit Universiti Kebangsaan Malaysia, 2000) 199.
12 Salleh Ben Joned, *Poems Sacred and Profane* (Kuala Lumpur: Pustaka Cipta, 2002) 39–44.
13 K.S. Maniam, *Haunting the Tiger* (London: Skoob Books, 1996) x.
14 Maniam, *Haunting the Tiger* 58.
15 Maniam, *Haunting the Tiger* 42.
16 Maniam, *Haunting the Tiger* 37.
17 Maniam, *Haunting the Tiger* 37, xii.
18 Maniam, *Haunting the Tiger*, 46.
19 K.S. Maniam. *Between Lives* (Petaling Jaya: Maya Press, 2003).
20 Maniam, *Between Lives* 4–7.
21 Maniam, *Between Lives* 108.
22 Maniam, *Between Lives* 289.
23 Maniam, *Between Lives* 188.
24 Maniam, *Between Lives* 115, 123, 125, 132.
25 Maniam, *Between Lives* 33.
26 Maniam, *Between Lives* 33.
27 Maniam, *Between Lives* 387–8.
28 Muhammad A. Quayum and Peter Wicks, *Malaysian Literature in English: a Critical Reader* (Petaling Jaya: Pearson Education, 2001) 81.
29 Lim, *Fistful of Colour* (Singapore: SNP International, 2003) 31.
30 Lim, *Fistful of Colours* 125.
31 Lim, *Fistful of Colours* 134.
32 Lim, *Fistful of Colours* 112.
33 Lim, *Fistful of Colours* 145.
34 Lim, *Fistful of Colours* 146.
35 Lim, *Fistful of Colours* 278.

Works cited

Ahmad, Shahnon. *Rope of Ash*. Transl. Harry Aveling. Kuala Lumpur: Oxford University Press, 1979.

Lim, Suchen Christine. *Fistful of Colours*. Singapore: SNP International, 2003.

Maniam, K.S. *Haunting the Tiger*. London: Skoob Books, 1996.

Maniam, K.S. *Between Lives*. Petaling Jaya: Maya Press, 2003.

Quayum, Mohammad A. and Peter Wicks, eds. *Malaysian Literature in English: a Critical Reader*. Petaling Jaya: Pearson Education, 2001.

Muhammad Haji Salleh. *The Mind of the Author*. Kuala Lumpur: Dewan Bahasa & Pustaka, 1991.

Muhammad Haji Salleh. *Beyond The Archipelago: Selected Poems*. Athens: Centre for International Studies, Ohio University, 1995.

Muhammad Haji Salleh. *Rowing Down Two Rivers*. Bangi, Malaysia: Penerbit Universiti Kebangsaan Malaysia, 2000.

Salleh ben Joned. *Poems Sacred and Profane*. Kuala Lumpur: Pustaka Cipta, 2002.

Tham, Claire. *Saving the Rainforest*. Singapore: Times Books, 1993.

Thumboo, Edwin, ed. 'General Introduction'. *The Fiction of Singapore*. Singapore: Unipress, 1990.

Thumboo, Edwin. *A Third Map: New And Selected Poems*. Singapore: Unipress, 1993.

Charting Malay Literary Studies and Malay Self-Identity

ROSLI TALIF and ABDUL RAHIM MARASIDI
UNIVERSITI PUTRA MALAYSIA

This chapter traces the influences of socio-cultural contexts such as colonialism and modernisation on the development of Malay literary studies, beginning with the struggle of the Malays to gain recognition through their traditional *Hikayats*. This struggle can be seen in the *Hikayats* being undermined as a genre which is merely confined to mythological places and characters. For modern readers, Dukuh Langka Dura (*Hikayat Dewa Mendu*) and Antah Berantah (*Hikayat Si Miskin*), for example, may be unfamiliar places but to Malay authors, these names were deliberately recorded from specific geographical locations identified in Malay chronicles such as *Hikayat Raja Pasai, Hikayat Banjar* and *Hikayat Aceh*.

To fit in with modernity, Malay authors needed to address topics of concern to Western readers. Colonial officers, for example, were very much concerned with and looked for a sense of humanity, the plot of the stories, their narrative expansion, geographical setting and the historical background of the works they were reading.

Some of the commentaries and criticisms of indigenous literature made by colonial officers in Malaya, such as R.O. Winstedt, found that Malay folklore borrowed most of its facts from the vast storehouse of Indian legends, its early crop stemming from the Hindu period and later, from the Islamic era. Winstedt, who was much influenced by his predecessors Sir Thomas Stamford Raffles, John Leyden and William Marsden, also referred frequently to the works of Portuguese and Dutch authors when writing about Malay culture, history and literature. It is the aim of this chapter to examine representations of the Malay in the writings of these colonial officers and other authors, and to show, in particular, how the different socio-cultural and historical contexts affect Malay literary studies and Malay self-identity.

In the sixteenth century, Europeans competed with each other to trade in

South-East Asian products. In the course of their trading activities, they recorded several aspects of the South-East Asian peoples, notably language, culture and literature, mainly for the purpose of colonialism and academic development.

The beginning of the influence of Western perspectives on Malay literary studies can be traced to the early colonial influence of the Dutch through the establishment of the Vereenigde Ost-Indische Compagnie (hereafter VOC), which replaced the trading and spiritual activities of the Portuguese in the Malay Archipelago. Earlier, the Portuguese had been responsible for building churches and promulgating Roman Catholicism among the non-Muslim Malays. It was during this time that the Dutch stereotyped Malays as lazy and unproductive. Ironically, this claim was reinforced by the fact that tin trading was monopolised by the VOC in the Malay states and the trading of agricultural products (sugar cane, coffee, and rice) in Java. These essential items were traded at very low prices, provoking negative responses among the Malays and Javanese. Consequently, they became less involved in these ventures, as they were not profitable.

From the eighteenth century onwards, scientific studies and theories of racial difference were also influential factors in the emerging discipline study of ethno-anthropology. The study of race in Europe was influenced by Charles Darwin's theories of the origin of species and of evolution, therefore shaping attitudes to cultural difference that was racially biased. According to this theory, the colonising races (mostly Europeans) possessed superior powers and were more gifted than other races. J.A. Hobson argued in a typical pronouncement that:

> probably everyone would agree that an Englishman would be right in considering the way of looking at the world and at life better than that of the Maori or the Hotentot, and one will object in the abstract to England doing her best to impose her better and higher view on these savages ... can there be any doubt that the white men must, and will, impose his superior civilization on the coloured race[1]

Alfred Russell Wallace, a naturalist, also came to believe in similar ideas about the origin of species and the theory of evolution as formulated by Darwin. He tried to demonstrate the truthfulness of his ideas in his book *Malay Archipelago* (1869).[2] From then onwards, colonial officers in South-East Asia continued to study the Malay race in the light of such received racial theory about cultural differences.

Earlier, when Thomas Stamford Raffles was the Lieutenant Governor of Java, he described the Javanese rulers as semi-barbarous and unaware of modern education and current technologies. They were unfamiliar with the invention of the printing press and knew little if anything at all about physiology and mathematics.[3] Elsewhere, Raffles elaborated on Javanese culture as having originated from India. The Brahmins, he noted, accompanied the Indian traders and introduced the Hindu gods, Indian literature and Sanskrit to the Javanese. The Javanese also adopted Indian mythology and shared their worldview. Therefore, as Raffles noted, anyone who studies Javanese will find many words borrowed from Indian languages.

Raffles also discussed the Malays in his memoirs. He noted that they constituted a single nation, speaking and communicating in a single language, but that they were scattered over a vast area extending from the Indian Ocean to Papua New Guinea.[4] 'They were not primitive or barbarous ... [and] the backwardness ... of the Malays was due to the lack of a legal system. The influence of Islam, Arabs, Dutch, and Chinese was also downgrading the Malays.'[5]

Marsden had previously motivated the Malay writer Lauddin to write his memoirs, including an account about the war between the EIC and the VOC in Western Sumatra, entitled *Hikayat Nakhoda Muda* (1791). Later, when Raffles was working in Penang, Marsden encouraged Ahmad Rijaluddin to write up his experiences and observations during a voyage to Calcutta in a manuscript entitled *Hikayat Perintah Negeri Benggala.* Both manuscripts were written under the influences of colonial notions to the effect that most of the Malay Hikayats were only fairy tales full of fantasies.

Raffles also trained a *peranakan*, Munshi Abdullah, to think like a British national[6]. Subsequently, the American Missionary in Singapore, Alfred North, encouraged Abdullah to write his trilogy, *Hikayat Abdullah*, *Hikayat Pelayaran Abdullah* and *Hikayat Pelayaran Abdullah ke Jeddah.* This trilogy appeared in lithograph and was distributed widely because of its importance to the Malay social history of the nineteenth century.

In this trilogy, Abdullah used a journalistic style of writing that was so far unknown to Malay authors. Abdullah criticised the negative habits of the Malays, their rulers and also their lack of understanding of the true nature of Islam. He also criticised the Dutch administration and certain British individuals like William Farquar who acted inhumanely in their treatment of Malays. The work of Abdullah gained considerable recognition and was therefore recommended as a textbook for colonial officers intending to serve in the Malay states.

To summarise, the appearance of the works of Lauddin, Ahmad Rijahuddin and Abdullah satisfied the primary objectives of the coloniser: that is, to train the native population in colonial ways of thinking and writing so as to act in accordance with the philosophy of imperialism. In other words, the intention was to civilise the coloured race by westernising their minds.

Another major work was Benjamin Keasberry's book *Hikayat Dunia* (1848), which dealt with historical accounts of the Malay world, the Malay Peninsula,

Sumatra, Java, Borneo, Sulawesi, Bali, Lambok and Australia. This book had a profound influence, directly or indirectly, on the content and style of the Malay historiographers[7] and other *hikayat* authors, especially on the subject of the Malays as a race or nation. While this text dealt with the influence of Hindu-Buddhists on the Malay culture, it had little to say on the contribution of Islam to the Malays or the accommodating nature of the Malays which eased the colonisation of the Malay archipelago.

According to the *Hikayat Dunia,* the peoples of the Malay world were lazy, stupid and dirty. They did not use their intelligence *(akal)* properly, whereas the European races did use their minds *(akal manusia)* effectively, so that it was the responsibility of the British colonisers of the Malay world to teach the Malays how to exploit their minds and deploy their reasoning skills, especially in their social activities and their writings.

Keasberry went on to criticise the views expressed in the *Malay Hikayats*, views that could not be believed by people endowed with intelligence and knowledge. In contrast to the *Malay Hikayat*, Keasberry asserts that 'whoever reads my *hikayat*, I remind you to think: Other foolish *hikayats* are only the products of the Malay mind, they are not established in truth'.[8] Whereas the focus of the *Hikayat Dunia* was on the historic and geographical origin of the Malay race, the traditional Malay *hikayats* had focused only on kings and governments *(Raja and Kerajaan)*, based on the idea that the king (Raja) descended from heaven to rule the Malays.[9]

The *Hikayat Dunia* was the logical continuation of Abdullah's trilogy in modernising Malay culture in accordance with colonial needs. It is for this reason that the colonial powers and the London missionary societies began to open schools for the Malays, especially for the children of the rulers. Most of these schools were built in Johor, Malacca, Penang and Singapore. The works of Abdullah and the *Hikayat Dunia* became school textbooks, serving as common readings for colonial officers in Malaya during the nineteenth century.

Missionaries like Keasberry tried to modernise and westernise the Malays by translating a number of books that stressed the superiority of the west by including articles in his *Cerita Ilmu Kepandaian* (The Story of Knowledge and Intelligence).[10] Keasberry attempted to persuade local readers to study European thought and to reject the teachings of Malay elders and religious leaders. Colonial officers and missionaries cooperated with the idea of westernising and secularising the minds of the Malays in order to expose them later to the teachings of Christianity, as Keasberry had intended when building schools for the local population.

The first step taken to westernise or modernise Malay minds was to develop the Malay school system and introduce Malays to western thought. In 1816, the

London Missionary Society built the Penang Free School.[11] In 1821, a branch of the school for Malay children was established in Gelugor. Shortly after, in 1823, Raffles built schools in Singapore for the children of British citizens and the Johor royal families who had settled there. Both Raffles and William Farquar encouraged the chieftains of other Malay states to send their children to those schools. The East India Company (EIC) later established the Anglo-Chinese School in Malacca.

The EIC and the London Missionary Society were both responsible for promoting western systems of education among members of Malay society in the Straits Settlements, in an effort to replace the Quranic Madrasah educational system. Chinese, Indian and Malay children, including the sons of the Sultan of Johor, attended schools established with this objective in mind. Textbooks set in such schools were comprised of teachings from the Judeo-Christian tradition, like the Ten Commandments and stories from the New Testament that had been translated into Malay. Keasberry had succeeded William Milne as teacher in the mission school, and was very determined to promote Christianity through education.[12] By 1855, Abdullah's trilogy and *Hikayat Dunia* were added to the list of school textbooks, together with the translated Malay translation of the Bible.

Another means of influencing Malay Culture was through journalism. The Malay language newspaper *Alamat Langkapuri* began publishing in 1869, serving readers among the Malay diaspora in Ceylon (Sri Lanka). This newspaper not only circulated there, but also found its way to the Malay Archipelago: that is, to the Malay homeland. In addition to the publication of local and international news, this paper also printed *syairs*, *pantouns* and other traditional poems. Some Malay newspapers made their way into the lists of recommended texts for students, especially those that appeared after an Indian-Malay *peranakan* had published the *Jawi Peranakan* in Singapore in 1876. The political orientation in this latter publication was pro-Malay; this paper supported the struggle of Malays for a Greater-Malay identity known as *Melayu Raya*.[13] The concept of *Melayu Raya* had its origin in the political struggle of Indonesian and Filipino activists. Indonesian leftists like Mas Marco, Tirto Adi Soerjo and Tan Malaka had envisioned a geographical area that was to include the Philippines, Indonesia and Malaya, encompassing all speakers of Malay languages. Similarly, Jose Rizal, the first Filipino nationalist, began to propagate Pan-Malay or greater Malay in his political struggle against American imperialism. Before that, he had criticised the Spanish for underrating the Malays by calling them lazy and categorising them as members of an inferior race.[14] All these issues motivated the trainees of Sultan Idris Teachers College (SITC) in the first three decades of the twentieth century to propagate the ideology of Malay nationalism, especially the concept of a greater Malay world among the Malay student body, and they achieved this aims through journalism, short stories and novels. The earliest novels representing Malay nationalism were *Iakah Salmah* (1928) by Abdul Rashid Talu, *Melur Kuala Lumpur* by Harun Aminurashid (1930) and *Percintaan Kasih Kemudaan* by Ahmad Bin Kotot (1927).[15]

The newspaper *Sekola Melayu,* edited by an Indian-Malay *peranakan*, was circulated in Singapore in the late 1880s and was eventually included among the texts recommended to students of the Malay Teachers College at Teluk Belanga. Muslim clerics such as Syed Sheikh Ahmad al Hady, Syeikh Tahir Jalaludin and Taha Abas also contributed to Malay journalistic writings during this period. Syed Sheikh Ahmad al Hady's Singapore newspaper *Al-Imam* tried to make Malays aware of the tactics of British colonialism in exploiting the Muslims at large. It also tried to influence Malay understanding of the fundamental teachings of Islam. The significance of *Al Imam* to the Malays was that it became the first newspaper to publish articles on Malay problems from an Islamic perspective. The *Al-Imam* was influenced by the writings of Jamaludin al Afghani, Muhd Abduh and Rashid Redha, all of which were published in the *Al Manar* and the *Al Urwat al Wutsqa* which circulated widely in the Middle East and Europe.

The growth of newspapers in the Malay language in the early nineteenth century reflected the role of Malay *peranakans* in the intellectual development of the Muslim-Malay society in the Peninsula and the Straits Settlements. There had been no social organisations representing the indigenous population, except for those dealing with welfare or sports activities like the *Kastam Zaria Club* in Kuala Kangsar and the *New Hope Society* in Johor Bharu founded in 1916.[16] The Malays had no other political organisations to present their social problems to the British Government. The new social organisations run by the *peranakans*, in turn, raised those issues and brought them to the consideration of the colonial government.

The Malays in Singapore had originally come from the Malay Peninsula, the Straits Settlements and the Malay Archipelago. They realised that there was no social organisation to serve as a platform for their problems. Eunos Abdullah, a former journalist from the *Utusan Melayu* (1907) and the *Lembaga Melayu,* encouraged Malays through his writings to unite and form an organisation, which was established in 1926 and became known as the *Kesatuan Melayu Singapura* (Malay Association of Singapore). Their memoranda to the Governor of the Straits Settlements, for example, succeeded in opening a Malay settlement in Singapore similar to the one at Kampong Baru, Kuala Lumpur.

The Malays in the *Kesatuan Melayu Singapura* were urban Malays who had originally come from rural areas of the Malay Archipelago. Living in the metropolitan state of Singapore exposed them to new ideas through their contact with western education, urbanisation and a legal system based on British jurisprudence.

Singapore had been, in 1900, a centre of Malay culture because most of the Malay language newspapers were published there. The growth of such newspapers in Singapore was also very encouraging: the *Neracha*, the *Lembaga Melayu*, the *Temasik* and the *Warta Melayu* were some of the newspapers published there. When the newspaper *Al Imam* suspended its publication in 1908, Muslim reformers shifted their activities from Singapore to the Malay states on the peninsula and to the Straits Settlements sites like Malacca and Penang. Apart from the newspaper writings, the early modern writings of Malays such as the work of Abdullah criticised their Malay rulers, especially with regard to their understanding of Islam. In the 1920s, Ibrahim al Madrasi wrote the short story 'Kecelakaan Pemalas' for the Islamic periodical *Pengasuh*, thereby creating a new literary genre. This development of a modern short story genre included the work of Syed Syeikh al Hadi who also wrote a novel, *Hikayat Faridah Hanum* (1925), that became famous for its criticism of the reformation of Islam as found in most of the articles published by the *Al Imam* during the years 1906–1908. Meanwhile, the teacher trainees of the SITC were exposed to English styles of writing. They also read a number of Indonesian novels, such as *Azab dan Sengsara* by Merari Serigar, *Siti Norbaya* by Marah Rosli, *Salah Asuhan* by Abdoel Moeis and others published in Jakarta by Balai Poestaka.[17] Students and staff were also exposed to new writings authored on the Malay Archipelago by academicians and colonial officers like Sir W.G. Maxwell, A.J. Sturrock, C.O. Blagden, R.O. Winstedt and many others, who were all interested in local affairs. The listing of SITC textbooks was now expanded to include such works as *Hikayat Dunia, Sejarah Melayu, Tawarikh al Islam by* Syed Syeikh al Hadi, *Hikayat Abdullah, Tarikh Tanah Melayu dan Pulau Percha* by R.O. Winstedt and *Sejarah Pulau Jawa*. Such works were mainly based on studies conducted by several Dutch scholars as well as by writers like Raffles, Marsden and Leyden.

The impact of modern education was notable at the SITC where students and staff became acquainted with the research supported by an influx of empirical data geared toward the acquisition of new thought patterns. The college authorities admitted selected students to join the college teaching staff. Some of those selected were Abdul Hadi Hassan, Buyong Adil, Harun Aminurashid and Ahmad Abdullah. They were the first group of the Malay SITC graduates who promoted the notion of Malay nationalism on the basis of the Greater Malay ideology of *Melayu Raya* among the trainees in the teaching college.

The notion of *Melayu Raya* was explored in a series of history books in six volumes by Abdul Hadi and Buyong Adil under the title of *Sejarah Alam Melayu*. This work was inspired by the writings of the Dutch, British, and French scholars, especially those in the fields of ethnology, history and archaeology and was studied at all Malay primary schools in Malaya, Singapore, Sarawak and Brunei.

A few young Malay officers, civil servants educated at the government English school, were attracted to Ibrahim Yaacob's ideas. This group of Malay intellectuals formed an association which was called *Kesatuan Melayu Muda* (Association of Malay Youths or KMM). The KMM was politically motivated to unite the Malays in Malaya, Singapore and Indonesia to subscribe to the pan-Malay ideology of *Melayu Raya*, also known as *Indonesia Raya* in the 1920s. The Malays in Malaya, Singapore and Indonesia planned a revolution, with the help of the Japanese Army, against British and Dutch rule in the Malay Archipelago.

Most of the Malay journalists who wrote and criticised the Indian and Arab descendants, were working for the *peranakan* newspapers.[18] They include Rahim Kajai, the first editor for *Utusan Melayu*, Onn Jaafar and Ishak Hj. Muhamad. Consequently, the rich and poor Malays in *Kesatuan Melayu Singapura* decided to set up a publishing company which could print a Malay language newspaper, the main objective of which was to function as a vehicle for Malay journalists to raise Malay issues and encourage readers to participate in the polemic political process spearheaded by the newspaper.

By 1939 the first wholly Malay owned newspaper, *Utusan Melayu,* was circulating in the Malay Peninsula and Singapore. Yusof Ishak, a former English language newspaper sports editor, was chosen to manage the company. The editorial board included prominent Malay reporters such as Rahim Kajai, Ishak Hj. Muhammad, Ahmad Boestamam, Zainal Abidin Hj. Alias and Sallehuddin. The circulation of *Utusan Melayu* increased as the paper gathered wide support from Malay readers. Its Sunday edition was called *Utusan Zaman. Utusan Melayu* survived until 5 February 2006 when it ceased publication because of waning numbers of readers. During the Japanese occupation, the Japanese military government closed all the Malay language newspapers and created a single newspaper, *Berita Malai,* that acted as a voice for Japanese military propaganda. The KMM went underground, working hand in hand with Indonesian revolutionaries to free the Malay Archipelago and Malaya, Singapore and Indonesia, in particular, from colonialism.

After the defeat of the Japanese Army, members of KMM from Malaya and Singapore joined the Indonesian Revolutionist Army against the Dutch in Indonesia. At the same time Ibrahim Yaacob escaped to Indonesia to avoid prosecution from the British because of his involvement and collaboration with the Japanese during the Second World War.

When the Crown Colony awarded open citizenship to non-Malays who claimed Malay states as their home land, many Malays rejected the policy of Malayan Union because they felt that the British government was attempting to eliminate the power of the Sultan and his individual sovereignty. The Malays refused to accept the idea of giving open citizenship to non Malays and especially to the Chinese, because loyalty to this country was in question because Chinese schools were still using syllabi which originally had been developed for primary and secondary schools in China. Similarly, the Tamils maintained cultural connections with India. To the Malays, however, the Malay world was their only homeland. Thus Malays used all available means, including media and social organisations, to protest against the formation of Malayan Union.

Malay intellectuals like Dato Onn Jaafar and Zainal Abidin Ahmad, called upon all the Malay social organisations to form a single political party to embrace the concept of Malayan Union. On 1 March 1946, a representative of forty-one social organisations established a Malay political party called United Malays National Organization (UMNO). The first leader of UMNO, Dato Onn Jaafar, persuaded the Sultan to boycott the inauguration ceremony of Malayan Union on 1 April 1946. The colonial office and the foreign office in London abandoned the concept of Malayan Union in July 1946 because of the criticism from the Malays and also from some retired British Malaya civil service officers in England.[19]

Chinese language newspapers such as *Qian Feng Bao*, and *Ting Hua Zhou Bao* published news on many issues concerning the language and culture of the Chinese community in Malaya and Singapore, the problems among the students in the Chinese schools, and the war between Chinese Communist Party and Kuomintang in China. The Malay newspapers such as *Utusan Melayu* under the editorship of A. Samad Ismail published news on the Indonesian revolution against the Dutch and encouraged the Malays to support the cause of Indonesian independence.

The leftists who were dominated by communist ideology began a campaign against colonial race by killing the managers of British-owned rubber estates and tin mines. Consequently, the British declared a state of emergency in FMS by mid June 1948. The British military imprisoned some Malay leftists such as Musa Ahmad. Ahmad C.D., and Rashid Maidin, who later joined their comrades who were mostly Chinese and escaped into the Malayan tropical rain forest from where they fought against the British.

Those who were fortunate enough escaped to Singapore where they were given an opportunity to work at the publishing house. Among the leftists who joined the publishing house were Keris Mas, Asraf, Dahari Ali and many others. Some of them later escaped to Indonesia where they joined the Indonesian

Revolutionary Army fighting for the Indonesian struggle for independence.

While the pro-western elites among the Malays maintained the respect of their former colonial masters, especially their love of the western way of life, sports and other social activities, numbers of low income workers, mainly Malay school teachers, low-paid government servants, literary activists and Malay writers, were attracted to socialist ideologies. The role of Malay journalists who worked in *Utusan Melayu* helped to change the minds of the rural Malays, uniting them through their writings on Malay issues, and identities, on the unification of the Malay Archipelago and poverty. In writing about these issues, they tended to blame the colonisers and immigrants for being responsible for the dispossession and displacement of the Malays in their own land.

Most of the Malay writers in the late 1940s were sympathisers of leftist ideologies. They were influenced by Indonesian writers of the *Pujangga Baru* group such as Sutan Takdir Alisjahbana, Armin Pane and Muhammad Yamin.[20] Most of their writings used terms originally borrowed from Indonesian writers such as '*Seni*' for the 'Arts,' '*Budaya*' for 'culture,' '*alat*' for 'tools,' and '*rakyat*' for 'people.' In 1948, when the Indonesians were in the midst of their revolution against the Dutch, Keris Mas or Kamaludin Mohamad wrote a novelette entitled *Pahlawan Rimba Malaya* which can be seen as equivalent to the revolutionary novels from Indonesian literature.

At the same time, Jymy Asmara formed a network of writers called *Sahabat Pena* (Pen Friend). The purpose of this group was to promote friendship and to encourage members to attempt literary writings such as short stories and poems in the Malay language. On 6 August 1950, these young writers formed a movement for the new generation of writers called *Angkatan Sasterawan 50* or *ASAS 50*. The leaders of the group were Mohammad Arif Ahmad or MAS and Keris Mas. The slogan promoted by these writers was 'Arts for Society' or '*Seni untuk Masyarakat.*'

ASAS 50 inspired a new trend in their writing, especially in short stories and poetry. Their thematic concerns were society, politics and culture, the promotion of the spirit of independence, and of self-reliance, stressing their roles as defenders of justice. *ASAS 50* criticised the colonisers, trying to reform Malay society and counter the influence of feudalism, superstition and deviant Islamic teachings, through the promulgation of leftist ideology and literature. Most of the *ASAS 50* members were formerly members of the KMM, the *Parti Kebangsaan Melayu Malaya* (Malay Nationalist Party of Malaya or PKMM), the *Kesatuan Rakyat Indonesia Semenanjung* (the Indonesian Citizens Union of the Peninsula or (KERIS), the *Angkatan Pemuda Insaf* (API) and *Angkatan Wanita Sedar* (AWAS) which rejected UMNO because of its colonial ties. Most of their works used Indonesian literary models especially the works of Pramoedya Ananta Toer, Achadiat Karta Mihardja and other such authors.

However, a group of conservative Malay authors with religious and Malay educational backgrounds such as Hamzah Hussin, Ahmad Lutfi, Rosemera and Harun Aminurashid opposed the radical writings of *ASAS 50.* Most of their works were published in the newspaper *Melayu Raya* and in magazines such as *Qalam, Hiburan* and *Harmy.* They promoted the slogan 'Art for Art's Sake' or '*Seni untuk Seni*'. The polemics between these two groups were published in their various newspapers. Thus, *Utusan Melayu, Utusan Zaman* and *Mastika* promoted 'Arts for Society,' while *Melayu Raya, Qalam* and *Hiburan* promoted 'Art for Art's Sake.'

Malay students at the University of Malaya (now the National University of Singapore) who were members of the Socialist Club also associated themselves with the writers of *ASAS 50*, delivering speeches and talks on modern Malay Literature which were published in '*Fajar*', the club's student newspaper. They mainly concerned themselves with the poverty and backwardness of the Malays which they claimed was due to colonial and capitalist economic practices together with the feudal mind set of the Malays. Many seminars were held on literature, culture, economics, education and social issues in order to reform and transform Malay Culture.

One of Malaysia's Literary Laureates who criticised the government on the issue of race relations was Shahnon Ahmad. According to Mohd. Yusuf Hassan, one of the major issues in Shahnon's novel *Menteri* is the economic advancement of the non-Malays who had little regard for the poverty of the Malays in their own country, revealing the racial tensions and prejudices that existed in the Malaysian community at that time. [21] Ungku Maimunah explains that the year in which *Menteri* was written is significant, in that it marked the end of a decade of independence which had not improved the social condition of the Malays.[22]

The problem of Malay poverty leading to the social unrest in 1969 has been written extensively by Malaysian social scientists such as K.J. Ratnam and R.K. Vasil.[23] Language also became one of the concerns of the educated Malays, who criticised the government when Parliament introduced the National Language Act in 1967 in which the status of the Malay language as the national language was not made clear. They expected the government to implement the Malay language as the national language, instead of simply positioning it as an official language, asserting that Malaysia is a country of the Malays.[24] In opposing the Language Act, university students, journalists, and professionals expressed their dissatisfaction by carrying Coffin 152 or '*Keranda 152*' to Parliament, symbolising the death of the Malays and the Malay language.

The Prime Minister at the time, Tunku Abdul Rahman persuaded the Malays to accept the Malay Language Act of 1967, with the promise that the government would protect both the Malays and other races as Malaysian citizens. The criticism against the government by Malays on language and land issues were captured by A. Samad Ismail in his novels *Kail Panjang Sejengkal* (1967), *Menduga Lautan Dalam* (1968) and *Detik-Detik Chemas* (1969).[25]

The self-identification of the Malays has been considered in this study from the differing socio-cultural contexts in the construction of the nation. At the end of the war when the British colonials returned to take over the reins of leadership, the confrontation between the Malays and the British turned into a struggle between European and indigenous values. The future progress of the Malays was understood as dependent upon their adaptability to European values, that is, their willingness to westernise. This can be observed through the changing patterns of writings by Malaysian writers in their effort to modernise and educate the Malays and to propagate modern literary styles. These modern literary styles allow writers to explore notions of Malay identity and Malay social issues, and for readers to have access to the development of Malay self-identity which has evolved from its early literary manifestations to its present conception.

Notes

1 Hobson (1902:158) is quoted in Robert Phillipson, *Linguistic Imperialism* (Oxford: Oxford University Press, 1992) 44–45.

2 Alfred Russel Wallace, *Malay Archipelago* (London: Macmillan, 1869).

3 Thomas Stamford Raffles, *The History of Java* (London: London University Press, 1817) 272: 273.

4 Syed Muhd Khairudin Al Junied, *Raffles and Religion: A Study of Sir Thomas Stamford Raffles' Discourse on Religions Amongst Malays* (Kuala Lumpur: The Other Press, 2004) 5.

5 Syed Muhd Khairudin, *Raffles and Religion* 6.

6 Right across the British Empire these practices can be identified. For example in India, Lord Macauley trained Sir Syed Ahmad Khan.

7 Such as Raja Ali Haji of Riau's work entitled *Tuhfat al Nafis* (1865) and Munshi Muhammad Ibrahim b. Munshi Abdullah's work entitled *Hikayat Pelayaran Muhammad Ibrahim Munshi* (1872).

8 Quoted in Anthony C. Milner, *The Invention of Politics in Colonial Malaya: Contesting Nationalism and the Expansion of the Public Sphere* (Cambridge: Cambridge University Press, 1995) 62.

9 Quoted in Milner, *The Invention of Politics in Colonial Malaya* 60.

10 Benjamin Keasberry, *Cerita Ilmu Kepandaian* (*The Story of Knowledge and Intelligence*, 1855: 74–76) quoted in Jan Van Der Putten 'Menyingkap Tempurung Orang

Melayu: Sejarah Melayu, Buku Teks dan Abdullah Munsyi', Seminar Sastera Cetak Abad ke 19, (Dewan Bahasa and Putaka, 14–15 December 2004) 9.

11 In 1816 Penang Free School was built with English as the medium of instruction, while later in 1821, another Penang Free school was built with Malay as the medium of instruction.

12 Farish Noor, *The Other Malaysia: Writings on Malaysia's Subaltern History* (Kuala Lumpur: Silverfish, 2002) 34.

13 Virginia Matheson Hooker, *Writing A New Society* (Honolulu: Allen and Unwin and University of Hawaii Press, 2000) 80.

14 Z.A. Salazar, '"Malay", "Malayan" And "Malay Civilization" As Cultural And Anthropological Concepts in the Phillipines from the Time of Rizal to the present'. Seminar at the International Conference on Malay Civilization (Kuala Lumpur, Malaysia, 26–28 August 1986) 10.

15 Ahmad Hj. Muhammad Rashid Talu, *Iakah Salmah* (Pulau Pinang: Jelutong Press, 1928); Harun Aminurrashid, *Melur* (Kuala Lumpur: Ahmad and Company, 1931); Ahmad Kotot, *Hikayat Percintaan Kasih Kemudaan* (Seremban: al-Matba'ah al Rawdzah al Islam wa Syarikah, 1927).

16 W.R. Roff, *The Origins of Malay Nationalism* (Kuala Lumpur: University of Malaya Press, 1967)184–5.

17 Merari Serigar, *Azab Sengsara* (Jakarta: Balai Pustaka 1920); Marah Rusli, *Siti Norbaya* (Jakarta: Balai Pustaka, 1922); Abdoel Moeis, *Salah Asuhan* (Jakarta: Balai Pustaka, 1928).

18 In 1900–1940s Malay journalists worked for *peranakan* newspapers. The Malay journalists criticised the peranakans (Indian and Arab descendents) for being opportunists in trying to displace the Malays from their own land through economy and leadership. Issues on Malay rights became the focus of these journalists.

19 Hooker, *Writing A New Society* 188.

20 Hooker, *Writing A New Society* 182–3.

21 Mohd. Yusuf Hassan, *Novels of the Troubled Years* (Kuala Lumpur: Dewan Bahasa and Pustaka, 1989) 38.

22 Ungku Maimunah, *Antara Kampung dan Kota Rural Bias in the Novels of Shahnon Ahmad* (Kuala Lumpur: Dewan Bahasa and Pustaka, 1989) 148.

23 Cheah Boon Kheng, *Malaysia The Making of a Nation* (Singapore: Inst of Southeast Asian Studies, 2002) 52–5.

24 Cheah Boon Kheng, *Malaysia The Making of a Nation* 50–1.

25 A. Samad Ismail, *Kail Panjang Sejengkal* (Kuala Lumpur: Utusan Melayu Sdn Bhd, 1967); *Meduga Lautan Dalam* (Kluang: Pustaka Pendidikan, 1968); *Detik-Detik Chemas* (Singapura: Penerbitan Pustaka Nasional, 1969).

Works cited

Ahmad Hj. Muhammad Rashid Talu. *Iakah Salmah*. Pulau Pinang: Ahmad, Abdul Rahman & Co., 1929.

Aminurrashid, Harun. *Melur*. Kuala Lumpur: Ahmad and Company, 1931.

Cheah Boon Kheng. *Malaysia The Making of a Nation*. Singapore: Inst of Southeast Asian Studies, 2002.

Hassan, Mohd Yusof. *Novels of the Troubled Years*. Kuala Lumpur: Dewan Bahasa and Pustaka, 1989.

Hooker, Virginia M. *Writing A New Society*. Honolulu: Allen and Unwin and University of Hawaii Press, 2000.

Kotot, Ahmad. *Hikayat Percintaan Kasih Kemudaan*. Seremban: al-Matba'ah al Rawdzah al Islam wa Syarikah, 1927.

Milner, Anthony C. *The Invention of Politics in colonial Malaya: Contesting Nationalism and the Expansion of the Public Sphere*. Cambridge: Cambridge University Press, 1995.

Noor, Farish. *The Other Malaysia: Writings on Malaysia's Subaltern History*. Kuala Lumpur: Silverfish, 2002.

Phillipson, Robert. *Linguistic Imperialism*. Oxford: Oxford University Press, 1992.

Raffles, Thomas Stamford. *The History of Java*. London: London University Press, 1817.

Roff, W.R. *The Origins of Malay Nationalism*. Kuala Lumpur: University of Malaya Press, 1967.

Salazar, Z.A. '"Malay", *"Malayan" And "Malay Civilization" As Cultural And Anthropological Concepts in the Phillipines from the Time of Rizal to the present'*. Seminar at the International Conference on Malay Civilization, Kuala Lumpur, Malaysia, 26–28 August 1986.

Samad Ismail, A. *Kail Panjang Sejengkal*. Kuala Lumpur: Utusan Melayu Sdn Bhd, 1967.

Samad Ismail, A. *Meduga Lautan Dalam*. Kluang: Pustaka Pendidikan, 1968.

Samad Ismail, A. *Detik-Detik Chemas*. Singapura: Penerbitan Pustaka Nasional, 1969.

Syed Muhd Khairudin Al Junied. *Raffles and Religion: A Study of Sir Thomas Stamford Raffles' Discourse on Religions Amongst Malays*. Kuala Lumpur: The Other Press, 2004.

Ungku Maimunah Mohd Tahir. *Antara Kampung dan Kota Rural Bias in the Novels of Shahnon Ahmad*. Kuala Lumpur: Dewan Bahasa and Pustaka, 1989.

Van der Putten, Jan. 'Menyingkap Tempurung Orang Melayu: Sejarah Melayu, Buku Teks dan Abdullah Munsyi' Seminar Sastera Cetak Abad ke 19, Dewan Bahasa and Pustaka, 14–15 December 2004.

Wallace, Alfred Russel. *Malay Archipelago*. London: Macmillan, 1869.

Humanity In Text/Intact: Malay Images in Selected Singaporean Writing in English

NOR FARIDAH ABDUL MANAF
INTERNATIONAL ISLAMIC UNIVERSITY OF MALAYSIA

Abstract

Race as a topic is always a problematic issue, not only in Malaysia but also in Singapore. It is problematic because of both governments' policies and, as well, the cultural constructions placed on the self by others. This paper explores how certain Singapore writers courageously deal with racial issues and demonstrate race concerns in their writings. This paper focuses on how some of these writers' racial sensitivities display elements of humanity in their texts as they address the need for intercultural and inter-racial communication with the 'other'. This paper looks at the projections of Malay image in writings in English, not only by Singaporean Malay writers but also by non-Malay Singaporean writers.

This paper examines Malay images in selected writings in English by Singaporean writers; the genres range from poetry to short story to drama/play. The writers come from various ethnic backgrounds. Whenever Malay issues emerge and a writer is asked to be named, most people might think immediately of Alfian Sa'at or Lily Zubaidah Rahim, but this paper is not just about them and what they write of Malay images in Singapore. This paper sets out to explore how certain Singaporean writers courageously deal with racial issues and demonstrate racial concerns in their writings, especially those of the minority. The focus of this paper is on how some of these writers' racial sensitivities display genuine elements of humanity (read human rights and justice) in their texts as they address the need for intercultural and inter-racial communication with the 'other'. It looks at the projections of Malay image in writings in English not only by Singapore Malay writers but also by non-Malay Singaporean writers so that some kind of cultural understanding is established, enabling people living in a multiracial and multicultural environment to connect without suffering from racial distrust and prejudice.

The history of a nation is often defined by those in power. Alfian Sa'at, in his response to Lily Zubaidah Rahim's *The Singapore dilemma: The political and educational marginality of Malay community* (1998) writes of the danger of privileging one history over another: ' ... attempts to privilege one history over another results in the oppression of minority voices. An African proverb states that, 'Until the lions have their histories, tales of the hunt will always glorify the hunter' (Alfian Sa'at).[1]

Alfian concludes by observing that it is not true to think that there are no more lions in the Lion City. This paper is about documenting these lions' voices.

Professor Hsu Yun-Ts'iao, in his article 'Singapore in the remote past', points out that it is erroneous to think that Singapore history began with her founding by Sir Thomas Stamford Raffles in 1819.[2] He highlights that the name Singapore derives from the Sanskrit word 'Singapura' or 'Simhapura', which means 'Lion City'. It first appeared with its previous name Temasek in *Sejarah Melayu* written in A.D. 1535 (revised in 1612). 'Temasik' (spelt Tumasik) also appeared in *Nagarakretagama* (written A.D. 1365) as well as in *Parraton*, a Javanese record of the fifteenth century. The Chinese sources give evidence of the existence of old Singapore going back from thirteenth century to as far as the third century.[3] Hsu Yun-Tsi'iao notes that Wang Ta-Yuan mentions the war between Tumasik and Siam in *Tao Yi Tchih Lueh* (written in 1330 A.D.), and further records that the war between Siam and Tumasik is also recorded in *Yuah Shih* (*History of the Mongol Dynasty*). Singapore was called Ma-Li-Yu-R by the Imperial Court of China which is believed to correspond to Marco Polo's Malaiyur.[4] For some, these accounts offer one version of Singapore history; for others, Raffles' version better explains that history. Raffles claimed that when he arrived in Singapore, there were few inhabitants, and only a handful of huts by the river. In his letter to his friend Colonel Addenbrooke (10 June 1819), he admitted that the fight for territory between East India Company and the Dutch was real. He wrote that the reason for the occupation was more on trade fulfilling the need for a station for their business trade with China:

> It was clear that the object of the Dutch was not only to command for themselves all the trade of the Eastern island but to possess the power in the event of future was of preventing our regular intercourse with China. By possessing the only passes to this Empire, namely the Straits of Sunda and Malacca, they had it in their power at all times to impede that trade; and of their disposition to exert this power, even in time of peace, there was no doubt. It was therefore determined that we should lose no time in securing, if practicable, the command of one of these Straits; and the Straits of Malacca on account of their proximity to our other Settlements appeared the most eligible.[5]

Raffles' claim that Singapore was not inhabited save for a few huts is refuted by many scholars, including W. Bartley who quotes Captain Newbold's account from 1839 noting that the Singapore population consisted about 150 fishermen and pirates, of whom about thirty were Chinese.[6]

In addition to this, a letter by Resident W. Farquhar to Raffles' secretary Lt. L.W. Hull gives evidence of the existence of a gambier plantation of a Chinese planter on the western side of the island.[7] Similarly, W.W. Skeat and H.N. Ridley write of the Orang Laut of Singapore—the Kallangs and Selitars.[8] The former lived on Kallang River, while the latter along the rivers on the Johore Strait. The Kallangs were removed by the Temenggong of Johore from the Kallang River to Pulai River when the island was ceded to Britain. According to Skeat and Ridley, there were about a hundred families but they were reduced to eight due to the spread of smallpox in 1847. They were said to have lived exclusively in boats and did not build huts or cultivate plants. Their language at that time appears to have been Malay.[9]

Singapore history continues to be written and rewritten, depending on the power of the day. Writers and 'historians' like Winstedt seem to find it difficult to separate historical facts from legends. For many people in modern and post-modern Singapore, such history is no longer important, because it challenges the idea of nationalism and nationhood based on a single race and one people, denying the rhetoric of policies like multiracialism and meritocracy. While economic dynamism is seen crucial to the growth of Singapore as a nation, social cohesion and political stability are seen as important for the Singapore economy to thrive. Lee Hsien Loong points out in 'Singapore of the Future' that these elements are important to make Singapore an outstanding home for all resident in Singapore.[10] The policies of multiracialism and meritocracy are implemented to consolidate the government's efforts to overcome the problem of persistent racial inequality. While these two policies are celebrated by many as directly responsible for the economic and political stability of Singapore, there are critics who challenge the relevance and justice of the policies in a multireligious and multicultural city-state such as that in Singapore. The policies are seen as necessary to manage Singapore's race relations, especially after Singapore's separation from Malaysia in 1965. S. Rajaratnam, then Foreign Minister, explained to the United Nations General Assembly in 1965 that PAP (People's Action Party) aimed to base national cohesion on a multiracial, multilingual secular society, stressing the richness of cultural diversity and at the same time seeking to superimpose a specifically Singaporean identity and sense of values:

> If we of the present generation can steadfastly stick to this policy for the next thirty

> years, then we would have succeeded in creating a Singaporean of a unique kind. He would be a man rooted in the cultures of four great civilizations but not belonging exclusively to any of them.[11]

Critics like Kuo Pao Kun (known as a playwright and a pioneer in multi-lingual theatre) writes in 'Contemplating an Open Culture: Transcending Multiracialism' that there is a need now to revise the policy for it was first set in the late 1970s to control racial conflict and hence it is not a master plan to move forward into the future. Kuo does not see the policy as proposing a vision to create a new people beyond race in which, 'everyone would have a qualitatively larger, sharable space in culture'.[12]

Kuo's concern for an Open Culture is shared by many other critics who see the flaws of the multiracialism policy. In an article 'Malays in Singapore' written by a group of researchers at the Center for International Development and Conflict Management (University of Maryland, USA), it is suggested that in spite of its well-meaning intentions, multiracialism does not allow the politicization of the identities of the Malay, Chinese, India and European communities.[13] Lily Zubaidah Rahim has pointed also that the existing policies (multiracialism included) are far from satisfactory. She also questions other policies like the ethnic residential quotas, population policies and educational programmes like the Special Assistance programme (SAP).[14]

It is not that the lions do not roar in Singapore, but we have not listened hard enough. Where Singaporean writers are concerned, some of the issues raised here are also represented in their writings. Admittedly, very few writers have written openly on race relations, racial conflicts or call for a freer space to negotiate race and culture. The subtle works if such earlier poets like Chandran Nair suggest that poetry is to be a safe mode to talk about race relations in Singapore (or Malaysia). We recall Nair's poem 'Sincerity' (which he wrote for Muhammad), in which he acknowledges the class and racial divides between the Chinese and the Malays as seen by his disillusioned Malay friend, Muhammad:

> … he saw middlemen collect
> the sweat
> of brothers in foreign banks
> and would not sit
> with those not brothers to the skin.

Nair also saw the futility of any attempts to reconcile racial and class differences:

So they called him
communal,
refused his love, burned his
poems.
only the cold wind pulled
nationality round him
so he walked the lonely path,

among jacaranda trees in
bloom,

in his country.[15]

We remember Lee Tzu Pheng's poem 'My Country and My People' was banned for a long time when she tried to address issues on nation, national identity and the modernisation of Singapore. However, things have changed since then; a generation of highly educated and wired young writers has emerged and has blossomed beautifully. They have their own means of getting heard. Many have resorted to publishing their writings online by creating their own websites or sending their works to e-journals. Others are happy to publish their works in small presses both in Singapore or abroad. Some of these writers include Alfian Sa'at, Haresh Sharma, Felix Cheong, Daren Shiau, Gilbert Koh and Eddie Tay. These young writers are willing to speak out directly about Singaporean reality. They depict a convincing multicultural and multiracial Singapore with all its irregularities and flaws. The romanticisation of the Singaporean landscape and people is now seen as a thing of the past. We hear one ethnic voice attempting a dialogue with another, sometimes blasting the pretense of the nation. Wesee images of the minorities written by the enviable 'other'. Since the focus of this paper is on Malay images in Singapore's writings in English, I will move now to consider some works by some of these writers.

Alfian Sa'at: Sometimes the most angry, loud and misunderstood writer

He is a writer you love to hate. He first trained as a medical doctor and now spends much time writing verse, fiction and in recent years, plays. In most of his writing he connects his readers (or his audience) to Singaporean contemporary scenes, ranging across social, cultural and political themes. Often the question of Singaporean identity is raised. Alfian is known for his portrayal of the subaltern voice—the voice of the marginalised, the minority voice. Alfian often writes of underprivileged Malays but does not criticise. While he takes the position of speaking for Malays, he also believes in self-criticism to promote self-help, a belief also held by Malay-Muslim community leaders in Singapore (especially those in the Islamic Religious Council (MUIS), MENDAKI and the Association of Muslims Professionals or AMP).

The voice of humanity in Alfian can be heard in his ability to point out what needs to be pointed out, which means going beyond race and embracing values beyond self-interest. Many of his critics think that he is a champion of Malay rights and uses every outlet to represent stories of the minority. Perhaps he is a champion writer of Malay rights in Singapore but in many of his works, he also satirises the pretense of his people. His short story 'Bugis' is a fine example in which he satirises Salmah, the 'tudung' woman, as one being more morally corrupt than her un-named tomboyish friend. Salmah is portrayed as someone who betrays her friendship and trust of her good friend in order to advance herself in the eyes of her boyfriend. The narrator friend sees through Salmah's pretense right from the very beginning:

> Salmah is wearing her tudung again.
>
> For those who don't know, the tudung is this scarf that good Muslim girls wear. People like Salmah just want to action, act like good girl; but later in school, she will meet her boyfriend, and hold hands with him. This wearing tudung also, I don't know who teach her or where she learn. Last month she never used to wear, her hair was always tied at the back with a red scrungee. She would often take it off to wear at her wrist, like a bracelet.
>
> Just one month and Salmah has found God.[16]

Alfian is not just self-critical of his own community but also of his nation. In many works, he speaks about the pretense of the nation, representing not only the Singaporean Malay voice, but also the voice of the silenced intellectuals of his nation. He has inspired others to react to his work, for example Felix Cheong, who dedicated one of his poems to Alfian in response to one poem in *One Fierce Hour* (1998), a work entitled 'Singapore You Are Not My Country':

> Singapore you are not my country.
> Singapore you are not a country at all.
> You are surprising Singapore, statistics-starved Singapore
> Soulful Singapore of tourist brochures in Japanese and hourglass kebayas
> You protest, but without pickering, without rioting, without Catherine Lim
> But through your loudspeaker media, through the hypnotic eyeballs of
> Your newscasters, and that weather woman who I swear is working voodoo

On my teevee screen.
Singapore, what are these lawsuits in my mailbox?
There are so many sheafs, I should have tipped the postman.
Singapore, I assert, you are not a country at all.
Do not raise your voice against me. I am not afraid of your anthem
Although the lyrics are still bleeding from the bark of my sapless
Heart
Not because I sang them pigtailed pinnafored breakfasted chalkshoed in
School
But because I used to watch telly till they ran out of shows.
Do not invite me to the podium and tell me to address you properly.
I am allergic to microphones and men in egosuits and pubicwigs.
And I am not a political martyr. I am a patriot who has lost his country
And virginity.
Do not wave a cane at me for vandalising your propaganda with
Technicolour harangues.
Red Nadim semen white Mahsuri menses the colourful language of my
Eloquent generation.
Your words are like walls on which truth is graffiti.
This has become an island of walls.
Asylum walls, factory walls, school walls, the walls of the midnight
Istana.
If I am paranoid I have learnt it from you, O my delicate orchid stalk
Singapore.
Always thirsty for water, spooked by armed archipelagoes, always gasping
For airspace, always running to keep ahead, running away from yourself.
Singapore why do you wail that way, demanding my IC?
Singapore stop yelling and calling me names.
How dare you call me a chauvinist, an opposition party, a liar, a
Traitor, a mendicant professor, a Marxist homosexual communist.
Pornograhy banned literature chewing gum liberty smuggler?
How can you say I do not believe in the free press autopsies flogging
Mudslinging bankruptcy which are the five pillars of Justice?
And how can you call yourself a country, you terrible hallucination of
highways and cranes and condominums ten minutes' drive from the
MRT? [17]

It is this long poem which has inspired Felix Cheong (poet, former television studio director of CNBC Asia, currently lecturer and freelance writer) to write 'The Obligatory Merlion Poem' (for Alfian) in *I Watch the Stars Go Out* (1999).[18] In his Zen-like poem, Cheong promotes the idea of accepting things as they are because no one has any control over the past or has the power to change innate human nature. Cheong asks:

> But what would you have done,
> given the freak of history
> and the quirk of circumstance,
> with this half-fucked city
> that was at once a meeting point
> and a point of contention?
>
> No name to call home,
> no home to our names—
> what would you have changed
> with hindsight and half a chance,
> to seize and size up our geography,
> herding a people into being? [19]

Part two of Cheong's poem offers a deeper understanding of Singapore as a nation explaining why Singapore has to be firm and brave in carrying out many of its policies (hence the lion section) and asking why its people are at the same time restless, having an urge to travel, to be as free as the fish element in the Merlion.[20] What is interesting in both poems is not just the ability of both poets to map Singapore and create a dialogue about a sense of home, but there is also another kind of dialogue, between two poets with different backgrounds. Both poems need to be read together to experience how the richness of one poem is enlarged by the other. Cheong makes no mention of race, hinting at everyone being equal (they are all people in transience—'No name to call home/no home to our names'). The idea of everyone having the migratory urgency to seek freedom also hints at the idea of the Malays in Singapore being regarded also as diasporic, just like other migrants to the island.

Where Malay image in writing in English in Singapore is concerned, Alfian's poem 'Autobiography' offers a fine example of a Malay home and Malay upbringing in the city-state of Singapore:

I didn't have radio-tuning parents
Who filled the house with music
Or instilled in me 'a love of the cinema'.
I never recalled my mother coming home
From the hairdressers' with a new hairdo
Or father teaching me fishing, or
Staying up to watch football on TV.
He did once bring a kite home but hung it
On my bedroom wall (he turned it into
A portrait, it wasn't his fault the wall
never became more of a sky)

Waking from a nap I would wander the rooms
To find mother copying cross-stitch designs
From a book or father watching a subtitled
Chinese re-runs. So I slept again, dreaming
Of playing toys away from the sunlight

When I awoke I was twenty, being asked
If I had a happy childhood. Yes, the one
We all have: filled to the brim
With the love of absent things[21]

In using autobiographical materials, Alfian manages to record the racial and class divides between those who have and those who have not, noting the economical, social and political divides that separate Chinese from Malays in Singapore). We should note a marked difference signalled by the writing of poems like these; given the experiences of earlier writers (like Nair/Tzu Peng), poets are no longer seen as threats to the political stability of the nation. The nation seems to have arrived.

There are other writers in Singapore who write of the Malay image, of race relations and of the need for inter-cultural communication: Gilbert Koh, Daren Shiau and Eddie Tay, most of them published by Ethos Books. As few women have been published by Ethos Books, it is difficult to record any women writers representing race issues. However, this does not mean that women are not writing at all. Alvin Pang, who was intimately involved in the founding of Ethos Books, has noted that established women writers like Catherine Lim, Leong Liew Geok, Lee Tzu Pheng or Claire Tham would have long signed up with other commercial publishers and hence have no need to switch to the newer (and smaller) presses. There are others who choose to be published abroad: Tan Hwee Hwee, Vyvyan Loh and Lau Siew Mei.[22] It is also a fact that Ethos Books has not been advertising for new manuscripts and the absence of new Singaporean women writers may reflect contemporary difficulties in finding publishing outlets.

Gilbert Koh's 'Train Ride to Singapore' is another poem which addresses racial and class differences in Malaysia. Koh was inspired by a story related to him by one of his friends, about racial discrimination in Malaysia where educational opportunities are concerned.[23] The Malaysian Chinese friend speaks of the fate of another Chinese friend who is poor and has done well in his university entrance exam but denied a place at the local university due to his race. Koh gives voice to this unjust phenomenon and empathises with the situation. The persona is that of a Malaysian Chinese on his way to study and work in Singapore where equal opportunities based on meritocracy are waiting for him, unlike the unfortunate Malaysian Chinese friend of his friend who has to stay back and work on his father's farm:

> The train pulled out slowly
> like a long sigh
> and I saw from my window
> how you stood alone at
> the station platform
> with hands in your pockets—
> you refused to wave
> but smiled a reluctant, sorry
> kind of goodbye.
>
> Five years ago we skipped
> the *bahasa melayu* class
> to play *chor dai di*
> in the dirty, deserted
> alley behind
> Ah Hin's coffeeshop,
> we talked about girls
> and about all the
> things we'd do
> when we were old enough
> to get a job or into
> university—

things were so much
simpler then.
Now we understand that
The colour of skin
Opens doors for some
In this country,
forever closes them
for others.
I'm going south
alone to chase a dream,
because I can,
you can't,
for this I'm sorry
and I really don't know
if I'm ever
coming back.

The image in this poem is of a Malay Malaysian being privileged because of his race ('the colour of skin') and what is hinted at here is the advantage of having an open system like Singapore's meritocracy policy in which rewards and positions are given only to those who earn them. However, Lily Zubaidah Rahim, in *The Singapore Dilemma* (1998), challenges this belief by citing findings made by Philip Brown (1990) on parentocracy, in which educational attainment and achievement are seen as determined by wealth rather than effort.[24] Children of rich parents have access to better schools—usually private ones—and are exposed to appropriate social skills and conduct as well as having the advantage of speaking and writing good English. Such background factors ensure them a place wherever they want to study. Lily is not convinced that this is appropriate for Malays in Singapore:

> Children from socially privileged backgrounds are thus equipped with the cultural capital to have a head start in deciphering the 'hidden curriculum' and general demands of school life. By contrast, those from socially disadvantaged family backgrounds are not adequately equipped to compete in the educational race with others who have had an educational head start. They are disadvantaged by having parents who are less adequately equipped with the cultural capital and material resources required for high academic achievement. Schools can thus be metaphorically viewed as a race between teams of pupils and parents who compete for the limited prizes.[25]

The situation of minorities in Singapore may be similar to Koh's view of minorities in Malaysia in his poem 'Train Ride to Singapore'.[26] However, this chapter is not about who deserves to get what and where to go to get more; it seeks to explore how Singaporean writers portray the Malay minority in their works. So far, such representations of Malays are motivated by the writers' sense of justice and human rights. It does not matter whose side they are on; their humanity is still intact. Destinations are not as important as the journeys they travel.

Writers like Daren Shiau and Eddie Tay demonstrate a spirit of openness and acceptance of the 'other'. Tay in *remnants* (2001) sees history as fragments of the whole truth and that the whole truth is always fictional. He looks back to historical sources when talking about Singapore as a nation. Using a post-colonial approach, he writes of British occupation in Singapore in the first part of *remnants*. In the second part of his work, he pays homage to his Chinese heritage through his readings of classical works of three Tang poets. Part three documents his 'asides', his comments and reflections of contemporary Singapore. Tay acknowledges the glorious past of the Malay rule when he includes the greatness of Seri Utama taking the enemy prisoner as mentioned in the Malay Annals. However, Tay believes that the way to move forward in Singapore is through making a spectacle of the ordinary; this he expresses in his poem 'ariel':

> For years I walked
> Among unreal figures, shuffled along corridors,
> made a tower of myself, to have arrived
> and discover I have been here, but worse,
> to find a dwarf capering in the mirror.
> So I learn to undo the grandeur, laugh at myself,
> and make a spectacle of the ordinary. This life
> needs no reward, no celebration, except a journey
> that shifts its rhythm, blends a scenery,
> and weaves a line with every emerging mood.[27]

Similarly, Tay's contemporary Daren Shiau acknowledges cultural difference which exists in Singapore. In his work 'Oral Tradition and the Wisdom in Numbers', he entertains his Malay friend's jest over Chinese obsession with wisdom of numbers. Instead of being offended or defensive of his Malay woman friend's disappointment at being sidelined at a big event (which is not the church reception) for not being able to offer the 'appropriate wedding gift money' which could either be S$168 (which means a single road of fortune to the newly weds) or S$88 (double luck), the poet wittily agrees to his friend's suggestion of offering

S$44 (4 is a bad luck number which means death) by juggling the numbers and bringing new meaning to the wedding gift money:

> how much do I give, Siti asked
> wedding *hongbaos*: it was difficult to tell
> '168', a single road of fortune; or double luck in '88'
> symbolizing the bride and groom
>
> she said,
> actually, that's too much for me
> i'm only invited to the church reception, you see –
> an old friend, she said it bitterly
>
> why not forty-four she jested
> yes, forty-four, I insisted
>
> you see: they add up auspiciously
> you will not bring less fortune, if you
> give this instead
>
> four plus four always equals eight[28]

What is apparent here is the portrayal of a Malay character as someone who is economically 'handicapped', limiting her access to social space (the big reception not at the church) despite her long friendship with the bride and groom. Whether Shiau intentionally writes of this scene as a social and political critique of minorities at risk in Singapore is not as important as the spontaneity of recording inter-racial relations in Singapore based on numerical superstition. His poem successfully portrays a genuine representation of inter-cultural communication between the races.

In a country like Singapore where the survival of a nation depends much on how well cultural diversities are managed, portrayals of the 'other' cannot be avoided. The poets mentioned in this chapter are writers sensitive enough to work out that the way to move forward as a nation is to connect with the past, present and the future. Whenever these writers speak, they speak for diversity, and it does not matter which side they are on; their humanity is still in text and intact.

Notes

1 Alfian Sa'at, *The Singapore Dilemma*. Accessed 1 July 2007 <http://www.freewebs.com/suaraanum/0401a03.htm> .
2 Yun-Ts'iao Hsu, 'Singapore in the Remote Past', Tan Sri Dato' Mubin Sheppard, ed., *Singapore 150 Years* (Singapore: Times Books International, 1953 [rep 1984])
3 Yun-Ts'iao Hsu, 'Singapore in the Remote Past' 1.
4 Yun-Ts'iao Hsu, 'Singapore in the Remote Past' 2.
5 T.S. Raffles, 'The Founding of Singapore', Tan Sri Dato' Mubin Sheppard, ed., *Singapore 150 Years* (Singapore: Times Books International, 1953 [rep 1984]) 89.
6 Raffles, 'The Founding of Singapore'117.
7 Raffles, 'The Founding of Singapore'117.
8 Raffles, 'The Founding of Singapore'118.
9 Raffles, 'The Founding of Singapore'118.
10 Hsien Loong Lee, 'Singapore of the Future', eds Arun Mahizhnan and Lee Tsao Yuen, *Singapore: Re-engineering Success* (Singapore: Oxford University Press, 1998).
11 Quoted in C.M. Turnbull, *A History of Singapore 18191988* (Singapore: Oxford University Press, 1989) 292.
12 Pao Kun Kuo, 'Contemplating an Open Culture: Transcending Multiracialism', eds Arun Mahizhnan and Lee Tsao Yuen, *Singapore: Re-engineering Success* (Singapore: Oxford University Press, 1998) 52.
13 Assessment for Malays in Singapore. Accessed July 1 2007. http://www.cidcm.umd.edu/mar/assessment.asp?groupID=83001#risk
14 Lily Zubaidah Rahim, *The Singapore Dilemma: The Political and Educational Marginality of the Malay Community* (New York: Oxford University Press, 1998).
15 Chandran Nair, 'Sincerity'. Homepage, accessed 3 June 2004. <http://www26.brinkster.com/chandrannair/poemsnallama.htm>.
16 Alfian Sa'at, 'Bugis', eds Dipika Mukherjee et al.,*The Merlion and the Hibiscus* (New Delhi: Penguin Books India, 2002) 1.
17 Alfian Sa'at, 'Singapore You Are Not My Country' in *One Fierce Hour* (Singapore: Landmark Books, 1998) 37–41
18 Felix Cheong, *I Watch the Stars Go Out* (Singapore: Ethos Books, 1999).
19 Cheong, *I Watch the Stars Go Out* 49–50.
20 Felix Cheong, 'Re:Felix Cheong'. E-mail to Nor Faridah Abdul Manaf. 20 May 2004.
21 Alfian Sa'at, 'Autobiography', eds Pang, Alvin and Aaron Lee, *No Other City: The Ethos Anthology of Urban Poetry* (Singapore: Ethos Books, 2000) 146.
22 Alvin Pang, 'Re:Fw:Felix Cheong', E-mail to Nor Faridah Abdul Manaf, 3 June 2004.
23 Gilbert Koh, 'Re:Fw:Spore poetry', E-mail to Nor Faridah Abdul Manaf, 23 April 2004.
24 Lily Zubaidah Rahim. *The Singapore Dilemma* 140–1.
25 Lily Zubaidah Rahim. *The Singapore Dilemma* 141.
26 Gilbert Koh, 'Train Ride to Singapore'.
27 Tay, *Remnants* 38.
28 Shiau, *Peninsular* 30–1.

Works cited

Alfian, Sa'at. 'Bugis'. Eds Dipika Mukherjee et al. *The Merlion and the Hibiscus*. New Delhi: Penguin Books India, 2002.

______ *One Fierce Hour*. Singapore: Landmark Books, 1998.

______ 'Autobiography'. Eds Pang, Alvin and Aaron Lee. *No Other City: The Ethos Anthology of Urban Poetry*. Singapore: Ethos Books, 2000.

______ The Singapore Dilemma. Accessed 1 July 2007 <http://www.freewebs.com/suaraanum/0401a03.htm>.

Bartley, W. 'The Population of Singapore in 1819'. Ed. Tan Sri Dato' Mubin Sheppard. *Singapore 150 Years*. Singapore: Times Books International, 1953 (rep 1984).

Cheong, Felix. *I Watch the Stars Go Out*. Singapore: Ethos Books, 1999.

Hsu, Yun-Ts'iao. 'Singapore in the Remote Past'. Ed. Tan Sri Dato' Mubin Sheppard. *Singapore 150 Years*. Singapore: Times Books International, 1953 (rep 1984).

Koh, Gilbert. 'Train Ride to Singapore'. Accessed 20 April 2004. <http://www.qlrs.com/issues/apr2002/poetry/trts.html>

Kuo, Pao Kun. 'Contemplating an Open Culture: Transcending Multiracialism'. Eds Arun Mahizhnan and Lee Tsao Yuen. *Singapore: Re-engineering Success*. Singapore: Oxford University Press, 1998.

Lee, Hsien Loong. 'Singapore of the Future'. Eds Arun Mahizhnan and Lee Tsao Yuen. *Singapore: Re-engineering Success*. Singapore: Oxford University Press, 1998.

Lily Zubaidah Rahim. *The Singapore Dilemma: The Political and Educational Marginality of the Malay Community*. New York: Oxford University Press, 1998.

Nair, Chandran. 'Sincerity'. Homepage. June 3 2004. http://www26.brinkster.com/chandrannair/poemsnallama.htm

Pang, Alvin and Aaron Lee (eds). *No Other City: The Ethos Anthology of Urban Poetry*. Singapore: Ethos Books, 2000.

Raffles, T.S. 'The Founding of Singapore'. Ed. Tan Sri Dato' Mubin Sheppard. *Singapore 150 Years*. Singapore: Times Books International, 1953 (rep 1984)

Sharma, Haresh. *Off Centre*. Singapore: Ethos Books, 2000.

______ 'Pillars'. Unpublished script by the Necessary Stage/Teater Kami, Singapore, 1997.

______ *This Chord and Others*. London: Minerva Press, 1999.

Shiau, Daren. *Peninsular*. Singapore: Ethos Books, 2000.

Skeat, W.W. & Ridley, H.N. 'The Orang Laut of Singapore'. Ed. Tan Sri Dato' Mubin Sheppard. *Singapore 150 Years*. Singapore: Times Books International, 1953 (rep 1984).

Tay, Eddie. *Remnants*. Singapore: Ethos Books, 2001.

Turnbull, C.M. *A History of Singapore 1819–1988*. Singapore: Oxford University Press, 1989.

Daring to Challenge the Status Quo: The Lateral Vision and Meandering Political Journey of Left Malay Nationalists from *Singapura*

LILY ZUBAIDAH RAHIM
UNIVERSITY OF SYDNEY

In the decades immediately preceding and following the Second World War, Singapore was a hot-bed of left-wing political activity. It was not coincidental that the staunchly anti-colonial Malay daily *Utusan Melayu* was founded in Singapore and left-wing organisations such as the Malay Nationalist Party and *Angkatan Pemuda Insaf* (API) attracted a sizeable following on the island. Singapore's cosmopolitan and highly politicised social environment produced visionary and progressive nationalists such as Said Zahari, Yusof Ishak and Samad Ismail. Inter alia, their vision for Malay and Malayan society extended beyond the narrow confines of ethnicity whilst maintaining their Malay nationalist sentiment. As socialists and social democrats of varying shades, they inevitably 'crossed swords' with British colonial authorities and the leadership of dominant political parties such as the United Malay National Organisation (UMNO) and the Peoples Action Party (PAP). As such, their political journey can be characterised by heady strides of political advancement, episodes of betrayal, periods of incarceration and shades of ideological contradiction.

As much of the mainstream historiography from both sides of the causeway tended to downplay or distort the ideals of radical Malay nationalists of this era, their contributions to Malayan, Malaysian and Singaporean society has been misunderstood and under-appreciated. This paper will attempt to re-examine the complex political visions of Said Zahari, Yusof Ishak, Aziz Ishak and Samad Ismail by analysing selected autobiographical and biographical texts. In this way, it is hoped that the paper will contribute towards illuminating their ideals and contradictions on issues pertaining to culture, colonialism, feudalism and social justice.

Singapore's geographic position at the very centre of the Malay World or *Nusantara* symbolises the pivotal role of the island not only as the economic and immigration hub, in the colonial and immediate post-colonial era, but also as the political and intellectual pulse of the region. Dating back to the formative years of British colonial rule, Singapore assumed the status of a religious, literary, theatrical and publishing centre in the Nusantara. Importantly, the island's stature as the regional intellectual hub was to a significant extent fuelled by its position as a major departure point for the Meccan pilgrimage. As such, many Muslims, particularly those from Indonesia, spent extended periods of time working on the island to save for their passage to Mecca or pay off their pilgrimage debts upon their return. Inevitably, some decided to make Singapore their home and did not return to Indonesia in a permanent sense.[1] Singapore's status as the hub for religious knowledge and activity in the Nusantara was buttressed further by the congregation of Islamic scholars on the island upon their return from their theological studies in the Middle East.

The organisational roots of modern Malay nationalism can also be traced to the 'European ruled Chinese city' of Singapore where the first Malay political organisation, *Kesatuan Melayu Singapura* (KMS, Singapore Malay Union) was formed in 1926.[2] In the British Straits Settlement of Singapore, where Malays were rapidly becoming a numerical minority with the steady influx of other Asian immigrants, the community was particularly vulnerable. Indeed, by 1860, the Chinese community had clearly outnumbered the Malay community in the region's colonial settler society. Malay insecurity was enhanced by the limited opportunities for social mobility and their declining socio-economic status. Most Malays held menial jobs as, for example, hired servants, peons, gardeners and security guards, and they were generally underlings of the dominant ethnic communities. In accordance with their declining socio-economic status, many Malays moved further away from the city in favour of the cheaper land on the outskirts of the island. There were only a miniscule number of successful Malay businesspeople such as Haji Embok Suloh, whose core business was centred on importing goods from Indonesia. Without doubt, the marginal status of Malays on the island spurred Eunos Abdullah, Tengku Abdul Kadir and Haji Embok Suloh to establish the KMS with a view to safeguarding the economic, educational and social interests of the Malays and represent the community's concerns to the colonial government.[3]

Motivated by political pragmatism, the largely English educated KMS leadership saw the colonial authorities as an effective ally in securing reforms to strengthen the socio-economic position of the Malays. In realising these ends, the KMS successfully lobbied the colonial authorities to establish a vocational institute for Malays in 1929 and secured 600 acres of land on the eastern outskirts of the city which was reserved for Malays. The KMS also founded a Muslim

Institute to assist poor Malays.[4] Just as importantly, leadership was successfully reclaimed from the Arab and Indian Muslim (Jawi Peranakan) communities by restricting membership of the KMS to Malays (*Melayu Jati*) and others indigenous to the Nusantara. The anti-Arab sentiment was likely to have been fuelled by the refusal of the Arab based organisation *Persekutuan Islam Singapura* (Muslim Federation of Singapore) to open its membership to Malays, reflecting a condescending attitude towards the poorer Malay community. Without doubt, their questionable claims of ancestry to the Prophet Mohammad, assumed religious knowledge, and expectation that Malays kiss the hand of a Syed as a mark of veneration, were sources of acute frustration to many within the Malay community.[5]

In upholding the *Melayu Jati* philosophy, a precursor to the ideology of *bumiputera*-ism later espoused by UMNO, the KMS leadership was also successful in advising the colonial authorities to appoint Malays, rather than Arabs or Indian Muslims, to represent the Malay community in the Legislative Council.[6] Before too long, other Malay Unions modelled on the KMS were established on the Peninsula with the expressed aim of representing Malay socio-economic and political interests. The ideology of bumiputera-ism thus emanates from the philosophy and concerns of the founding fathers of the KMS in promoting the interests of the marginalised *Melayu Jati* in Singapore.

The first Malay owned and managed nationalist newspaper, *Utusan Melayu*, was founded in 1939 by Yusof Ishak in Singapore. After a brief tenure at the Arab owned *Warta Malaya* in the mid-1930s, Yusof became disillusioned with the paper's commercial focus, and general lack of interest in nationalists struggles in the region.[7] Moreover, *Warta Malaya*'s neglect of issues concerning Malays and tendency to blame them for their socio-economic marginality convinced Yusof that a Malay language paper that was not only owned and managed by Malays but also dedicated to the future of the community was urgently needed. Fired up by this mission, Yusof worked tirelessly to raise funds from within the Malay community and realise his ambitious dream of founding a Malay daily. *Utusan Melayu*'s motto of upholding religion, people and country and a pledge, made in the maiden issue, that 'These three causes are what the *Utusan Melayu* stands for, and for these *Utusan Melayu* will live for and fight to the death for" reflected the Malay nationalist ideals of the paper's founder.[8]

Renowned for having nurtured a generation of radical Malay nationalists who played a pivotal role in raising the political consciousness of Malayans, the paper radicalised the nationalist struggle for independence and served as a training ground for future leaders, intellectuals and activists who played an important role in shaping the political destiny of Malaysia and Singapore. Suffice to say, their intellectual vision continues to shape and inform contemporary debates on nation-building in both states.

Here I shall focus on the complex political ideals and meandering political journeys of *Utusan Melayu* journalists and radical nationalists Said Zahari, Samad Ismail, Yusof Ishak and Aziz Ishak. In many respects, the complexity of their ideals, meandering nature of their political journey, rejection of feudalism, socialist leanings and association with leftist organisations across ethnic lines rendered them vulnerable to misrepresentation, political betrayal, character assassination and incarceration. Said Zahari was detained for seventeen years by the PAP government in Singapore while Samad Ismail was detained in 1946 and 1951 by the British authorities. In 1976, Samad was detained by the Malaysian government shortly after receiving the highest literary prize, the *Pejuang Sastera*. Having served in Tunku Abdul Rahman's Cabinet as a Minister for more than seven years, Aziz Ishak's detention without trial rocked both UMNO and the larger Malaysian political scene. By contrast, the founder of *Utusan Melayu* and Singapore's first Yang Di-Pertuan Negara and President, Yusof Ishak, has been commonly perceived as a political turncoat for 'turning his back' on the Malay nationalist struggle by ostensibly aligning with the Chinese-dominated PAP government in Singapore. His place in the history of Malaysian nationalism and role as the father of *Utusan Melayu* has been downplayed. I shall attempt to better understand their complex ideals and meandering political journey by analysing Said Zahari and Aziz Ishak's autobiographies, *Dark Clouds At Dawn: A Political Memoir* and *Special Guest*, Yusof Ishak's biography, *A Biography of President Yusof Bin Ishak* by Melanie Chew and Samad Ismail's anthological biography *A. Samad Ismail: Journalism and Politics* edited by Cheah Boon Kheng.[9]

Political autobiographies can be an effective means of better understanding the mind-set, motivation and actions particularly of unorthodox political actors 'ahead of their time'. While narratives from the 'horse's mouth' can serve as a potent means of dispelling myths and setting the record straight, they can also act as a textual vehicle for rationalising, glossing over and sanitising past errors in political judgment. It is thus crucially important for the researcher to sensitively discern fact from fiction and 'fact-ion' (a combination of fact and fiction). This process of deciphering can be assisted by placing the narrative within broader historical, social, political and economic environments.

Similar challenges are also inherent in political biographies that have been commissioned by governments to promote a preferred national historiography and identity. Indeed, Melanie Chew's attempts at drawing a strong correlation between Yusof Ishak's worldview and his Minangkabau ancestral heritage reveal a distinct tendency to project culture and identity in essentialist terms.

This approach bears marked similarities to the PAP government's culturalist discourse widely promoted in the 1980s and 1990s.[10] Moreover, Lee Kuan Yew's complex political relationship with Yusof Ishak appears to have been sanitised of its instrumentalist political motives and opportunism. Having convincingly portrayed the spirit of the youthful and academic high-achieving Yusof at Raffles Institution, his burning idealism that led to his founding of *Utusan Melayu* and subsequent frustrations with the Alliance leadership on issues related to press freedom, Chew's grasp of the political thinking of post-*Utusan Melayu* Yusof in Singapore is disappointing. Mirroring the PAP leadership's political rhetoric about the boundless opportunities in immigrant and supposedly meritocratic Singapore, Chew writes: 'We are, in the main, immigrants, as Yusof Ishak was himself, an immigrant. But his life tells us that in this country, we can come from nowhere, and prove ourselves worthy'.[11] Yusof's post-Utusan years are arguably the most complicated, misunderstood and contradictory aspects of his political journey. This period represents a major lacunae in the history of Singapore and Malaysia and this aspect of historical recovery or rediscovery awaits future research.

Political biographies such as Cheah Boon Kheng's insightful edited volume on Samad Ismail has contributed much towards understanding his complex and chequered political journey. The varied but complimentary chapters have served as jig-saw puzzles in piecing together Samad's colourful political life, enormous contributions to journalism and the dilemmas confronting left nationalists at that tumultuous juncture in Malayan history. Notwithstanding the penetrating insights of the various chapters in the book, the reader is left with as many unanswered as answered questions. Unanswered questions relate to Samad's 'break' with the PAP, the machinations behind his 'exile' to Jakarta and the sinister manoeuvring within UMNO and the PAP that culminated in his third detention in 1976. My intention in this chapter is to shed some light on these political intrigues.

Anak Melayu Modern di-Singapura

Multiracial consciousness

Despite the British 'divide and rule' approach of encouraging the various ethnic communities to live in separate residential enclaves, form separate social organisations and accept the ethnic based economic division of labour, the highly cosmopolitan and modernising dynamic of the island contributed to inter-ethnic interactions which extended beyond the boundaries of the Furnivallian plural society, where the various ethnic communities were supposed to 'mix but ... not combine'.[12] In particular, many working-class Malays and Chinese living and working in close proximity in Singapore's frontier-like society forged relationships that were both functional and social. Recounting his grandparents' close friendship with a Hailamese couple, who also worked as servants for the same European employer and shared many Saturday nights playing card games, Said Zahari wrote:

> All members of the group had the same background of poverty and hardship. Essentially, it was this that bound them together in warm and sincere friendship, despite differences in race, language, culture and religion.[13]

Said's childhood experiences in the predominantly Malay village of Kampung Kebun Bunga in Singapore demonstrates the way in which commercial relations between the ethnic communities often extended into social relations of trust and friendship. Apek, the Chinese night soil carrier and hawker of vegetables and seafood by day, was also a trusted and integral member of the Kampung Kebun Bunga community:

> The villagers never tried to bargain down the prices set by Apek. They just paid, deeming his prices reasonable because they trusted him implicitly. And when some housewives did not have enough money to pay him immediately, they could still get the vegetables and fish they wanted. They would pay him the next day.[14]

Apek's son Ah Thong was also very much in his element playing with Said and the other Malay children while his father hawked his foodstuffs in the village.

The close inter-ethnic interactions between students in English medium schools reflected and reinforced the island's cosmopolitan and multiracial complexion. This cosmopolitism was embedded in the youthful experiences of Yusof Ishak and Aziz Ishak, who were educated at Victoria Bridge School and then at the prestigious Raffles Institution for their secondary education. Both excelled at their academic studies and were actively involved in sporting and extra-curricular activities. Without doubt, they were acutely aware that their academic prowess and social standing had the powerful effect of proving to their non-Malay colleagues that Malays could be as academically competent as non-Malays, thereby dispelling the pervasive and unflattering stereotypical colonial myths about Malays.[15] Indeed, the consciousness that their personal performance would have wider ramifications undoubtedly prompted them to strive towards excellence in their academic endeavours. The fusing of the personal with the political and setting ambitious standards and goals for themselves continued well after their youthful endeavours in Singapore and goes some way towards explaining their myriad achievements later in life.

Yusof's leadership and social skills in the multi-ethnic school setting were identified and developed by his appointment as school prefect. His intellectual prowess was demonstrated by attaining distinctions in his Senior Cambridge examinations and entry into the exclusive Queens Scholarship class at Raffles Institution. His flair for critical analysis and lateral intellect were nurtured during his tenure as co-editor of the school paper *Rafflesian*. He excelled in the National Cadet Corp (NCC) and was the first student in the NCC to be made an officer with the rank of Second Lieutenant. A gifted sportsman, Yusof participated in various sporting activities and became Lightweight Boxing Champion in 1932.[16] Acknowledging the social benefits of his education in the multi-ethnic Raffles Institution, Yusof was to note in the 1960s:

> It was in Raffles Institution well over 30 years ago that I first began to be associated with non-Malay boys ... It might be said that I had unconsciously become, at a very early age, first a Malayan and second a Malay ...[17]

Paralleling the experiences of Yusof Ishak and Aziz Ishak, Samad Ismail's English medium education at Victoria Institution moulded a mind-set that was comfortable in both Malay and non-Malay social settings. Demonstrating the importance of intellectual compatibility in the forging of meaningful friendship, Samad's closest friend throughout his schools years at Victoria Institution was Devan Nair, Singapore's future trade union czar, President and finally political exile. Their interlocking intellectual journey continued well after their formal education when both became actively engaged in left-wing political activity and were detained by the colonial authorities at St. John's Island in 1951. Like incorrigible recalcitrants emboldened and radicalised even further by their detention, upon their release in 1953 they flung themselves even further into the clutches of left-wing activism. It was during this time that they helped to establish the Peoples Action Party (PAP) by providing it with the left-wing trade-union and mass-base support it needed to convincingly win the 1959 elections and form government.

Elaborating on the close friendship between Samad and Devan, Samad's wife Hamidah Hassan wrote:

> A. Samad Ismail was very close to Devan Nair ... helped Nair get married, and when Nair was detained a second time, A. Samad Ismail contributed financially to help Nair's family tide over their problems.[18]

In the 1955 elections in Singapore, Samad mobilised resources of the *Utusan Melayu* to support Devan Nair's electoral campaign as a PAP candidate in Farrer Park.[19] Samad's personal experience of forging meaningful friendships with leftists across ethnic lines led him to believe that ethnic tensions between the

Chinese and Malays was a consequence of colonial policies and encouraged by other parties with an interest in keeping the ethnic communities apart.[20]

One of the positive experiences of the Japanese Occupation years for the youthful Said Zahari was his successful admission into the selective Japanese Teachers Training College (*Sihan Gakko*). Of the 100 youthful multi-ethnic applicants who sat for the entrance examination, Said was one of the twenty that was selected. Having performed well in his earlier studies at Tanglin Tinggi Malay School where he was selected as a teacher trainee, Said's successful enrolment into Sihan Gakko and exposure to non-Malays in a formal educational setting was to hold him in good stead for the hurly-burly of left-wing politics in cosmopolitan post-war Singapore and Malaysia.[21] Just as importantly, Said's entry into the competitive Sihan Gakko is likely to have engendered a consciousness and self-confidence that he was the intellectual equal of any other non-Malay.

Distilling republican and anti-colonialism sentiments

Well before Yusof and Aziz Ishak had been ideologically exposed to republican ideas, their early experience of rejection from the prestigious Malay College at Kuala Kangsa, presumably due to their non-aristocratic family background, had a profound impact on their perception of feudalism. The experience of rejection from the Malay College contributed to their perception of feudalism as inherently unjust and a hindrance to the development of Malay society. This perception was reinforced by their academic achievements at the highly competitive Raffles Institution. Yusof's inability to study law in England, after narrowly missing out on the prestigious Queen's Scholarship, reinforced his view that the colonial government did little to assist *rakyat* like himself to further themselves whilst entrenching the feudal privileges of the Malay aristocracy.

Denied the opportunity of fulfilling his childhood ambition of studying law, Yusof accepted a position at the Police Academy in Kuala Lumpur. This tenure did not last long as he was dismissed after reprimanding a member of the royal family, employed at the Police Academy, for mistreating his servant. Yusof returned to Singapore even more contemptuous of the retarding effects of feudalism and colonialism on Malayan society.[22]

The anti-feudal mentality of brothers Yusof and Aziz was echoed in print during their tenure with the *Utusan Melayu*. In the paper's monthly journal *Mastika* in the late 1940s, Aziz was to provocatively pronounce that neither Tunku Abdul Rahman nor Datuk Onn would be able to truly achieve independence for the *raayat* because of their aristocratic background.[23]

Yusof's disdain for feudalism strengthened further when as Singapore's Head of State (Yang Di-Pertuan Negara), he was treated with disrespect by the other royal Heads of State at the Conference of Rulers, presumably because of his *rakyat* origins. Moreover, he was acutely conscious of the fact that in terms of protocol at the Rulers Conference, he was consistently accorded the lowest rank, given the least important seat on the extreme left and subjected to the usage of royal terminology such as *patik* (I) and *hamba* (slave).[24] For Yusof, the colonial collusion and manipulation of Malay feudalism was starkly illustrated by the higher protocol accorded to the European Governors of Penang and Malacca over him.

In contrast to Yusof and Aziz, Said Zahari's and Samad Ismail's limited regard for the feudal system in Malay society and enthusiasm for republicanism can be attributed to their humble Javanese migrant family background, strongly Javanese social environment within the Malay community in Singapore and support for the nationalist struggles for independence in Indonesia. Indeed Samad's wife Hamidah Hassan has observed that whilst growing up in the Javanese dominated Kampung Melayu in Singapore, Samad 'was more Javanese than Melayu during those days'. He was brought up on the Javanese *Bangsawan* classics and folk-lore by his parents, joined a *Keronchong* band in his youth and believed in Javanese superstition despite his progressive left politics.[25]

Samad's republicanism was nurtured when in his capacity as assistant editor of *Berita Malai* during the Japanese Occupation, he befriended radical Malay nationalists such as Ibrahim Yaacob, Ishak Haji Mohamad, Dr Burhanuddin Helmi and Ahmad Boestamam and supported their republican *Indonesia Raya* ideal. This ideal advocated the political union between the colonial territories of the Dutch Indies and British Malaya.[26] So committed was Samad to the Indonesian anti-colonial nationalist struggle that he assisted Indonesian nationalists in Singapore to smuggle arms and foodstuffs to Indonesia.[27] He also passed reports to Indonesian nationalists and acted as a part-time correspondent of the Indonesian *Antara* news agency from the *Utusan Melayu* office. As Antara's correspondent, Samad developed friendships with future Indonesian post-colonial leaders such as Sutan Shahrir, Agoes Salim, A.K. Ghani and Adam Malik.[28]

Under the influence of Samad's guiding hand, *Utusan Melayu* by the mid-1940s no longer referred to Indonesian nationalist fighters as *pengganis* (terrorists) and gave wide coverage to the Indonesian struggle for independence.[29] To be sure, the paper's support for the Indonesian nationalist struggle reflected the attitude of the wider Malay community in Singapore. Recalling the pro-Indonesian nationalist stance of many Singaporean Malays and the propensity of Malay customs and immigration officers to be lax about the entry of Indonesians without legal documentation into the island, Suryono Darusman wrote: 'It was as if the Indonesian struggle for independence brought out feelings of confidence in the eventual realization of their own national aspirations in the future'.[30]

Despite *Utusan Melayu*'s leading position in the nationalist movement for independence after the Second World War, Yusof and Samad decided to take the paper's anti-colonial stance to an even higher gear. Illustrative of this radical turn, Yusof Ishak boldly but perceptively predicted in an *Utusan Melayu* article in 1948 that Malaya would attain independence within ten years.[31] This lurch to the left was roundly endorsed by *Utusan Melayu*'s left-oriented journalists who were not only actively involved in left organisations and political parties like the Malay Nationalist Party, but some, like Dahari Ali, had also fought in the Indonesian War of Independence.[32] *Utusan Melayu*'s anti-colonial stance struck a chord with the public as evidenced by the dramatic increase in the paper's circulation in the late 1940s. By 1957, its circulation had sky-rocketed to 40,000 from 6,000 in 1948, heralding *Utusan Melayu* as the highest circulating Malay newspaper in the British colony.[33]

To be sure, *Utusan Melayu*'s popularity with the Malay masses stemmed from its acute sensitivity to the difficulties confronting both urban and rural Malays. The large network of *Utusan Melayu* reporters and stringers throughout Malaya and the Straits Settlements ensured that the paper was 'on the pulse' of the masses.[34] Through *Utusan Melayu* the cutting edge debates in Singapore were transmitted to the Peninsula and debates on the Peninsula were relayed back to Singapore.[35] The paper's human interest stories, which highlighted the plight of the poor and destitute, were well-received by the public and invoked generous donations, culminating in the establishment of a special fund for the poor called *Tabung Penderitaan*.[36] Suffice it to say, *Utusan Melayu* had captured the imagination of the community and achieved its core objective of giving voice to the Malay *rakyat* and progressive nationalist forces within the wider society. Recalling his youthful veneration for the paper which reflected the robust community support for it, Said Zahari wrote:

> I looked on the *Utusan Melayu* as the voice of the Malays, the newspaper that was fighting for my people who had been colonized for centuries. To work for the *Utusan Melayu* at that time was to work for my people and my country.[37]

Utusan Melayu's tilt to the left was dealt a blow with the detention of its Deputy Editor, Samad Ismail, from1951-1953, together with Abdullah Majid, James Puthucheary, Devan Niar and P.V. Sharma, for their supposed involvement in the Singapore Anti-British League, allegedly linked to the Malayan Communist Party. *Utusan Melayu* was branded by the colonial authorities as a troublesome 'pink' paper, and its journalists were placed under surveillance by Special Branch; the paper was banned from military camps, police departments and other arms of the colonial state largely manned by Malays.[38] Much to the annoyance of the colonial authorities, the paper became even more staunchly anti-colonial when Samad resumed his position at *Utusan Melayu* upon his release from detention in 1953. By then, *Utusan Melayu* began to devote much coverage to anti-colonial struggles in the region and around the world.[39] The paper's insights into anti-colonial struggles and guerrilla warfare were no doubt sharpened by the brief assignments of its journalists to war-torn Indonesia, Vietnam, Laos and Cambodia.[40]

An illustration of *Utusan Melayu*'s bolstered confidence in confronting the colonial government was the fracas over the British High Commissioner Gerald Templer's abuse of Aziz Ishak because of his less than deferential coverage of Queen Elizabeth's coronation in 1953. Templer's denunciation of Aziz as a 'cowardly rat' was splashed on the front pages of *Utusan Melayu*, enhancing further the anti-colonial profile of the paper for daring to directly take on the High Commissioner. This incident served as a turning point in Aziz's political career as he henceforth 'became a minor hero among the people, particularly among UMNO members'.[41] In less than two years Aziz was to become a Cabinet Minister in the Alliance government.

Nerve-centre of the intellectual left

In many respects, *Utusan Melayu*'s reputation as the premier anti-colonial newspaper contributed to its role as the nerve-centre of both the Malay and non-Malay nationalist movement in the 1940s and 1950s.[42] In particular, the paper's insightful stories and analysis of the plight of rural and urban Malays from a historical and political economy perspective raised the consciousness of non-Malay left intellectuals. R. Rajakumar, a former leader of the University of Malaya Socialist Club, recalled that it was fashionable for left intellectuals to identify themselves with the Malay peasantry:

> They spoke to each other in English about the need to have Malay as the common language and exploded with rage at the fashionable explanation for poverty that the Malay peasants were lazy. In 1954, the Chinese students under left-wing leadership made a resolution demanding that Malay should take the place of English in their schools ... Chinese intellectuals spoke of the responsibility of the Chinese working-class to fight for the oppressed Malay peasants.[43]

Without doubt, *Utusan Melayu*'s nerve-centre role can be strongly attributed to the tireless political activities and the intellectual magnetism of the paper's Deputy Editor Samad Ismail. Political activists, student leaders, trade unionists and politicians, literary and cultural figures and educationalists congregated at the *Utusan Melayu* office to discuss politics with the doyen of the left, Samad

Ismail. They included Lee Kuan Yew, Lim Chin Siong, UMNO leaders such as Jaafar Albar and Hamid Jumat and Dr Burhanuddin al-Helmy.[44] Samad Ismail brought Malay writers into contact with non-Malay writers from the University of Malaya where literary discussions of a political tone were conducted in bazaar Malay and local English. Samad can also be credited for introducing Malay writing to a larger audience through articles he penned for the *Singapore Standard* and the formidable Malay translations of Tolstoy, Checkov and Alberto Moravia in *Utusan Melayu*'s monthly journal *Mastika.*[45] Samad's extensive contacts with the left coupled with *Utusan Melayu*'s anti-colonial credentials allowed the paper's reporters easy access to student leaders, trade unionists and others from the left. At the height of the Chinese middle-school agitation and the Hock Lee Bus workers riots, *Utusan Melayu* reporters were the only ones to be accorded access to the protesting students and workers.[46]

Lee Kuan Yew and the PAP leadership owe Samad Ismail a debt of gratitude for assisting the fledgling party to forge links with the Chinese and Malay left in Singapore. Samad and Devan Nair were some of the founders of the PAP in 1954. In its formative years, the PAP relied heavily on Samad, Devan and Lim Chin Siong to procure the mass support required for the 1955 and 1959 elections. Until his departure from the PAP in 1956, Samad was a major recruiter of Malays into the party, with numerous *Utusan Melayu* journalists such as Samani Mohamad Amin among the first Malay members of the PAP.[47]

The End of an Era—Samad's Departure from *Utusan Melayu*, Yusof's Return to Singapore

In many respects, *Utusan Melayu*'s success and dynamism can be attributed to the partnership between its visionary founder Yusof Ishak and the intellectual dynamo Samad Ismail. Notwithstanding their markedly dissimilar temperaments, they were obsessively committed to ensuring that the paper played a pivotal role in charting the course of Malaya's political destiny. Both were immensely proud of the fact that *Utusan Melayu* was nurtured on the sweat and tears of the Malays. Ali Salim has aptly captured this synergistic partnership in the following way:

> While Yusof could be aloof and temperamental, Samad was more sociable and affable...Samad Ismail absorbed shocks and pressures like a sponge absorbs water. Yusof became excited in difficult situations. Samad's brain ticked like a well-oiled clock in crisis ... For Yusof Ishak, the world revolved round *Utusan Melayu*. A. Samad Ismail looked beyond the *Utusan Melayu*, the world was his stage.[48]

Sadly, this dynamic partnership came to an abrupt end when Samad was re-assigned to Jakarta as *Utusan Melayu*'s correspondent in 1957 after working in *Utusan Melayu* since the paper's inception in 1939. The political machinations behind Yusof's decision in re-assigning Samad to Jakarta remain shrouded in mystery, perplexing even Samad's wife Hamidah Hassan who acknowledged that 'both were almost like twins. Then suddenly, they separated. Even today, he has not told us the full story ...'[49] There are several plausible explanations for Samad's mysterious 'exile' to Jakarta. The most straightforward explanation was advanced by Yusof when explaining to the *Utusan Melayu* staff that Samad had to be sent to Jakarta before the paper moved its headquarters to Kuala Lumpur because the Alliance government would not renew the paper's printing license with Samad still in a senior position.[50] Endorsing this perspective, Melanie Chew asserts that Tunku was supposed to have written a note to Aziz Ishak, then a Minister in the Federal cabinet, asking for Samad to be removed as Deputy Editor.[51] Coupled with Tunku's well known dislike for Samad's left-wing political views and activities and the deep-seated suspicions held by the British colonial authorities about Samad's influence on left-wing activists and trade-unionists, this explanation is likely to have been grudgingly accepted by many of the *Utusan Melayu* staff.[52] Also to be considered is Hamidah Hassan's proposition that Samad's transfer to Jakarta may be partly attributed to a clash of egos arising from Yusof's growing uneasiness over Samad's rising stature in *Utusan Melayu*:

> Consciously or unconsciously, A Samad Ismail began to overshadow his boss as the number one man, and finally, A. Samad Ismail had to pay the price for relegating Yusof into the shadows.[53]

Another convincing explanation which includes Lee Kuan Yew in the behind-the-scenes manoeuvring, and augments rather than contradicts the earlier perspectives, is purported by Said Zahari. According to his perspective, the PAP leadership were determined to win government in the 1959 elections but did not want Samad in Singapore before or after the elections. Samad had already left the PAP but was still a major political force within left-circles and the Malay community. Lee was aware that Samad's contempt for him was well known, with Samad pronouncing that Lee would one day be revealed as the 'number one enemy of the people'.[54] As such, his presence in Singapore was potentially a major hindrance to the PAP's goal of winning the 1959 elections.

The animosity between the two was intensified when Samad joined Berita Harian of the *Straits Times* Press Group in 1958 and accepted the Chairmanship of Singapore UMNO. Explaining Lee's rancour at Samad's acceptance to head Singapore UMNO, Chew stated that he 'regarded it as a defection, a betrayal of the PAP and a personal betrayal'.[55] Lee's fear that Samad's political skills would allow him to influence public opinion and the UMNO leadership against the PAP's goal of merging with the larger Federation goes some way towards explaining his determination to try and short-circuit Samad's journalistic career at Berita Harian.[56] In a series of public talks entitled 'The Battle for Merger' in 1961, Lee alleged that Samad (using the code name Zainal) had informed him in the early 1950s that he was a communist and connected with the Malayan Communist Party.[57] Lee's determination to crush Samad has been confirmed by A. C. Simmons, General Manager of the *Straits Times* Press in KL, that he was under pressure by 'certain Singaporeans' to sack Samad from Berita Harian.[58] The proposition that Lee had instigated Yusof Ishak to remove Samad from both the Singaporean and Malayan political arena is supported by Samad's own investigations into the matter. When Samad made enquiries to Jaafar Albar about whether Tunku or other UMNO leaders had pressured Yusof into preventing Samad from moving to the paper's new headquarters in KL, Jaafar apparently stated that he did not believe that Tunku did not want him in KL.[59]

To some extent, the dynamism and direction of *Utusan Melayu* began to lose momentum after Samad was exiled to Jakarta in 1957 and finally left the paper in 1958. Yusof had lost his sounding board and right-hand man who had insider links to UMNO leadership and was adept in dealings with them. While *Utusan Melayu*'s anti-establishment views were supported by the UMNO leadership before *Merdeka* (political independence) in 1957, criticism from the press was barely tolerated after *Merdeka*. Commenting on this irony, Aziz Ishak, former *Utusan Melayu* journalist and Cabinet Member during this period, noted:

> On the whole, in respect of freedom of the press, my late brother agreed with me that we had much more freedom in the editorial column in the days before Merdeka. Before Merdeka, *Utusan Melayu* not only co-operated with the Alliance by projecting its policy but also spearheaded the attack on British exploitation of the country and the people ... But on achieving Merdeka, the Alliance leaders were intolerant of fair comments and criticism by the *Utusan Melayu* and later the press generally.[60]

Politically disillusioned and emotionally exhausted by unrelenting pressure from the UMNO leadership which culminated in a 1959 directive from Tunku effectively demanding an end to *Utusan Melayu*'s editorial independence, Yusof decided to sell off his equity in the paper to Tunku and return to Singapore.[61] Confiding to Said Zahari about his lack of will in continuing the struggle to safeguard press freedom, Yusof declared 'I can't take it any more, Said. It's too much ... Enough is enough ... I am past fifty now. I no longer have the strength to fight this blight'.[62]

Yusof's departure signalled the impending demise of an independent *Utusan Melayu* and the end of an era in Malay journalism. Yet, would the story have ended differently if Samad was still with the paper? Would Yusof have been able to negotiate more effectively with the UMNO leadership with Samad's assistance? Just as importantly, to what extent was Yusof's decision to sell off his equity and move back to Singapore influenced by Lee Kuan Yew? As *Utusan Melayu*'s long serving legal adviser who had been privy to many of Yusof's heated discussions with UMNO leaders, Lee was acutely aware of the pressures that Yusof had sustained.[63] Furthermore, in anticipation of merger, the PAP government would eventually have to appoint an appropriate person for the position of Yang Di-Pertuan Negara. To be sure, there would not have been a more appropriate person for the job than Yusof. Indeed, shortly after Yusof's return to Singapore, he was appointed Chairman of the Public Service Commission, became Yang Di-Pertuan Negara in 1963 and President of the Republic of Singapore in 1965.

Yusof Ishak's successor as *Utusan Melayu*'s Editor-in-Chief, Said Zahari, remained just as defiantly committed towards maintaining the paper's editorial freedom and upholding its original aims of serving religion, people and country.[64] The paper gave wide coverage to social issues such as the struggle of landless farmers from Sungai Sirih in Kuala Selangor who decided to work on state land after tiring of waiting for land from the government. Prominence was also accorded to allegations that bureaucrats maintained a colonial mentality in dealing with farmers.[65] In particular, the paper's sympathetic stance towards the anti-colonial struggles in Asia and Africa and criticism of US and Western military interventions around the world irritated the Alliance leadership due in no small measure to their pro-Western foreign policy orientation. The paper criticised the Malayan government for not supporting Indonesia's claims on West Irian particularly after the Malayan delegate abstained from voting on the issue in the United Nations. The murder of Congo leader Patrice Lamumba by Belgian colonial agents was roundly condemned in an editorial urging the government to expel the Belgian ambassador from Malaya.[66]

The Malayan government finally decided to put an end to *Utusan Melayu*'s editorial independence by demanding that the paper cover the activities of Alliance Ministers and support policy statements of the government in mid-1961. Rejecting these demands on the grounds of defending the principle of press freedom, *Utusan Melayu* workers and the Printing Workers Union went on a strike which lasted for six months (from July to October 1961).[67] This strike is historically significant as Malays, prior to this episode, were not known for their involvement in labour struggles, commonly associated with Indians and Chinese workers. Importantly, the strike was not over material or working conditions but about the principle of safeguarding press freedom.[68] Without doubt, the strike was severely undermined when Said was refused re-entry into Malaya after visiting striking *Utusan Melayu* workers in Singapore. The ban on Said was only lifted by the Malaysia government in May 1989.

Not willing to jeopardise the proposed merger of Singapore into the Federation, the PAP leadership were reluctant to support the *Utusan Melayu* strikers. However, Lee did issue a public statement expressing 'sympathy' for Said and held out vague assurances that his government would help resolve Said's problems with the Tunku shortly after the order was issued prohibiting his re-entry into Malaya.[69] The PAP leadership's hands-off approach towards the strike was clearly demonstrated by the failure of Devan Nair as leader of the trade union movement in Singapore to support the *Utusan Melayu* strikers in Singapore even though they belonged to the Singapore Printing Workers Union. Said also failed in getting Lee to stop Othman Wok, then senior *Utusan Melayu* executive in Singapore and known PAP supporter, from undermining the strike. Recollecting his disillusionment with the PAP leadership, Said wrote:

> ... I failed to get the hoped for co-operation from the PAP leaders, the 'pro-worker socialist' party! ... This was a let down to the *Utusan Melayu* Strike Action Committee in Kuala Lumpur and to all the workers on strike in Kuala Lumpur and Singapore.[70]

The only support for the beleaguered strikers came from left-wing trade unionists, students and political activists. Without doubt, the whole episode was a major political turning point for Said, precipitating his direct involvement into the rough-and-tumble of left-wing party politics, and eventually the leadership of Partai Rakyat Singapura (Peoples Party of Singapore).

Although Said had received ongoing overtures to join the PAP and the Barisan Socialis, he decided to throw his lot in with the Partai Rakyat Singapura in the belief that it was the only party with the potential to unite Malays whilst working with other left parties in Singapore in striving towards the independence of Malaya and Singapore.[71] Of particular anxiety to the PAP leadership was the likelihood that Said's credible reputation would have rendered PRS electorally attractive to many Malays, who Said believed were not particularly attracted to the PAP and tended to be 'sitting on the fence'.[72] Failure to attract more Malay support for the PAP would have been potentially disastrous for the party as its political footing was already made precarious by the mass defection of left-wing elements from the PAP to form the Barisan Socialis in 1961. By then, the PAP maintained only a razor thin majority in the legislature and was perpetually deluged by opposition party sponsored motions of no-confidence against the

PAP government. Acknowledging the imperative of merger in the face of its cliff-hanger position, former PAP stalwart Toh Chin Chye noted: 'So the [PAP] government was on the verge of being toppled! We had to hang on grimly, until merger took place'.[73] To add to the PAP's sense of siege, the leadership would have also felt threatened by Said's plan for PRS to 'look for points of political agreement with UMNO and the PMS (Peninsula Malay Union), two right-wing political parties, to unite the Malays in Singapore …' and ambitions to 'represent the Malays of Singapore in negotiations on the future of the country with the other political parties and with the British colonial authorities'.[74]

Said's bold plan of transforming the PRS into a potent political force was short-circuited by his detention less than six hours after he had accepted the leadership of PRS on the night of 1 February1963. He was detained together with Barisan Socialis leaders and more than 100 left-wing political activists in a joint assault undertaken by the PAP and Alliance government in cooperation with the British authorities, in an operation code named Operation Cold Store (OCS). Benefiting from OCS's paving the way for Singapore's merger into the Federation and exploiting the near decimation of the left-wing opposition parties, the PAP leadership opportunistically held general elections shortly after the merger in September 1963. Revealing a mercenary zero-sum attitude that was willing to crush the already fractured political opposition, three successful Barisan Socialis candidates, including Chia Thye Poh, were arrested under detention without trial laws.

Initially accused of being a leading member of the communist united front, then an agent of a foreign power, Said was subsequently denounced as a communist by the PAP leadership.[75] This final allegation served to justify his incarceration without trial for seventeen years. Ironically, his fate would have been markedly different if he had accepted the overtures to join the PAP. Said, together with Chia Thye Poh, who was detained for twenty-seven years, remain the longest serving political prisoners in Singapore.

Aziz Ishak's Fall from Grace

> '…an injustice to one is an injustice to all … If we allow ourselves to become afraid of truth then the time will come when we will bitterly regret our indifference'.[76]

Aziz Ishak's tumultuous tenure as a Cabinet Minister for more than seven years (1955–1963), followed by an equally heady period within the ranks of the political opposition and incarceration (from 1964 to his unconditional release in 1971), in many ways captures the contradictions and paradoxes of Tunku's Alliance government and the different conceptions of independence within the Malay nationalist movement. His ability to reach the highest offices of government despite an overtly left-wing nationalist and socialist orientation is indicative of the many ideological streams within UMNO during this period. Indeed, Tunku was known to make light-heated banter about Aziz being the socialist representative in his Cabinet.[77]

Appointed as Minister of Agriculture in 1955, Aziz took up this challenge with enthusiastic gusto and resolved to initiate reforms within the rural economy that would improve the socio-economic conditions of the majority of Malays who were then rural dwellers. His belief that Malaya had not attained complete sovereignty because economic independence had not been achieved was espoused in a 1959 parliamentary speech which advocated the imperative of striving towards achieving economic, scientific and technological independence.[78] Aziz's popularity within the bureaucracy was not bolstered by his allegation that many government officers in rural areas had maintained a 'colonial mentality' in dealing with farmers.[79] Dictated by the ideals of restructuring the country's political economy and changing the colonial mind-set, Aziz initiated a range of agricultural reforms which put him at logger-heads with his Cabinet colleagues and vested interests that had long benefited from the economic and political status quo.

The policy initiative that was to contribute to his eventual resignation from the Cabinet was the establishment of a Urea Fertilizer Plant which would provide low cost fertilizer to farmers. Despite the plan being fully endorsed by the UN's Food and Agriculture Organization (FAO) experts and popular with farmers and the wider public, Tunku refused to endorse it. Not surprisingly, Western diplomats also criticised the plan for its socialist tilt.[80] Armed with data from the British multinational Imperial Chemical Industries (ICI), who had been supplying the bulk of fertilizers to Malaya, Tunku criticised the plan at the UMNO Annual General Assembly in May 1961.[81] Much to Tunku's surprise, his dismissal of the plan provoked considerable discussion amongst UMNO delegates, highlighting its popularity. Some UMNO delegates went as far as to warn the government not to fall into the hands of vested economic interests.[82] Despite the obstacles placed in front of him and an almost pariah status in Cabinet, Aziz continued to doggedly push for the Urea Plant plan. Eventually, Tunku offered support for the Urea Plant plan on condition that Esso hold a 51% interest in the plant. After this offer was rejected by the Board of the Fertilizer Society of Malaysia, Aziz was transferred to the Ministry of Health.[83] Disillusioned with the Alliance government, he resigned from Cabinet in early 1963 and shortly after formed the National Convention Party which unsuccessfully took part in the 1964 elections.[84] Not long after the elections, Aziz was detained under the ISA, along with many left-wing Malay nationalists and PMIP (Pan Malayan Islamic Party) leaders, such as Ishak Haji Mohamed and Dr Burhanuddin El-Helmy, for allegedly colluding with Indonesia in its *Konfrontasi* campaign against Malaysia.

The multiracial, republican, nationalist, regionalist and internationalist orientation of progressive Malay nationalists from Singapore has been much misunderstood, particularly by official historiographies that have a vested interest in interpreting events of the tumultuous late colonial and post-colonial period. This was the period of the Cold War, the Emergency and Konfrontasi, characterised by a bitter clash of ideologies particularly evident in the newly independent and soon to be independent states. In this environment radical nationalist forces were systematically marginalised by Western powers, colonial authorities and conservative nationalist forces intent on maintaining their hold on political power in the post-colonial era.

Yusof, Ishak, Samad Ismail, Said Zahari and Aziz Ishak were more than just Malay nationalists caught up in the politics of de-colonisation. They were radical Malay nationalists whose identity transcended the narrow confines of ethnic identity but encompassed identification with the Malay and non-Malay *rakyat* and included a perspective that was regionalist, internationalist and anti-colonial in a political and economic sense. Their lateral vision meant that they were willing to support and cooperate with UMNO, particularly during the lead up to Merdeka, but were also supportive of other anti-colonial nationalist movements that sought to challenge other embedded manifestations of colonialism. Such vision also contributed to a meandering political journey which included intermittent and in some instances circular forays into a broad spectrum of nationalist parties. This meandering may appear ideologically contradictory at first glance, but reasoned when placed in the context of the tumultuous political environment which thrust up new possibilities whilst closing others. We can learn and be enriched by the daring and idealistic spirit of radical Malay nationalists. This is perhaps their most precious gift to us.

Notes

1 William Roff, *The Origins of Malay Nationalism* (New Haven: Yale University Press, 1967).
2 C.M. Turnbull, *A History of Singapore, 1819–1875* (Kuala Lumpur: Oxford University Press, 1977) 100.
3 Raden Soenarno, 'Malay Nationalism 1896-1941', *Journal of Southeast Asian History* 1.1 (1960): 10.
4 Melanie Chew, *A Biography of President Yusof bin Ishak* (Singapore: SNP Publishing, 1999) 67.
5 Chew, *A Biography of President Yusof bin Ishak* 51.

6 Eunos Abdullah represented the Malays in the Legislative Council until his death in 1934. He was succeeded by Haji Embok Suloh.
7 Chew, *A Biography of President Yusof bin Ishak* 71.
8 Cited in Said Zahari, *Dark Clouds at Dawn: A Political Memoir* (Petaling Jaya: INSAN, 2001) 53.
9 Said Zahari, *Dark Clouds at Dawn;* Aziz Ishak, *Special Guest* (Kuala Lumpur: Oxford University Press, 1977); Chew, *A Biography of President Yusof bin Ishak;* Samad Ismail, *A. Samad Ismail: Journalism and Politics*, ed. Cheah Boon Kheng, *A Samad Ismail: Journalism and Politics* (Kuala Lumpur: Singamal Pub, 1987).
10 For a critical analysis of the Asian Values culturalist discourse, refer to Lily Z Rahim, 'In Search of the Asian Way: Cultural Nationalism in Singapore and Malaysia', *Journal of Commonwealth and Comparative Politics* 36.3 (1998).
11 Chew, *A Biography of President Yusof bin Ishak* 7.
12 John S. Furnival, *Colonial Policy and Practice* (New Yok: University Press, 1956).
13 Said Zahari, *Dark Clouds at Dawn* 11.
14 Said Zahari, *Dark Clouds at Dawn* 12.
15 For an insightful discussion of these myths, refer to Syed Hussein Alatas, *The Myth of the Lazy Native* (London: Frank Cass, 1977).
16 Chew, *A Biography of President Yusof bin Ishak* 69.
17 Chew, *A Biography of President Yusof bin Ishak* 70.
18 Hamidah Hassan, 'A Consummate Actor', ed. Cheah Boon Kheng, *A Samad Ismail: Journalism and Politics* (Kuala Lumpur: Singamal Pub, 1987) 8.
19 Ali Salim, 'A Pioneer in Malay Journalism', ed. Cheah Boon Kheng, *A Samad Ismail: Journalism and Politics* (Kuala Lumpur: Singamal Pub, 1987) 53.
20 Said Zahari, *Dark Clouds at Dawn* 97.
21 Said Zahari, *Dark Clouds at Dawn* 15.
22 Chew, *A Biography of President Yusof bin Ishak* 58-70.
23 Aziz Ishak, *Special Guest* (Kuala Lumpur: Oxford University Press, 1977) 8.
24 Chew, *A Biography of President Yusof bin Ishak* 115.
25 Hassan, 'A Consummate Actor' 20.
26 Cheah Boon Kheng, 'Introduction', ed. Cheah Boon Kheng, *A Samad Ismail: Journalism and Politics* (Kuala Lumpur: Singamal Pub, 1987) xvi.
27 Cheah Boon Kheng, 'Introduction' xviii.
28 Hassan, 'A Consummate Actor'1–3.
29 Hassan, 'A Consummate Actor'11.
30 Suryono Darusman, *Singapore and the Indonesian Revolution 1945-1950* (Singapore: ISEAS, 1992) 13.
31 Said Zahari, *Dark Clouds at Dawn* 52.
32 Ali Salim, 'A Pioneer in Malay Journalism' 56.
33 Chew, *A Biography of President Yusof bin Ishak* 77.
34 Ahmad Sebi, 'Samad's Influence', ed. Cheah Boon Kheng, *A Samad Ismail: Journalism and Politics* (Kuala Lumpur: Singamal Pub, 1987) 90.
35 Ahmad Sebi, 'Samad's Influence' 91.
36 Ali Salim, 'A Pioneer in Malay Journalism' 69.
37 Said Zahari, *Dark Clouds at Dawn* 38.
38 Said Zahari, *Dark Clouds at Dawn* 55.
39 Said Zahari, *Dark Clouds at Dawn* 56.
40 Said Zahari, *Dark Clouds at Dawn* 45–6.
41 Aziz Ishak, *Special Guest* 9.

42 Ahmad Sebi, 'Samad's Influence' 89.
43 R. Rajakumar, 'Malaysia's Jean-Paul Satre', ed. Cheah Boon Kheng, *A Samad Ismail: Journalism and Politics* (Kuala Lumpur: Singamal Pub, 1987) 40.
44 Ali Salim, 'A Pioneer in Malay Journalism' 54.
45 Tim Harper, *The End of Empire and Making of Malaya* (Cambridge: Cambridge Uni. Press, 1999) 304.
46 Hamidah Hassan, 'A Consummate Actor' 18.
47 Said Zahari, *Dark Clouds at Dawn* 109.
48 Ali Salim, 'A Pioneer in Malay Journalism' 52–4.
49 HamidahHassan, 'A Consummate Actor' 8.
50 Ali Salim, 'A Pioneer in Malay Journalism' 73.
51 Chew, *A Biography of President Yusof bin Ishak* 95.
52 Said Zahari, *Dark Clouds at Dawn* 81.
53 Hamidah Hassan, 'A Consummate Actor' 18.
54 Quoted in Said Zahari, *Dark Clouds at Dawn* 81.
55 Chew, *A Biography of President Yusof bin Ishak* 96.
56 Said Zahari, *Dark Clouds at Dawn* 82.
57 Said Zahari, *Dark Clouds at Dawn* 82.
58 Said Zahari, *Dark Clouds at Dawn* 83.
59 Said Zahari, *Dark Clouds at Dawn* 84.
60 Aziz Ishak, *Special Guest* 19.
61 Said Zahari, *Dark Clouds at Dawn* 59.
62 Said Zahari, *Dark Clouds at Dawn* 59.
63 Aziz Ishak, *Special Guest* 21.
64 Said Zahari, *Dark Clouds at Dawn* 63.
65 Said Zahari, *Dark Clouds at Dawn* 63–5.
66 Said Zahari, *Dark Clouds at Dawn* 72.
67 Said Zahari, *Dark Clouds at Dawn* 74.
68 K.S. Jomo, Foreword', in Said Zahari, *Dark Clouds at Dawn* xxxii.
69 Said Zahari, *Dark Clouds at Dawn* 111.
70 Said Zahari, *Dark Clouds at Dawn* 111.
71 Said Zahari, *Dark Clouds at Dawn* 123.
72 Said Zahari, *Dark Clouds at Dawn* 135.
73 Cited in Chew, *A Biography of President Yusof bin Ishak* 112.
74 Said Zahari, *Dark Clouds at Dawn* 134.
75 Said Zahari, *Dark Clouds at Dawn* 120.
76 Aziz Ishak, *Special Guest* x.
77 Aziz Ishak, *Special Guest* 16.
78 Aziz Ishak, *Special Guest* 40.
79 Aziz's allegations were taken up by *Utusan Melayu* in an editorial calling on the government to take action against such government officers. Refer to Said Zahari, *Dark Clouds at Dawn* 65.
80 Said Zahari, *Dark Clouds at Dawn* 67.
81 Aziz Ishak, *Special Guest* 29.
82 Aziz Ishak, *Special Guest* 30.

83 Aziz Ishak, *Special Guest* 38.

84 The party was based on socialist principles and included seasoned radical Malay nationalists such as academic Syed Husin Ali and journalist Dahari Ali. The NCP were engaged in an electoral alliance with the Socialist Front but failed to win any seats in the 1964 elections.

Works cited

Ahmad Sebi. 'Samad's Influence'. *A Samad Ismail: Journalism and Politics,* ed. Cheah Boon Kheng. Kuala Lumpur: Singamal Pub, 1987.

Ali Salim. 'A Pioneer in Malay Journalism'. *A Samad Ismail: Journalism and Politics,* ed. Cheah Boon Kheng. Kuala Lumpur: Singamal Pub, 1987.

Aziz Ishak. *Special Guest.* Kuala Lumpur: Oxford University Press, 1977.

Cheah Boon Kheng. 'Introduction'. *A Samad Ismail: Journalism and Politics,* ed. Cheah Boon Kheng. Kuala Lumpur: Singamal Pub, 1987.

Chew, Melanie. *A Biography of President Yusof bin Ishak.* Singapore: SNP Publishing, 1999).

Darusman, Suryono. *Singapore and the Indonesian Revolution 1945–1950.* Singapore: ISEAS, 1992.

Furnival, John S. *Colonial Policy and Practice.* New York: University Press, 1956.

Hamidah Hassan. 'A Consummate Actor'. *A Samad Ismail: Journalism and Politics,* ed. Cheah Boon Kheng. Kuala Lumpur: Singamal Pub, 1987.

Harper, Tim. *The End of Empire and Making of Malaya.* Cambridge: Cambridge Uni. Press, 1999.

Jomo, K.S. "Foreword', in Said Zahari, *Dark Clouds at Dawn: A Political Memoir.* Petaling Jaya: INSAN, 2001

Rajakumar, R. 'Malaysia's Jean-Paul Satre' *A Samad Ismail: Journalism and Politics,* ed. Cheah Boon Kheng. Kuala Lumpur: Singamal Pub, 1987.

Roff, William. *The Origins of Malay Nationalism.* New Haven: Yale University Press, 1967.

Said Zahari. *Dark Clouds at Dawn: A Political Memoir.* Petaling Jaya: INSAN, 2001.

Soenarno, Raden. 'Malay Nationalism 1896–1941'. *Journal of Southeast Asian History.* 1.1 (1960): 10.

Syed Hussein Alatas. *The Myth of the Lazy Native.* London: Frank Cass, 1977.

Turnbull, C.M. *A History of Singapore, 1819–1875.* Kuala Lumpur: Oxford University Press, 1977.

Zubaidah Rahim, Lily. 'In Search of the Asian Way: Cultural Nationalism in Singapore and Malaysia'. *Journal of Commonwealth and Comparative Politics* 36.3 (1998).

Some Personal Reflections on Political Culture in Contemporary Singapore Malay Novels

ISA KAMARI

One day my child, who was eight years old at the time, came back home from school crying. She hugged me tightly and would not let go. I responded by caressing her hair and waited for her to speak. After a few moments she asked me this question: 'Am I Chinese, daddy?' I was dumbfounded. I did not expect such a question from her. She repeated it. 'Am I Chinese, daddy? My friends in school called me Chinese.'

I said spontaneously, 'No dear, you are Malay'. But deep inside me I knew I had not fully answered her question.

It is true that I registered her as Malay on her birth certificate. But I know that my mother-in-law is Chinese. A Malay family adopted her during the Japanese occupation. My late father-in-law's mother is Japanese. His father is Malay. I have both Malay and Javanese blood running in my veins. So what type of blood runs through my daughter's veins?

More questions crept into my mind. Is blood type, skin type or ethnicity important to one's identity? Are they important to one's development and sense of humanity? Is home upbringing the determining factor? Is the culture that permeates one's life the main influencing factor? As it turned out my daughter's simple question has become mine. I venture to say that it is the same question that many of us might ask.

I sought my dear wife's attention on our daughter's plight. She did not give me an answer. Instead she handed me the draft of her PhD dissertation entitled 'Trends in Malay Political Leadership' and asked me to read it. At that point I was rather annoyed because I thought she had ignored my anxiety. But her smile made me read her work and I found the answers to some of the questions that were disturbing me about our daughter's predicament. As always, a wife knows better.

What the dissertation gave me is the insight that political culture plays a major role in developing one's view of life, thus affecting the development of one's character and orientation. It greatly affects one's aspirations and actions. I have always viewed identity from the viewpoint of ethnicity, myth, tradition and morality. It never crossed my mind that who or what I am is affected by the political culture that is created by the political system I am exposed and made to respond to. I was thus moved to read more on the political culture that pervades our society. Not surprisingly I discovered one important and recurring factor.

The issue of inter-racial integration has been the corner stone of the development of political culture of Singaporeans like me. Right from the Japanese Occupation, Separation, Confrontation and Independence, the same sensitive issue has given rise to struggle, disharmony and tension. I asked myself, is there a better view to this? How can we instil hope and harmony instead of fear and discord?

That is how I was moved to write my first novel *Satu Bumi* or *One Earth*, which was published in 1998.*Satu Bumi* begins in the Bidadari Muslim cemetery, where Irman, an engineer, is visiting his grandmother's grave for the last time before her body is exumed. There Irman meets an old gravedigger, Jati, and the two spend the night together at the Bidadari mosque. Each has a story to tell. As the stories unfold, it becomes evident that the storytellers share a common destiny. The novel, beginning right after the Japanese Occupation of Malaya, represents a yearning for understanding between ethnic groups in Singapore. It is a testament of hope and faith that by sowing the seeds of love, humanity will survive and flourish. After all, our ethnicity is just skin-deep, literally.

In an interview for *Dewan Sastera* Malaysia in June 1999, I was asked whether I would be writing on my experiences as an architect.[1] I said, 'God willing! I will try'. I also promised that it would be a sequel to *Satu Bumi*

Since *Satu Bumi* related the life of the Singapore Malays from the Japanese Occupation until the independence of Singapore, I felt challenged to explore the development of the community after Singapore moved towards the status of a developed nation. The desire to delve into the social and psychological conditions of the community in the post-independence era had already surfaced in my poems and short stories. Many writer friends had also noted that there was a consistency to my thoughts so far. I felt the need to develop my ideas in a coherent work.

In my poems, published in the collection *Sumur Usia* in 1993, I had delved into the spiritual as the basis of life to counteract the feeling of alienation experienced by the modern Malay. I had been trying to find the relationship between our aspirations and desires with the social, political and economic conditions of society. This psychological approach was my answer to the alienation and erosion of values that were affected by the onslaught of modernity and technology.

In my collection of short stories (*Sketsa Minda*, published in 1994), my analyses of society addressed the multiple levels of alienation that affect the lives of the modern Malay. Among the sub-themes I explored were the loss of freedom (*'Gagak'*), the fading of humanity (*'Celupan'*) the conflict between creativity and production (*'Pengukir'*), the misguided aims of education (*'Pekebun'*), the shallowness of worldly life (*'Seladang'*), the harshness of automation (*'Pertemuan'*), religious extremism (*'Klinik'*) and the erosion of love (*'Arca'*).

These early explorations prompted me to write a novel based on similar sub-themes. I decided to employ a simple plot, exploring the realm of hallucinations and dreams to relate different ideas on alienation.

The modern and post-modern lives of the Singapore Malays are rather precarious and shallow. All of us have experienced some form of 'psychosis'. We play different roles and are involved in multiple activities that do not bring much meaning to our lives. What is worrying is that we are not really concerned about the conflicting aspects of our lives and have lost touch with concepts of humanity.

What do we need to understand about this phenomenon, and how do we bring back the peace to our souls and minds? How do we rediscover ourselves? These are some of the issues that I investigated in *Menara* or *The Tower*, which was published in 2002.

Menara relates the last few days in the life of an architect who has felt alienation. The protagonist experiences some sort of psychosis or hallucination when he climbs the tower that he had just built. He begins to question which is more real—the hallucinations he is experiencing or the tower?' *Menara* represents the struggle between his physical and spiritual worlds. The tower is an image both of his success and failure.

The architect is a symbol of development. The main question in *Menara* is what kind of development do we want? What type of *menaar* or tower do the Singapore Malays want to build?

Through the eyes of my fellow Singaporean writer Suratman Markasan (born 1930), in *Penghulu Yang Hilang Segala-galanya (The Village Head Who Lost Everything)*, published in 1998, the Malays are represented as owning the land because they are indigenous to it and have administered it for 100 years. But the island Pulau Sebidang is taken away by the government together with the rights of the Malays (symbolised by the Penghulu) to administer it. The reason for the transfer of Singapore: Raffles, SNP Editions, 1999. rights and power is for development.

Another fellow Singaporean writer, Mohamed Latiff Mohamed (born 1950) has also deliberated on the issue of the rights and power of the Malays. In his philosophical novel *Dalam Keasingan (In Alienation),* published in 1989, Latiff's protagonist, Pemada, is about to be hanged by *Yang Berkuasa* (The One in Power). The strange thing is that Pemuda does not know why. Readers are invited to follow Pemuda on his quest to answer the ultimate question: who is 'The One in Power'? It seems that those who do not have the 'desire' to understand their rights deserve to face extinction (death by hanging).

In his later novel, *Batas Langit* (*Limit of the Sky*), published in 1996, Latiff shares his experiences and perceptions on the social and political development in Singapore more directly. Here he represents incidents that occurred in the years immediately before and after the separation of Singapore from Malaysia in 1965. Through the eyes of the teenage character Adi, Latiff explores the pain of expulsion.

In this novel Latiff is engrossed with the issue of rights and power which defined relationships between different ethnic groups at that time. The tension that enveloped life then is characterised by suspicion and fear. Incidents like the demonstrations held by the Chinese students, the strikes of the workers of the Hock Lee Bus Company and the riots that tore the peace and harmony between different races were signs of the uncertain times.

Latiff exposes the weakness of his society. The suffering of Adi's family is taken to represent the suffering of the Singapore Malays at that time. This was an historical phenomenon. The backwardness of the Malay community went beyond the physical sphere; it resulted in the paralysis of the psyche and soul of the community, which Latiff portrays as disillusioned, misguided and out of touch with reality. Latiff reflects the weakness in the foundation and political leadership of the Singapore Malays through the character of Abang Dolah, an aspiring leader who had abandoned his religion and run away and cohabited with another man's wife. If all these weaknesses and low morals did not stun the reader, the willingness of Adi to take Abang Dolah as his role model would surely convey the low status of the Malay community then. Clearly, the political struggle of the Singapore Malays had been misguided.

The main issue that Latiff tried to highlight through *Batas Langit* is why had the Singapore Malays suffered and stooped so low? Was it because of the politics then that did not favour the Singapore Malays? Or, was it because of the lack of unity of the Singapore Malays and the self-centredness of their political leaders? Or, was it the inability of the Singapore Malays themselves to penetrate the 'Limit of the Sky' that had enveloped and suppressed their lives? What is this 'Limit of the Sky'?

In my opinion the true meaning and strength of this novel are not in the factual recording of history and the political conditions then. In this realistic novel, Latiff has actually focused on the limits of the mind and soul of the Singapore Malays that resulted in backwardness, suffering and deprivation in their lives. It is quite clear that *Batas Langit* reflects the tragedy and frailty of the Singapore Malays.

The claiming of 'rights and power' over a territory or domain rests on the premise that such belong to the indigenous people of the land or domain. Plainly, since the Singapore Malays are the indigenous people of Singapore, as stipulated in the Constitution, they should be entitled to 'rights and power'. This must be the premise postulated by both Suratman and Latiff in their novels. However the realities of minority status of the Singapore Malays and the canons of multi-racialism and meritocracy have made this claim appear 'ideological'.

In my own novel *Satu Bumi,* the issue of 'rights and power' of the indigenous *Orang Seletar,* who lived at the shores near the causeway but were not given Singapore citizenship status, is offered for reflection. However the same issue as applied to the mainland Singapore Malays has taken a dramatic shift.

First, it takes the reality of Singapore's expulsion from Malaysia as a basis to re-evaluate the political and social positions of the Singapore Malays. Second, it accepts the sovereignty of Singapore as a starting point to define the claims to 'rights and power' of any group in the citizenry.

Whatever rights the Singapore Malays had over the other ethnic groups after Separation were not taken for granted but had to be justified and rationalised through the canons of multiracialism and meritocracy. In *Satu Bumi* this reconstruction of premises and values is conveyed through the creation of a family and community, represented by all ethnic groups helping one another in times of trials and tribulations.

Rights and Development

While Suratman Markasan makes symbolic gestures towards the connection between rights and development in *Penghulu Yang Hiland Segala-galanya,* as does Mohamed Latiff Mohamed in *Dalam Keasingan*, there is little that is concrete in these works to underpin the struggle; nor is a development programme suggested through the thoughts and actions of the characters.

In my own work, characters participate more directly in political processes. In *Satu Bumi*, Jati returns to Singapore from Johore to join in the political process that resulted in the formation of Malaysia and finally expulsion of Singapore from Malaysia. He sees the need to be involved and to fight for the rights of his community. He sees this as a duty despite being labelled as *pengkhianat* and *kafir* when he switches political affiliations from 'KERIS' to 'Parti Angkatan Baru'.

He sees the PAB as focussing on development while KERIS kept drumming up the issue of 'rights and power' without any concrete plans to uplift the status of the Singapore Malays.

The effects of the rapid development of modern Singapore on the Singapore Malays are deliberated in detail in my novel *Menara*. The formation of the self-help group Mendaki was a government effort to divert the attention of Malay youths away from the global Islamic resurgence in the late 1970s and early 1980s towards an endeavour closer to the political and political aspirations of the country. I represent Mendaki as a crucial milestone in the effort to uplift the educational performance of Malay students, thus propelling the Singapore Malays towards development. The effects of this political agenda on the psyche and identity of the Singapore Malays are tremendous. *Menara* is my attempt to address the problems faced by the Singapore Malays squarely through practical observations on the different facets of their lives. *Menara* is a novel that has 'moved on' and offers some reflections on conflicts and resolutions.

Multiracialism

Apart from the discomfort of having a Chinese neighbour who plays loud music, issues of multiracialism are not really elaborated upon by Suratman Markasan in *Penghulu Yang Hilang Segala-galanya.* Likewise, in Latiff's *Dalam Keasingan*, the issue of multiracialism is only mentioned in passing, as polemic rather than discourse, through the extraordinary journey of Pemuda into the minds of characters like *Bayang Merah, Bayang Putih, Pemimpin and Seniman.* However, in *Batas Langit*, Latiff explicitly explores the tension that arose between the different ethnic groups before the independence of Singapore. Some semblance of multiracialism philosophy is revealed through the actions of Mak Timah in accepting and raising a Chinese baby, rejected by her family. The actions of *Bibik* in protecting her Malay neighbour during the racial riots are also testament to the 'feeling' of multiracialism.

In my own work *Satu Bumi*, I have brought the issue of multiracialism to the forefront by eradicating stereotypes and reconstructing unfamiliar scenarios in the plot. Tan Swee Lin, for example, is adopted into a Malay family and becomes a Muslim. Malek becomes a communist and joins Ah Sin (Hashim) who can converse fluently in Malay. Swee Lin's father donates materials for the construction of the village mosque. The imam of the mosque is of Indian origin. Swee Lin works as a samsui woman while still a Muslim. All have to face the trials and tribulations of the day, not based on their ethnicity but because of the values that they uphold. This all happens prior to the independence of Singapore, pre-empting the new social structure and political culture that would evolve.

Religion and Politics

The intervention of politics in the religious life of the Singapore Malays is a sub-theme in *Penghulu Yang Hilang Segala-galanya*. Suratman explores the issue through the character of Syed Farid, who manipulates the understanding and interpretation of Islam to fit into the agenda of Maiden, enabling him to gain support from the community. This is a sharp criticism by Suratman on the administration of religion in the country. Incidentally, the Malays are the only community in Singapore to have the privileges of a statutory board, which administers Islam in the country, and a Minister in-charge of Muslim affairs.

In *Dalam Keasingan, Bayang Putih* is a symbol of religious leadership that is helpless against the onslaught of politics. The religious leaders are represented by Latiff as bigots who only care for themselves and not the community. In *Batas Langit*, the Natrah incident and the riots that erupted during the celebration of Prophet Muhammad's birthday highlight the tenuousness of the relationship between politics and religion.

I feature the same incidents in *Satu Bumi*. In addition, loyalties to either religious beliefs or political and ethnic positions are tested through the characters of Malek, who abandons his religion for communism, and Aminah, who sticks to Islam despite her sufferings and associations with her samsui sisters. Aminah is killed by a group of Chinese men because she has *masuk Melayu* or become Malay. The interrogation and tracking of movements of the main character by the authorities, because of his alleged religious and political involvement, are also illustrated in the novel.

Language and Politics

There is no deliberation on the issue of language and politics in Suratman's *Penghulu Yang Hilang Segala-galanya*. Latiff, however, records the founding of the first Malay secondary school, *Sekolah Menengah Sang Nila Utama,* in *Batas Langit*. Adi is overjoyed to have been chosen to enrol in the school. He sees the future of the Malay community in championing the Malay language through the founding of the school. (*Sekolah Menengah Sang Nila Utama* was closed down in the 1990s due to low enrolment. The Singapore Malay families had generally accepted the fact that English as the medium of instruction in schools gave a better chance of employment to their children. The Malay language was defined as a 'mother-tongue' in the context of the bilingual policy implemented in schools in the 1970s.)

In *Satu Bumi* I acknowledge the status of Malay language as the national language by portraying it as a *lingua franca* of the other ethnic groups. However, *Satu Bumi* also shows the short-sightedness of the Malay Teachers Union in rejecting the implementation of the English language in schools in the 1960s through fear that the Malay students would lose their Malay identity. This had resulted in the lagging behind in educational performance of a generation of Malay students.

Political Leadership

In *Penghulu Yang Hilang Segala-galanya*, Suratman brilliantly portrays the conflict between traditional and modern political leadership through his characters Pak Suleh and Maiden. Traditional leadership is shown as unable to compete with the machinery and manoeuvrings of modern political leadership. There was no place for traditional leadership for the post-independence Singapore Malays.

In *Batas Langit*, Latiff represents some semblance of political leadership through the character of Abang Dolah. The leadership, portrayed authentically, did not stand on a firm moral ground. Although he had vision, Abang Dolah was not a model political leader for the Singapore Malays. The community that he led was economically and socially decadent.

In *Satu Bumi*, I created Jati as a staunch fighter taking risks for the sake of the community. A practical and realistic leader, he sees the need to uplift the living conditions of his community instead of 'crying over spilt milk'. He has the courage to face the realities of the day and move forward. Although branded as a traitor and infidel by some members of his community, because of his decision to shift political alliances, he stands by his principles.

As can be seen, novelists have startling differences on the way they perceive issues on political culture and the Singapore Malay identity. Suratman and Latiff come from a generation that had directly experienced the trauma of expulsion of Singapore from Malaysia. Both are witnesses to tragic events that remained fresh in their minds and are recorded in their works. Both are inheritors of the legacy of Malay 'rights and power' when Singapore was part of Malaysia. Both are also former educationists who taught and championed the Malay language and literature.

Latiff went to the first Malay secondary school, *Sekolah Menengah Tun Sri Lanang*, while Suratman pursued further training at the Sultan Idris Teachers Training College at Tanjung Malim and became a prominent and influential educator. Suratman was also appointed Chairman of a mosque committee some time after his retirement from the educational service.

I did not experience the trauma of the Separation although I was born just before Singapore became part of Malaysia. I vaguely remember the effects of the racial riots when my whole family stayed indoors for protection, but this faint memory did not impact greatly on my life. Furthermore, I was not part of the educational system that championed the Malay language and literature. Instead I was thrown into the educational system that promoted the philosophy of bilingualism, regarding Malay as a second language. I am also the product of a political system that emphasised material and technological advancements as the cornerstones of development of a nation.

In summary, Suratmn, Latiff and I went through quite different political cultures that shaped our disparate aesthetic tendencies and convictions. I do not carry the emotional baggage from the traumatic years that might still influence and burden both Suratman and Latiff[2]This is understandable and justified by the context of our respective experiences.

Suratman and Latiff see the Singapore Malays as a homogenous community who are part of the larger geopolitics of the region. I, however, have tried to mould my views and perception of the Singapore Malay identity in the context of a multiracial and multireligious Singapore. The effects of modernity and technology on the Singapore Malays are also apparent in my works.

Latiff has not departed much from championing Malay 'rights and power'. Since his seminal work *Segumpal Api Selingkar Pelangi*, (*A Fist of Fire, An Arc of Rainbow*, 1978), until his latest work *Bagiku Sepilah Sudah*, (*For Me It Has Always Been Desolation*, 2003) he has been loyal to this struggle and philosophy.[3] To Latiff, Malay is everything, even if it means that the 'Malay problem' stays with the community.

Suratman, on the other hand, is more introspective. Lately he champions the Islamic way of life in his works.[4] The context of 'rights and power' in his mind is the world of the Singapore Malay/Muslim vis-à-vis Islam and the 'ummah'. In that sense Suratman has found some resolution to the 'Malay problem' that has suppressed his community all these years. Nevertheless, some observers note that Suratman is rather simplistic in his deliberations. This has resulted in works that are predictable, didactic, ideological and even pedestrian for some.

I have tried to move on and accept the realities that have affected the Singapore Malays and offered writings that delve into psychological and spiritual dimensions. As a first step, as attempted in *Satu Bumi*, I have tried to demolish stereotypes in perception and offered windows of interpretation that could shake and remould the Singapore Malay identity based on the realities and challenges of the day. Islam is also featured in all of my works but I have presented its living rather than ideological nature.[5] Even thoughts about Islam are shaped by the political culture of the times.

My deliberations on the chosen novels so far are preliminary. I hope to have convinced the reader that political culture is a strong determinant of identity.

The topics and framework of this book offer fresh grounds for further research on the evolution and definition of the Singapore Malay identity, or even of the identities of Malays elsewhere. The convenient criteria of the Malay language, customs and Islam as determinants of Malay identity no longer suffice. While these may be applied to the larger Malay diaspora, the criteria fail to differentiate the context and reveal the peculiarities of groups of Malays living under different political systems or cultures.

The Singapore Malays have developed along different lines from other Malays in the region, largely due to the different political culture that has influenced and shaped their lives through the years. And the Singapore Malay novelists, having been influenced by the changing political culture, have come forward to capture this evolving Malay identity effectively and intensely in their works.

Notes

1 *Dewan Sastera* Malaysia, June 1999.

2 See Hadijah Rahmat, *Mengesan Jejak, Batas Langit, Satur Bumi Pada 9 Ogos 1965.* Seminar Antarabangsa Asia Tenggara Ke-2, Kuala Lumpur, 27-29 Ogos 2001.

3 Mohamed Latiff Mohamed, *Segumpal Api Selingkar Pelangi* (Singapore: Solo Enterprises, 1978); Mohamed Latiff Mohamed, *Bagiku Sepilah Sudah* (Singapore: Pustaka Nasional, 2003).

4 See Suratman Markasan, *Kembali Kepada Al'Quran* (Kuala Lumpur: Pustaka Jaya, 2000)

5 See my *Tawassul* (Singapore: Pustaka Nasional, 2002) and *Munajat Sukma* (Singapore: Pustaka Nasional, 2003).

Works cited

Bedlington, S.S. *Malaysia and Singapore.* Ithaca: Cornell University Press. 1978.

Betts, R.H. *Multiracialism, Meritocracy and the Malays of Singapore.* PhD Thesis: Massachusetts Institute of Technology, 1975.

Blondel, Jean. *Political Leadership.* London: Sage Publications, 1989.

Brown, David. 'The Corporatist Management of Ethnicity in Contemporary Singapore'. Ed. Rodan. *Singapore Changes Guard,* New York: St. Martins Press, 1993.

Chen, Peter S.J. and Fawcett, James T. *Public Policy and Population Change in Singapore.* New York: The Population Council Inc., 1979.

Cheng, Goh Phai. *Citizenship Laws of Singapore.* Educational Publications Bureau, August 1970.

Clutterbuck, Richard. *Conflict and Violence in Singapore and Malaysia 1945–1983*. Singapore: Graham Brash, Pte Ltd, 1984.

Hussin, Wan. *The Singapore Malays*. Singapore: Kesatuan Guru-guru Melayu Singapura, 1990

Kamari, Isa. *Menara*. Singapore: Pustaka Nasional , 2002.

Kamari, Isa. *Munajat Sukma*. Singapore: Pustaka Nasional, 2003.

Kamari, Isa. *Tawassul*. Singapore: Pustaka Nasional, 2002

Kamari, Isa. *Satu Bumi*. Singapore: Pustaka Melayu, 1998.

Karni, Athsani and Dzafir, Ridzwan. 'Singapore Malays and Employment Opportunities'. Eds Sharom Ahmat and James Wong. *Malay Participation in the National Development in Singapore*. Singapore: The Central Council of Malay Cultural Organizations and Community Study Centre, 1970.

Latiff Mohamed, Mohamed. *Bagiku Sepilah Sudah*. Singapore: Pustaka Nasional, 2003.

Latiff Mohamed, Mohamed. *Batas Langit*. Kuala Lumpur: Pustaka Cipta Sdn Bhd, 1996.

Latiff Mohamed, Mohamed. *Dalam Keasingan*. Kuala Lumpur Marwilis Publisher & Distributor, 1989.

Latiff Mohamed, Mohamed. *Segumpal Api Selingkar Pelangi*. Singapore: Solo Enterprises, 1978.

Li, Tania. *Malays in Singapore*. Singapore: Oxford University Press, 1989.

Markasan, Suratman. *Penghulu Yang Hilang Segala-galanya*. Kuala Lumpur: Fajar Bakti, 1998.

Markasan, Suratman. *Kembali Kepada Al'Quran*. Kuala Lumpur: Pustaka Jaya, 2000.

Minchin, James. *No Man is an Island: A Study of Singapore's Lee Kuan Yew*. Australia: Allen & Unwin Pty Ltd, 1986.

Nam, Tae Y. *Racism and Nation-Building in Malaysia and Singapore* India: Sadha Prahashan, 1973).

Rahmat, Hadijah. *Mengesan Jejak, Batas Langit, Satu Bumi Pada 9 Ogos 1965*. Seminar Antarabangsa Asia Tenggara ke-2, Kuala Lumpur, 27–29 Ogos 2001.

Sukmawati Sirat. *Trends in Malay Political Leadership*. Phd Thesis: University of South Carolina, 1995.

Turnbull, C M. *A History of Singapore*. Singapore: Oxford University Press, 1977.

Vasil, George. *Successful Singapore*. Singapore: SSMB Publishing Division, 1985.

One x Four: Representing Malay Identity In Singaporean Theatre

ROBERT YEO

SINGAPORE MANAGEMENT UNIVERSITY

In the years following Singapore's separation from Malaysia on 9 August 1965, the island state pursued a policy that emphasised its multiracial and multilingual nature. Four official languages were adopted, Chinese, English, Malay and Tamil. Governmental communication had to be conveyed in the four languages whether in the written, oral or visual media. Representation in government on quasi-governmental committees had to have members of the four major language groups.

My own experiences as chair of the Drama Advisory Committee (DAC) of the Ministry of Culture, and later the Ministry of Community Development, from 1977–1991 confirms this. The committee was charged with the responsibility of promoting drama and in it were two representatives each, who saw to the development of drama in their respective language groups. I was the neutral chairman who, although English-educated, was given the task of ensuring that the interests of the four groups were adequately represented. I had no qualms or problems about what I considered to be politically correct.

I wrote in the programme of the 1980 Festival of Arts:

> Except for the occasional visits by professional groups and one or two professionals who participate in locally produced plays, theatrical activity in Singapore is amateur in status. It takes place in English, Malay, Mandarin and Tamil. Performance in the four official languages is not the result of conformity to governmental policy but arose naturally out of the post-colonial, multilingual situation.[1]

The point I was making here is that official policy in the arts respected the actual reality on the ground and produced the '1 x 4' equation. This reflected the relationship between the norm and the real and their mutual influence on one another.

A publication that gives a good idea of the multilingual situation of drama around 1991 is *Modern ASEAN Plays Singapore* (1991), for which I was the general editor.[2] The selection of plays was a negotiated process and eventually the four editors representing the four languages—Raman Daud (Malay), Naa Govindasamy (Tamil), Choo Woon Hock (Chinese) and Max Le Blond (English)—chose the following plays:

Malay:	*Enchong* by Nadiputra
Tamil:	*After Us* by P. Krishnan
	Singapore Bridegroom by S.U. Shanmugam
Chinese:	*Alien* by Han Lao-da
	Inside and Outside the Door by Liu Miu-Zhou
English:	*The Silly Little Girl and the Funny Old Tree* by Kuo Pao Ku
	Emily of Emerald Hill by Stella Kon

The selection largely pleased all four communities and demonstrated governmental parity of the acceptance of the 1 x 4 cultural paradigm.[3]

But circumstances changed. Parental pragmatism leads to the dominance of English as the preferred medium of instruction in educational institutions like schools, junior colleges, polytechnic and universities. English-language writing, including theatre, which began with Act 3 becoming the first theatre company in 1983 to employ theatre people full-time, followed by TheatreWorks, The Necessary Stage and others. These first two were English-Language companies and the third bilingual Chinese and English.

The rise of English-language theatre

The preference for English and professionalisation privileged writing in English, and in the mid-eighties a succession of playwrights began to make their names, writing play after play. The playwrights included, among the older writers, Kuo Pao Kun, Robert Yeo and Stella Kon. Younger playwrights followed, among them Haresh Sharma, Michael Chiang, Ovidia Yu, Eleanor Wong, Elangovan, Eng Wee Ling, Desmond Sim, Alfian Sa'at and Chong Sze Chien.

The majority of these playwrights did not feel obliged to address the 'representation of Malays.' Their writings stemmed from their experiences and interests and could be said to fall into two categories. The first category is plays in which the main characters are Chinese because the playwrights are Chinese and belong to the 75% Chinese majority of Singapore's population. In the second category are plays by English-educated playwrights. Because they are English-educated, their experiences and their plays, insofar as experiences fuel plays, are more likely to show their dramatic world as multiracial. The issue here is not whether the plays have centralised one racial group and marginalised others, but whether their plays present the truth as the playwrights see it. In my *Singapore Trilogy*, for instance, possibly the central character is the opposition politician Reginald Fernandez, an English-educated, Singaporean of Malayali extraction.[4]

It would never have occurred to me to be asked whether I was engaged in the 'representation of Indians.' I was attempting to show the reality as I knew it, and the reality boiled down to the fact that quite a number of opposition politicians in Singapore through a certain period were of Indian/Malayali origin.

English language theatre was preoccupied with themes that challenged official ways of giving priority to some issues and not others. I openly took on Singaporean politics and political detention as themes for my plays, Eleanor Wong overtly explored lesbian issues, Michael Chiang and Russell Heng presented transvestites on stage, Tan Tarn How created gay characters, Eng Wee Ling and Ovidia Yu addressed feminist issues, Elangovan scrutinised marginalised people in relation to class race and religion while Desmond Sim addressed the theme of paedophilia. Adopting their own agenda, these playwrights put on the table topics which, in some cases, the government would rather not see discussed or had not discussed themselves. Censorship tightened and controversies resulted.

A full-length book on the Singapore theatre entitled *Theater and the Politics of Culture in Contemporary Singapore* by William Peterson (2001), covered this exciting period very well. Peterson wrote:

> English language theatre has been chosen as the primary lens through which to view the politics of culture in Singapore, not just because it is a field in which I am trained but also because throughout the 1990s, theatre in English showed itself to be the single most dynamic and volatile form of cultural expression. The visual arts, music, or—most likely—film may someday supplant English-language theatre as the form that provides the sharpest insights into the effect of government politics on emerging cultural formations, but for the moment, theatre reigns supreme. I would argue that it is English-language theatre more than any other form that was the most actively and consistently engaged with and controlled by Singapore's political culture throughout the 1990s. It merits detailed consideration also because it was the first largely indigenous theatre to become professional, and by this I mean simply that a significant number of Singaporeans now make a full-time living creating it. Finally, it is clearly English-language theatre that the government is 'banking on' in terms of developing cultural institutions at home and promoting Singapore's brand of the 'New Asia' overseas. In this last capacity, Singaporean theatre in English is also the form that most aggressively promotes interculturalism, a force that has emerged during the last two decades as one of the most significant cross-currents in world theatre.[5]

Nonetheless, if one looks closely at the plays written and produced from around the early 1990s to the present, it is possible to make a case for a third group of plays that consciously engage with the 'representation of Malays.' These are plays by Haresh Sharma, Elangovan, Kuo Pao Kun and Robert Yeo.

Haresh Sharma

Haresh Sharma (1965—) is the resident playwright of The Necessary Stage (TNS), a leading professional company in Singapore. Of Indian origin, Sharma has written/devised nearly thirty plays. Of these, three directly address Malay theme/character within a multicultural context and they are *Off Centre* (1993/94), *Rosnah* (1995) and *Pillars* (1997). As *Pillars* does not exist in published form, I will discuss *Off Centre* and *Rosnah*.

Off Centre, first staged in 1993, is a brave, innovative and controversial play. It takes as its subject schizophrenia, and presents in stark terms two young sufferers, Vinod (a male Indian) and Saloma (a female Malay). Using the strategy of collaboration which marks the theatrical preference of TNS, *Off Centre* 'was devised by the cast and playwright Haresh Sharma in a process led by director Alvin Tan.'[6]

Note the phrase, 'devised by the cast ... ' In this method of preparing a play for the stage, it appears that much of the credit goes to the actors, the director becomes the facilitator, and the playwright the servant. The twelve-person cast is multiracial and their individual contributions are negotiated, presumably with the director coordinating and the dramatist recording, writing and rewriting. Such a process provides for a plurality of voices to be heard while at the same diminishing the role of one person (the playwright or the director) as the pre-eminent representative of all of them.

The questions to be asked here are, firstly: how adequately has the theatre company represented the community of the mentally ill? A second question is: as Vinod is Indian and Saloma Malay, is race a factor in the representation? Through my examination of the process of staging the play Rosnah, I shall attempt to answer these questions.

Rosnah dissects the experience of a Singaporean Malay woman who goes to London to study in the 1990s. She faces a cultural dilemma which she defines in this way: 'It is not easy for Malay girl to go to university. Foreign university somemore.'[7]

One might ask, why is it not easy for a Malay girl to go to university? And what does 'foreign university somemore' mean? A Malay girl (or boy, for that matter) usually comes from a financially poor family who cannot afford to send a child to university. A Malay girl is unlikely to be educated to a level that qualifies her for university admission and furthermore, a Malay girl is likely to be too traditional to think of going to a foreign university. If these reasons are accepted, they reinforce notions of Singapore Malays as being impoverished, undereducated, conventional—and marginalised.

Can we imagine English-educated Chinese girls from Singapore saying: 'It is not easy for a Chinese girl to go to university. Foreign university somemore'? Is Haresh Sharma the playwright being Orientalist? Is he presenting Malays in Singapore in the 1990s in stereotypical terms? The evidence in the play says 'no' to these questions. The dialogue is authentic:

> STEPHEN. Stephen Edwards. Thirty years old. Philosophy major. President of Student Union ... University of London. I met him ... My first winter there was terrible. Somemore I just moved to my new bedsit. So, in February, when the sun started shining, one day, I went to Leicester Square. I made an egg mayonnaise sandwich at home. I went there, sat down and started eating and looking at the pigeons. Then one pigeon kasihan ... walk in front of me, just pecking on the ground, but nothing there. So I did a very simple thing. I took a bit of the bread and throw at him. Sekali ... alamak ... attack! Two million pigeons from don't know where all started flying, kee kaw kee kaw ... and I am in the middle. I am screaming. Then suddenly, this hand ... this white hand appear ... and this ... this white voice ... and the next thing ... I am at a café with a man ... a white man.[8]

The characterisation is convincing in depicting accurately Rosnah's state of being in transit while abroad; in fact, it is partially based on journals kept by the actress Alin Mosbit who went to Glasgow in 1994 for workshops/improvisations with a Scottish theatre company. Mosbit played the roles of Rosnah in the first production in 1995 and again in 1996 and 1997 and together with the playwright and Alvin Tan, the artistic director of TNS and the director of the play, engaged in the process of devising the play through its three transformations. Mosbit's input as a Malay woman, mediated no doubt by Sharma's rewrites and Tan's direction, ensured accurate representation of Rosnah as both stereotypical, in the sense described earlier, as well as recognisably typical: a young woman going to a Western capital who is torn between two cultures, between the need to change or not change. This theme had been taken up by early Singapore playwrights writing in English, notably Lim Chor Pee in his plays *Mimi Fan* (1962) and *One Year Back Home* (1974).[9] Negotiation across cultures guards against bias and is more likely to produce truer representation. Sharma attests to this:

> The joy of collaboration, especially in Singapore, whose multiracial reality is strongly reflected in its theatre, is in its discovery of people from different backgrounds, with different worldviews, ready to share with experiences, their cultures and their histories.[10]

But critic Lee Weng Choy has expressed caution about the claims of TNS with respect to self-representation. He asks:

> Must a Malay man always represent his race, ethnicity, gender and identity? So despite all their intentions to develop a theatre of collaboration, the fundamental issues TNS has to work through concern the politics of representation. That is, they must fully confront what it means to represent others, what it means to represent oneself, and what it means to do a play about a community.[11]

Elangovan

While collaboration goes a long way to safeguard multicultural representation in the works of Haresh Sharma, Alvin Tan and the cast of TNS, the plays of the prolific bilingual Tamil Singaporean Elangovan (1957) are largely one-man shows. He is highly conscious of living in a multicultural environment that is Singapore and of his own status as a member of the Indian minority. His largely non-realist plays interrogate the basis of Singapore's multiculturalism, and valorise ethnically marginalised people. His characters show command of the lowest register of Singapore English, and spew out expletives generously (across language and dialect); this has made most of his plays RA (Restricted Artistic), that is, for those above eighteen only. He is an angry young man who has refused to grow up because if he does, he will undoubtedly lose his passion.

Writing on his own, he has nonetheless developed a sensitive awareness of the plurality that is his environment. Three plays, in particular, are relevant to themes of identity: *Talaq* (1998), *Oxygen* (2001) and *Mines* (2002).

Elangovan is aware of the 1 x 4 equation but does not write in accordance with, or in resistance to it. He does not set out deliberately to write about or include specifically Malay persons but insofar as he demonstrates multiracial awareness, there is bound to be wide, ethnic representation. He is interested in controversial issues of social relevance and the fault lines in race relations in Singapore provide him, in *Oxygen* and *Mines*, with sufficient material.

In *Talaq*, his most controversial play, Elangovan takes up arms against female oppression and a brutal patriarchy that is linked to religion. The only character in this challenging monodrama is not Malay, but an Indian Muslim woman who resists the physical and verbal harassment of her husband by reporting him to the authorities. The Muslim practice of allowing a man to divorce his wife by pronouncing *Talaq* three times is exposed as a male chauvinist weapon used to morally browbeat women. The problem is not race but religion.

However, in *Oxygen*, Elangovan is keener to make theatre out of conflicts in which race intersects with religion. Race, by itself, may not be the cause; thus Ali, the oxygen man, the main character who works for a company supplying oxygen to medically ill people, could be Malay or Indian Muslim. In fact, the name Ali is very likely derived from the actor who plays him, Ahmed Ali Khan, who is of Pakistani origin. Faizal, one of his Malay customers, sees him not as a Muslim but as an Indian and yells at him, 'Stupid keling.'[12] His Chinese customers also regard him as an Indian and a smelly one.

The people in Elangovan's plays display intolerance of the other, the other often being people of another race. The picture presented of Singapore is not a flattering one; beneath the official and public expressions of inter-ethnic harmony, Elangovan's characters discover virulent strands of racism that show in their scurrilous language.

Nowhere is this more evident than in *Mines*. Here, literally, in 'No man's land'[13] according to the stage directions, three soldiers, a Malay from Malaysia, a Chinese and an Indian from Singapore face one another in a border area which is land-mined. The Malay and Chinese soldiers are in mortal danger of being blown up at any moment when along comes an Indian soldier who claims he laid the mines, insults them, warns them of the threat of death and leaves. An Apache helicopter belonging to the Singapore Armed Forces appears and the commander orders his subordinate to fire on the remaining two men despite protestation from the subordinate that one of the men is Chinese. The order is carried out.

The situation provides the playwright with an opportunity to criticise Singapore companies that manufacture and export landmines, and for all three men to hurl insults at one another in very stereotypical terms:

> MALAY SOLDIER. [To Chinese Soldier] Don't listen to this Indian dog.
>
> INDIAN SOLDIER. Fuck you. Hey Abang Kerbau [Brother buffalo]! Your religion gives permission to hate infidels. Peace groups give permission to hate militarists. Conservatives hate liberals. Straights hate Gays. Hate is a virtue my brother. You only fuck thousands of cunts in your imagination but you end up dying fucking one miserable cunt all your life. Your wife's. But in war … hate gives you the chance to break every other women's hymen.
>
> CHINESE SOLDIER. Oh God! I don't want to hear this rubbish!
>
> IS. Oh God! Whose God? Is there enough space in the sky for all our Gods? How many heavens? How many Hells? Your God is my Devil and my Devil is your God. You have seen coughing and sneezing but have you seen the GERM?
>
> MS. Yes. I am hearing from it from the Germ's mouth. You must be the think-tank or septic tank for your country. You dogs make the best loudspeakers when the Chinese switch on your petty power. You dogs only bark with Chinese batteries.
>
> CS. Hey hey hey … you are the ones who use more loudspeakers and blast the neighbourhood five times every day to chase our Gods away.[14]

Their long speeches are necessary to keep them awake because a wrong movement opens them to the risk of being blown up, given the fact that they are strapped to landmines. The Indian soldier is a ghost whose deliberate insults keep them alert. There are, generically, a Malay soldier, a Chinese soldier and an Indian soldier; the characterisation is not intended to distinguish them as individuals. The soldiers remain stereotypes sharing similar personality traits: foul-mouthed, ethnically intolerant, authority-hating and suspicious, no matter which ethnic group they belong to.

In fact what sets Elangovan's plays apart from those of other Singaporean playwrights who write in English is his preference for creating proletariat characters who are marginalised. Decentred, labouring under notions of being opposed, they often show a command of the low register of Singapore English, which is full of negative and ethnically-loaded borrowings from languages and dialects spoken by Singaporeans, in particular Malay, Hokkien and Tamil. In this respect, there is parity of treatment according to the representation of the main communities of Singapore, which marks his plays as products of a multiracial society who because of their disadvantages vent their anger at their own class and the classes on top of them. They represent the minority, whether ethnically or financially, and as the character Ali, the oxygen man says in the play of the same name, 'a minority has no right to become the majority.'[15] Elangovan must be praised for daring, in his plays, to defecate on political correctness, presenting racial issues as he starkly perceives them.

Kuo Pao Kun

Kuo Pao Kun (1939-2002) is widely regarded as the writer who stretched multilingualism in plays to its limit by literally writing his plays in a variety of Singapore languages and dialects, to the extent that they can no longer be described as English plays. He began this in 1988 with his production of *Mama Looking for Her Cat.* The play, about an elderly Chinese grandmother alienated from her family and her urban environment, employed a multilingual cast of eleven persons who spoke the following languages/dialects: Hokkien, Mandarin, English, Teochew, Cantonese and Tamil.

The impetus for this bold linguistic stroke is undoubtedly Kuo's multicultural worldview. The play involved input from his cast. As he explains:

This play is written with materials contributed by a group of 11 actors during an intensive workshop directed by the author who finally structured the play. Most of the materials used in the play were contributed by the team of 11. However, the author remains responsible for the play artistically.[16]

The test of the play's linguistic plurality is the extent to which there are passages completely spoken in Hokkien, or Teochew, as this example shows:

> [They start writing letters in English and Mandarin, simultaneously translating in Hokkien. They share the letters and translations aloud, each taking a couple of sentences]
>
> W. Dear Mama, I've just arrived at the airport. The winter is very cold here and I think I will find it a bit difficult to adapt myself
>
> [The Hokkien version follows]
>
> V. Mr and Mrs Leconte came to meet me at the airport. You know what? There was an accident at the airport. You packed too many things in my bag and it burst open at the customs and all the sambal belachan and haybee hiam came out.
>
> [The Hokkien version follows]
>
> JH. I'm finding life in France very interesting. And I'm learning new things all the time. I'm even learning how to drink wine and eat cheese.[17]

Mama Looking for her Cat does not include an important Singaporean language, Malay. To put this another way, there is no Malay character in Kuo Pao Kun's dramatis personae. This situation changed when Kuo Pao Kun devised, wrote and directed the play *OZeroOI* in 1991. He staged the English version play after workshopping with four actors, among them two Malays, Zai Kuning and Lut Ali, and two Chinese, Cindy Sim and Ang Gey Pin.

OZeroOI is a play that fuses memory and myth. All four characters return to their childhood past and for the Malays, the past includes growing up in kampongs which were on the verge of disappearing in the year of performance. Both Zai and Lut now live in Housing and Development Board flats, and though they do not bemoan the move from kampong to apartment, the fact that these things are mentioned reinforces typical images, especially for Singaporean Malays. Zai also recalls his migrant roots from Indonesia.

Thus, Zai, who could be Zai himself, or a projection of collective racial memory, says:

> 'I love climbing trees, coconut trees, in my kampong. When I hate school, I run to Jardine Steps. Smoke cigarette. Smoke ganja. And my brother always come look for me. "Go home lah, Mak waiting for you … "
>
> 'Now I am five, Mak bring me to school first time. "Jangan jahat jahat, ya? Nanti Mak ambil Nani balik, ya?" School finish, Mak no come. I cry. Kakak come. "Mak give birth to baby girl. Little sister is called … " We laugh …
>
> 'Now I am … on the beach … water very warm … wave not big … silent … no sound … I AM FROM SULAWESI, I SAIL THE SEAS OF NUSANTARA! … Sail! … sail! … sail! … '[18]

Robert Yeo

I shall now refer to my own practice as a playwright dealing with the representation of Malays. In 1992, my play *The Eye of History* was performed in Singapore. It was a play that asked: If Sir Stamford Raffles, the founder of modern Singapore, was to come back to life and pay a courtesy call on Lee Kuan Yew, the first Prime Minister of Singapore, what would they talk about?

To frame the encounter within its past and present setting, I decided to use the historical character of Munshi Abdullah, author of the famous nineteenth text *Hikayat Abdullah.* To achieve absolute verity, I used Abdullah's own words:

Sometime later a rumour was heard in Malacca that the English were going to attack Java. Two or three months after we heard the news Mr Raffles and his wife came to Malacca, with an English copying clerk named Mr Merlin and a Malay clerk named Ibrahim, a half-Indian from Penang ... [19]

In addition, I also fictionalised Abdullah by making him return to Singapore in the early nineties to engage Prime Minister Lee Kuan Yew:

PM. Come, Munshi Abdullah, take this seat. (He points to a seat. Abdullah sits.)

ABDULLAH. Allah be praised, Perdana Mentri. I did not expect to be back to see a Singapore so transformed. When I left for Malacca in 1837, I did not believe I would set foot again on this beloved soil in which I spent so many happy years.[20]

I also thought I would provide my take on the 1 x 4 equation and wrote scenes in which three workmen, a Malay, a Chinese and an Indian, under the supervision of their Eurasian boss, put up the statue of Raffles by the Singapore River. It was obviously meant to be tongue-in-cheek, a humorous and lightly ironic comment on the Speak Mandarin campaign and its effects on those who have difficulty learning their mother tongues:

INDIAN. Hey, got words. See what it say. (He bends to read.)

(The Malay and Chinese workmen walk around.)

MALAY. Yes, this side also got. Malay words.

CHINESE. This side also, in Chinese lah.

INDIAN. What it say, ah?

CHINESE. Sorry lah, in Chinese, I cannot read Chinese.

INDIAN. Susah lah you, Chinese cannot read Chinese.

CHINESE. What you think you so clever ah? Here got all those curly, curly words, must be Tamil. Ok you read, smart guy.

INDIAN. [peers] Sorry lah, I also cannot read Tamil.[21]

To summarise then, I believe it is possible to discuss Singaporean theatre in the English language, from the mid-eighties to the present, in terms of overlapping phases each with a specific focus. In the first phase, playwrights wrote about what engaged them, uncoerced by governmental policy that emphasised the 1 x 4 racial/linguistic equation. Overlapping this phase, dramatists/directors in the nineties boldly set their own agendas and addressed topical problems of the day like politics, gay and lesbian rights, feminism, minority identity and transvestitism. They responded to their milieu and conveyed in their works images of multi-ethnicity, including Malay representation. In particular, the contrived nature of the plays of Haresh Sharma and Kuo Pao Kun, working with a diverse cast, made multiculturalism inevitable. Kuo transformed English into a multilingual language and extended the potential of Singaporean theatre. Speaking for myself, I employed and at the same time fictionalised a historical character while taking a light-hearted look at the comic consequences of language policies in multilingual Singapore.

Notes

1 Robert Yeo, 'Drama in Singapore' (programme of the Singapore Arts Festival, Singapore, 198O), 21.
2 Yeo (Ed.), *Modern ASEAN Plays Singapore* (Singapore: Ministry of Information and the Arts, 1991).
3 William Peterson, *Theater and the Politics of Culture in Contemporary Singapore* (Middletown CT, USA: Wesleyan University Press, 2001), 4. He is critical of this 1 x 4 equation as 'a kind of formulaic trap' (64).
4 Yeo, *The Singapore Trilogy*, (Singapore: Landmark Books, 1991).
5 Peterson, *Theater and the Politics of Culture*, 3.
6 Haresh Sharma, *Off Centre* (Singapore: Ethos Books, 1999). 127.
7 Sharma, *This Chord and Others* (London: Minerva Press, 1999), 176.
8 ibid., 175.
9 ibid., xii.
10 ibid., xii.
11 Lee Weng Choy, 'Imaginary Front: The Necessary Stage and the Problem of Representation,' In The Necessary Stage, *Nine Lives: 10 Years of Singapore Theatre, 1987-1997* (Singapore: The Necessary Stage, 1998), 223.
12 Elangovan, 'Oxygen.' In *Flush* (Singapore: Self-published, 2002), 80.
13 Elangovan, *Mines*, (Singapore: Self-published, 2002), 11.
14 ibid., 41.
15 Elangovan, 'Oxygen,' 82.
16 Kuo Pao Kun, *The Coffin is Too Big for the Hole* (Singapore: Times Books International, 1990), 103.
17 Kuo, 'Mama Looking for Her Cat,' in Quah Sy Ren (Ed.), *The Complete Works of Kuo Pao Kun* (Singapore: Practice & Global, 2005).

18 Kuo, *Images at the Margins* (Singapore: Times Books International, 2000), 319.
19 Yeo, 'The Eye of History' (Unpublished MS.), 1. Play performed 9–12 January 1992, Victoria Theatre. Singapore.
20 Yeo, 'The Eye of History,' 35.
21 Yeo, 'The Eye of History,' 7-8.

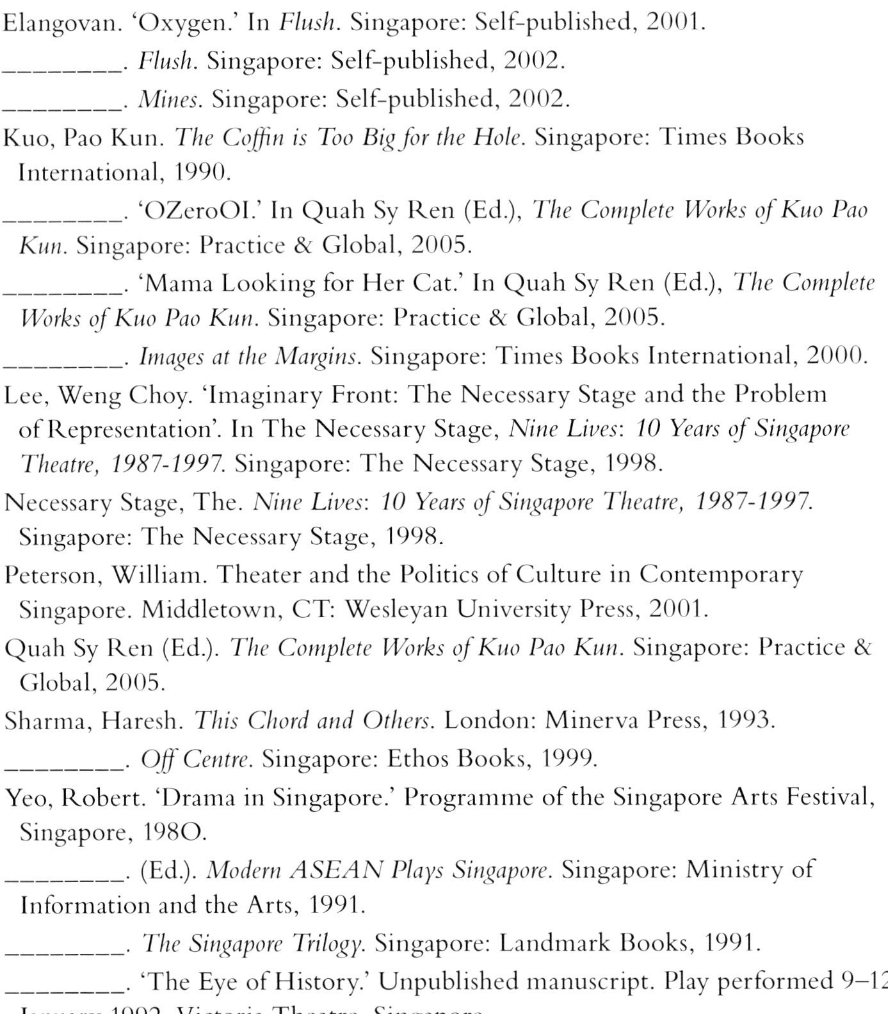

Works cited

Elangovan. 'Oxygen.' In *Flush*. Singapore: Self-published, 2001.

________. *Flush*. Singapore: Self-published, 2002.

________. *Mines*. Singapore: Self-published, 2002.

Kuo, Pao Kun. *The Coffin is Too Big for the Hole*. Singapore: Times Books International, 1990.

________. 'OZeroOI.' In Quah Sy Ren (Ed.), *The Complete Works of Kuo Pao Kun*. Singapore: Practice & Global, 2005.

________. 'Mama Looking for Her Cat.' In Quah Sy Ren (Ed.), *The Complete Works of Kuo Pao Kun*. Singapore: Practice & Global, 2005.

________. *Images at the Margins*. Singapore: Times Books International, 2000.

Lee, Weng Choy. 'Imaginary Front: The Necessary Stage and the Problem of Representation'. In The Necessary Stage, *Nine Lives: 10 Years of Singapore Theatre, 1987-1997*. Singapore: The Necessary Stage, 1998.

Necessary Stage, The. *Nine Lives: 10 Years of Singapore Theatre, 1987-1997.* Singapore: The Necessary Stage, 1998.

Peterson, William. Theater and the Politics of Culture in Contemporary Singapore. Middletown, CT: Wesleyan University Press, 2001.

Quah Sy Ren (Ed.). *The Complete Works of Kuo Pao Kun*. Singapore: Practice & Global, 2005.

Sharma, Haresh. *This Chord and Others*. London: Minerva Press, 1993.

________. *Off Centre*. Singapore: Ethos Books, 1999.

Yeo, Robert. 'Drama in Singapore.' Programme of the Singapore Arts Festival, Singapore, 198O.

________. (Ed.). *Modern ASEAN Plays Singapore*. Singapore: Ministry of Information and the Arts, 1991.

________. *The Singapore Trilogy*. Singapore: Landmark Books, 1991.

________. 'The Eye of History.' Unpublished manuscript. Play performed 9–12 January 1992, Victoria Theatre, Singapore.

Writing Place and Voice in a Multicultural Society

SUCHEN CHRISTINE LIM

I am a writer, and as a writer, I observe, absorb, imagine, shape and create using language as the tool of my craft. I am fascinated by the way people communicate within a complex multilingual environment. As a child I observed how my family spoke the Penang Hokkien and Cantonese dialects at home and switched to speaking pasar Malay in the market. I was especially struck by the way my mother used her hands and rolled her eyes, looking heavenwards when she was intent upon striking a good bargain with the Che'Dah selling spices. Growing up in a Chinese-speaking family, the first two Malay words that I learnt were 'Berapa?' (How much?) and 'Merdeka!' (Independence) I must have been five or six years old when I first saw life-sized posters of Tungku Abdul Rahman, the founding Prime Minister of the Federation of Malaya, with his fist raised. Later, on the radio, I heard his shouts of 'Merdeka! Merdeka!' and imagined him punching the air with his raised fist. In school, however, I failed my Malay language and was often in disgrace. Such childhood observations and experiences must have been absorbed into the marrow of my bones, seeping out into my writing years later, when I wrote *A Bit of Earth*.

Language is the place from which we write. Living as we Singaporean writers do, in a multi-ethnic environment, we cannot help but notice the multilingual landscape, and be part of it. The linguistic landscapes of Singapore and Malaysia offer the writer rich possibilities, experiences, attitudes and memories, influencing the way we use language to express our imagined realities. In this, we are not alone. Irish writers and poets before us like James Joyce and Seamus Heaney, Jewish American writers like Bernard Malamud, Indian writers like Vikram Seth and African writers like Chinua Achebe have dug deep into their memories of non-English languages spoken or heard during their childhood to mine the rich lode of linguistic resources and experiences.

For the Singaporean and Malaysian writer, the linguistic landscape is far more complex than that of the Irish writer dealing with the English and Gaelic languages or the Protestant and Catholic religions. In his general introduction to *The Fiction of Singapore* (up to 1990), professor and poet, Edwin Thumboo, gives an illustration of the linguistic complexity that the fiction writer, writing in English, faces: in Southeast Asia where characters from other communities—Malay, Chinese, Tamil, Eurasian, ex-Colonial—each with its types and sub-types people the landscape.

This expansion in the range of types is exacerbated by linguistic and other changes across the generations, and within the ethnic groups. Among Chinese, it is not unusual to find dialect-speaking grandparents, bilingual parents and grandchildren competent in English and Mandarin but not dialect. Grandparents and grandchildren do not therefore share any language. Include similar linguistic variations in the families of Tamil and Malay characters, and then imagine the writer moulding the English language like clay to represent the discourses of these characters, you will then have an idea of the problems involved.

Even with the three generation Chinese family and with two uncles added, and limiting the fiction to one ethnic group, the writer would need to invent an appropriate language for each character in the different, permutating social and linguistic setting they inhabit and operate in ... The mathematics of the discourses involved in coping with a larger range of types is obviously infinitely daunting.[1]

If I had read this passage before I wrote my novels, or had I stopped to analyse Singapore's linguistic complexity, I would not have written *Fistful of Colours* or *A Bit of Earth*.[2] It would have been too daunting. In these two novels, I was writing across race, language and culture. Therefore I am glad that cognitive critical analysis is the work of the critic while the work of the poet, playwright and novelist is simply to follow his or her own intuition and imagination.

The Malay and Chinese voices in *Fistful of Colours* and *A Bit of Earth* span two to three generations with the first generation speaking mainly non-English languages. I depended a lot on imagination and on the inner ear, as well as my reading of historical texts, when I created the Malay characters in *A Bit of Earth*. For example, in the case of Datuk Long Mahmud, Menteri of Bandong in the state of Perak, 1873, I read up on the history of the Sultanate of Perak. The place and time are significant. In the nineteenth century, Perak was rich in tin deposits. It attracted English and Chinese adventurers, miners and traders to whom land was a commodity to be exploited for profit. But to a Malay chief like the Menteri of Bandong, land was more than a commodity; it was his blood and his heritage.

His bloodline was impeccable. The descendant of a long line of noble families in the Celebes and Aceh, he was linked, on his mother's side, to the legendary Tun Perak, the greatest chief minister of the Malaccan sultanate … Thanks to Allah's most gracious mercy and compassion, his late father had succeeded in persuading the sultan to cede to the family in perpetuity the whole of Bandong Valley, a feat repeated by only one other chief, the menteri of Larut. It was a legacy he had to preserve, he thought. And his eyelids drooped like a veil over his dark eyes, hiding all signs of what he might be thinking.

After a long time in which he seemed plunged into deep thought, he raised his handsome profile and sniffed the fragrance of jasmine perfuming the air in his compound. His eyes travelled to the distant hills surrounding his beloved valley. Bequeathed to him by his father. Bequeathed to his father by His Royal Highness. The land of his children and *Insya Allah*, God willing, the land of his children's children and all their descendants. Not just an acre of earth for digging and planting, or measuring and selling by the white men and the Chinese.[3]

Was I creating a fictional type when I created the proud and powerful Datuk Long Mahmud? Characters like Datuk Long Mahmud existed in Malay fiction and Malay narratives long before *A Bit of Earth* was published. However, I believe his appearance in my Singaporean novel written in English was a first. I must confess that I have not met any Menteri Besar in real life; I did not know anyone like Datuk Long Mahmud. But, having read the history of Perak, the Malay state that had drawn up a legal code of 99 laws before the arrival of the British, it was unthinkable to me that all Malay chiefs were either like children or fools and scoundrels (as portrayed in the history books I read as a student, written by British historians). In the course of my research for *A Bit of Earth*, I stumbled upon Sir Hugh Clifford's novel, *Salleh: A Prince of Malaya,* first published in 1926.[4] Sir Hugh Clifford was the former British Resident of the state of Pahang. The narrator's patronising attitude towards Malay culture and society annoyed me no end. In his excellent introduction to the novel, J.M. Gullick cited some examples of the narrator, Jack Norris' superior attitude. Prince Salleh's English education was said to have only made him 'as near an approximation to a decent white man as a Malay can be'.[5] Back in Pelasu, Salleh was perceived as '*dropping back* more and more into a Malay'.[6] In hindsight, I think my creation of Malay characters of nobility like Datuk Long Mahmud and Datuk Ibrahim could have been, in part, a reaction to novels such as Clifford's, who, to be fair to him, was 'a man of his time, viewing the world from a conscious position of assumed superiority.'[7]

While that may be the case, I must also add that a part of me knows that in the process of writing, a writer is not always conscious of the choices she is making. I did what I did because intuitively it felt right for the time and place I was describing, and I went along with the feeling. Perhaps it is because, having grown up in a place or understanding its social history, instinctively the writer knows that certain places, in memory and experience, induce a certain attitude or sensibility in characters.

The Malay voices in *A Bit of Earth,* reflected the particular time and place in Malaya's history. Datuk Long Mahmud was a chief or menteri before the English colonisers came This pride of the indigene and his deep feeling for the land of his forefathers was something I discovered in the course of my writing. It was new to me, a writer of Chinese immigrant stock, who had grown up with different perceptions of land and place. My own experience of place is that of the temporal and transient. The constant erasure of place and memories in the city of Singapore, through the tearing down of old buildings and the putting up of new buildings, reveals an attitude towards land as investment and dispensable commodity, something that Omar, the grandson of Datuk Long Mahmud, observed when he spoke to Kok Seng, son of the tin mining tycoon, Wong Tuck Heng.

Omar was looking out the window at the passing hills and jungle beyond the River Bandong.

> 'I grew up here. When I was a boy, this was all jungle. Now … look.' He pointed to the orange-tiled roofs of the Chinese shophouses coming into view. 'You Chinese work very hard to buy and own land. Then you sell. It's like what you own, you also disown. We Malays are different. We're part of the land. We can't disown it and it can't disown us. Just like the forest cannot disown the trees.'[8]

In the context of the language of place, Omar's comment expresses, in essence, the difference between the attitude of the indigene and the immigrant towards place or land. This difference affects a country's political landscape and the relationship between communities. The Chinese immigrants of the nineteenth century, like the British colonials, did not have the kind of relationship with the land that someone like Datuk Long Mahmud had; this was something not quite understood by the author of *Salleh: Prince of Malaya.* In Singapore's history, from the time of Raffles to the 1980s, place denoted ethnicity. When Stamford Raffles planned the city of Singapore, he followed the colonial practice of the English empire builders, which was to divide and rule. He marked out on a map where each ethnic community would live: the Malays in Geylang Serai, the Chinese in Chinatown along South Bridge Road, the Indians in Little India along Serangoon Road and the Europeans in Tanglin along Tanglin Road, Napier Road and the Botanic Garden. Although we still have Geylang, Little India and Chinatown today, some things have changed since the 1980s.

In *Fistful of Colours* I suggest the significance of place.

> The Geylang neighbourhood where Zul had spent most of his boyhood had changed.Gone were those familiar landmarks which had given his boyhood a sense of stability because he had once thought they were eternal, suspended in time even though the rest of Singapore was changing. But those totems of his youth, like everything else, had been bulldozed and demolished to make room for the new concrete boxes erected in place of the Flame trees, the angsanas, the lallang patch, the muddy ditch (where he'd caught his first guppy) and the roadside barber's stall under the angsana tree. Ah Seng, the Chinese barber, in khaki shorts and cotton singlet cut the hair of all the neighbourhood boys, right there where the shops were now. Coarse white powder flying in the air, joking, scolding and cajoling the boys, where was the man now?
>
> ... Geylang market, a cluster of ramshackle stalls covered by flapping canvases and tar paper, used to be round the corner from where the church was standing now. It was a place of endless entertainment especially when the koyok or Chinese medicine man demonstrated his gongfu skills to sell medicated oils.
>
> This market was Zul's playground where he kicked stones and tin cans with his siblings, but the place and memories of its people like the Chinese medicine man have been erased.
>
> When he looked up, the view before his parked car was the neat row of two-storey HDB shophouses which had taken the place of the zinc and wood shops of the Chinese grocers and Indian dhobis. With a sharp pang, he recognised what he had known all his life. That, as always, it is the outer physical rim of our social hub which changes faster than its core of age-old prejudices, cock-eyed perceptions and irrational fears. For as long as we mix and mingle in the comfortable confines of the marketplace, all is well; move beyond that into the personal and the intimate areas, then the hub quivers and shakes like a machine into which one has accidentally poured water instead of oil.[9]

With hindsight, I would say that I chose Geylang as the setting for the activities of Zul, the English-educated Malay journalist in *Fistful of Colours*, because Geylang used to be the area where most of the Singapore Malays lived during the 1950s and 1960s. That area has now changed, like Zul in my novel.

Place is memory and ethnicity in *Fistful*. It evokes a sense of roots, but roots, in reality, are transient. What has been rooted in the earth is often uprooted in Singapore. The geographical landscape is always subject to change. The Geylang experienced in *Fistful* by Zul, when he was a boy and later a wistful young man, no longer exists. Chinese grocers and barbers seldom know how to speak Malay these days. Geylang, as seen by Zul in *Fistful,* is a place that registers loss and social change in Singapore.

The language that Datuk Long Mahmud spoke in nineteenth century Perak, at a time before the English had colonised it, was the language of traditional Malay nobility, a courtly formal language. Years later, when Datuk Ibrahim, his son, became the British-appointed Penghulu (village chief) of Bandong, his speech to the villagers was in a less formal register. His Malay speech was closer to that of the commoner. By the time of the third generation in the early 1900s, Omar, the grandson of Datuk Long Mahmud, had attended the Penang Free School and acquired the habit of speaking English with his classmate, Ong Kok Seng.

Writing in a multicultural context, the writer has to grapple with the question of how best to reflect non-English voices and the various speech registers, as well as switching from non-English to English speech. In the following scene from *A Bit of Earth,* Ibrahim has replaced his father, Datuk Long Mahmud, not as the Menteri of Bandong, but as its District Officer. On this occasion, he has been invited to address the junior Malay civil servants in the colonial service. His speech has none of the archaic formality of his father. It reflects the changes taking place in Malay society at that time.

> '... Look around you. Bandong has too many Malay punkah pullers, Malay gardeners, Malay constables, Malay postmen and Malay junior clerks! In the whole country, there're too many Malays in jobs like peons and road sweepers. Inside our hearts we want a fair share of higher appointments in the government service. You who've passed the English examination, don't you want to be trained for a higher post?' ... .
>
> '... Begging Tok's pardon.' The chairman was very apologetic. 'We can't talk about politics here. We don't want the government to think that we're a political or secret society.'
>
> Cowards! Their English education had changed them into mincing little courtiers dancing to the tune of their masters, lowing like cows led by the nose ring! Please, Allah in your mercy, don't let Omar become one of them.
>
> He stood up and, raising his voice to make himself heard above the persistent drumming on the tin roof, (Ibrahim) declared, 'Tonight I'm here not to talk about politics but to talk about my acre of earth and my place in it.' He picked off the clump of mud ... and held it up for all to see. 'Look this bit of earth belongs to you and me.'[10]

Ibrahim's speech contrasts with that of Wong Tuck Heng, addressing his clansmen on the occasion of the founding of the Republic of China:

> Great rejoicing this New Year! Everywhere all over Southeast Asia, Chinese people are letting off firecrackers. China belongs to the Han people again! ... Yam seng, my brothers! My countrymen! At last we Chinese can look the foreign devils in the eye as equals! We're no longer slaves of the Manchus. Walking with our heads in perpetual kowtow! Today we walk with our heads up![11]

Both speeches, however, reveal a common desire for dignity and equality of treatment. I did not plan this. It was only on reflection that I saw the common thread that linked Ibrahim and Wong Tuck Heng, the one an indigene, the other an immigrant.

In *Fistful* there is a focus on the relationship between Janice and Zul, and the reaction of their parents when the young people want to marry.

Joseph Wong, the father of Janice, reacts negatively. He blames his wife and threatens to disown his daughter because she is leaving home to marry Zul.

> "We have brought up a right proper Christian, let me tell you," Joseph Wong glared at his wife ... "What kind of a mother are you? Tell me I want to know ... What for I work my butt off to send her to a good school? A good Christian school! ... What for? The son's a hopeless bum. The daughter's a spineless bitch! No backbone! If she has any backbone, she will insist on her own beliefs! Are you happy now Martha? Proud of your two children? She is leaving. Disowning us! I can do the same, let me tell her! From this moment, pooi!", he spat, "I have no daughter!"[12]

Zul's father warns his son of the potential problems for the children of mixed marriages. Both sets of parents react with fear and anxiety because they are aware of the communal and religious tensions that are likely to exist if a Christian Chinese marries a Muslim Malay.

> "*Air yang tenang jangan sanka tiada buaya* (don't think there are no crocodiles because the water is calm) ... My son, I dread the day when the Malays and the Chinese clash, like on May 13, which I pray with all my soul, Isya-Allah, will never happen again. But, if the dreaded unforeseen should happen, what will become of your children, my grandchildren? Will my grandchildren be torn and be distrusted by both sides ?... Please forgive an old man his pessimism ... You have not told us very much about the parents of Janice Wong. Mak and I think that they are not happy about their daughter's plan to marry you. You are Muslim; they are Christians. And this can be one big area of trouble."[13]

More problems are raised than solved in my representation of the relationship between Janice and Zul. The voices heard here are not meant to comfort and reassure the reader, nor to gloss over the problems of a mixed marriage such as that between Zul and Janice, a Muslim and a Christian respectively.

The writer's place in a multicultural society makes him or her more acutely aware of the diversity of non-English voices and the need to honour these voices so that they are heard alongside English speech. My way of incorporating this awareness may not be the best way. As we Singaporeans mature as a writing community we will find better ways of developing different voices into an aesthetic that will mirror our society as it is, not as perceived through the aesthetics of a monoculture.

Some years ago, an academic in Singapore accused me of not having a consistent voice in my fiction. At the time I had no reply to this criticism and I dutifully noted my failing. But now, four novels later, with my last two deploying different voices, I recognise that a consistent voice does not suit my artistic purposes and what I feel as an artist, rooted in a multicultural society. We need to develop a polyphonic aesthetic for reading and writing the different voices and languages that reflect the different points of view and shifting perspectives in a multicultural society. Perhaps this will be Singapore's literary contribution to the world of literature in English, while many writers in the West still write within their own ethnic community for fear of being accused of cultural misappropriation. Singapore literature in English, as reflected in the works of our poets, dramatists and novelists, has shown that the ethnic borders in our society are porous. The English language is the malleable clay used to create the verisimilitude of the various languages in our midst.

I conclude this chapter with Zul's recollection of his father and Ah Hock, the Chinese man whom his father had saved during the Japanese Occupation of Singapore. This passage exemplifies the practice of representing diverse voices in a multicultural context.

> 'Telima kasih, telima kasih,' Ah Hock cried when he woke up after a long sleep.
>
> 'Boleh cakap Melayu?' my father asked.
>
> 'Sikit boleh, sikit, sikit!'
>
> My father spoke quietly to Ah Hock in pasar Malay, I think, and as I imagine the scene now, I believe it must have dawned on my father then that the essence of our communication lies not so much in words as in the feelings behind the words. 'Hati yang baik.' (A heart that's good.) My father's kindly look and tone were received with gratitude; Ah Hock grasped his hand and murmured 'Telima kasih' over and over again, mispronouncing his Malay words and getting the intonation all wrong. However, that did not bother my father. Neither did it bother Ah Hock that my father's Hokkien had sounded terrible. Their feelings of sympathy as fellow sufferers gave their words a force which accurate pronunciation could never have.[14]

Notes

1 Edwin Thumboo (Gen.Ed), *The Fiction of Singapore* (Singapore: Unipress, The Centre for the Arts, National University of Singapore, 1990) xvii–xviii.
2 Suchen Christine Lim, *Fistful of Colours* (Singapore: SNP International, 2003) 1st published in 1992; Suchen Christine Lim, *A Bit of Earth* (Singapore: Times-Marshall Cavendish, 2001).
3 Suchen Christine Lim, *A Bit of Earth* 30–31.
4 Hugh Clifford, *Salleh: A Prince of Malaya* (Singapore: Oxford University Press, 1989 [1st published 1926]).
5 J.M. Gullick, 'Introduction', in Hugh Clifford, *Salleh: A Prince of Malaya* (Singapore: Oxford University Press, 1989 [1st pub. 1926]) 99.
6 Clifford, *Salleh*. 216.
7 Clifford, *Salleh*.
8 Suchen Christine Lim, *A Bit of Earth* 336.
9 Suchen Christine Lim, *Fistful of Colours* 142–44.
10 Suchen Christine Lim, *A Bit of Earth* 326–27.
11 Suchen Christine Lim, *A Bit of Earth* 364–65.
12 Suchen Christine Lim, *Fistful of Colours* 153-154.
13 Suchen Christine Lim, *Fistful of Colours* 278-279.
14 Suchen Christine Lim, *Fistful of Colours* 272.

Works cited

Clifford, Hugh. *Salleh: A Prince of Malaya*. Singapore: Oxford University Press, 1989 (1st pub. 1926).

Gullick, J.M. 'Introduction', in Hugh Clifford, *Salleh: A Prince of Malaya*. Singapore: Oxford University Press, 1989 (1st pub. 1926).

Suchen, Christine Lim. *Fistful of Colours*. Singapore: SNP International, 2003 (1st published in 1992).

Suchen, Christine Lim. *A Bit of Earth*. Singapore: Times-Marshall Cavendish, 2001.

Thumboo, Edwin (Gen.Ed.). *The Fiction of Singapore*. Singapore: Unipress, The Centre for the Arts, National University of Singapore, 1990.

The Hushed Identity: Malay Ethnicity and Sexuality in Malaysian and Singaporean Literature in English

LILY ROSE TOPE
UNIVERSITY OF THE PHILIPPINES

In Alfian Sa'at's short story, 'Project', a Malay boy, Salim, hangs out with his non-Malay friends in a McDonalds joint eating French fries. He proudly considers Wei Cheng his best friend. This picture of multicultural perfection is tested when Salim goes to the toilet and is confronted by a mentally handicapped boy who is apparently afraid of being alone in a cubicle. The boy asks Salim not to leave and to wait for him while he 'shee-shees'. The boy is Chinese. Salim taunts the boy and refuses to stay.

> Salim clutched the hefty boy by his left shoulder and tried to push him. He resisted. Salim realized that he did not want to see the boy's penis. He was a Chinese boy, there was foreskin on his penis.[1]

This powerfully discursive scene raises some preliminary points that are worthy of discussion. First, ethnicity is performative. Traditional notions of ethnicity link it with race and imbue the term with physical markers such as colour of skin, eyes and hair, shape of nose, physical build and so forth. Such physical rendition of ethnicity has been proven to be limiting, even unjust, but unfortunately it continues to persist. Meantime, more recent studies have begun to look at ethnicity not only as a set of biological features but as performance. One's looks should not matter. In the story, Salim has to decide whether or not to help the Chinese boy. His decision is informed by his cultural conditioning. It is an ethnic performance, a marker of identity.

A second point is that sexuality can be a site of ethnic performativity. Anne-Marie Fortier points out that ethnicity can be both visible and invisible. Visible markers would include racial features and performed activities such as the use of language and the practice of religion. These are shared and recognized by members of the community as signs of membership and belonging. Because of familiarity and usage, these markers are eventually naturalized and, within the community, become invisible. But this definition also includes markers that are hidden, understood but not spoken of. These include the secret, the forbidden, the private performance that cannot be carried out in front of an audience. Sexuality is an example of an invisible marker. Its performance is confined to the private domain—in the body and in the mind.

I borrow here Fortier's working definition of sexuality which includes not only desires (who wants whom) or sex acts (who has sex with whom and how) but in a more Foucauldian fashion of thinking about a series of practices and injunctions that are part of the widely discursive formation called 'sexuality': these include not only bodily dispositions that perform the genders of the 'heterosexual matrix', but also love, affection and other feelings (such as those tied to notions of romantic love) that are part of the discursive system of sexuality.[2] Thus sexuality includes not only wanting, but also rejecting. Both inclusions can be manifestations of natural human emotions but they can also be practices of power.

The cited incident in the short story 'Project' does not illustrate desire; rather it depicts rejection and exclusion based on ethnic notions of bodily functions. In the public domain, Salim is an ordinary boy whose sole ethnic marker is his name. He moves within a politically correct circle of non-Malay friends. But his real identity test is given him in a public toilet where he must choose between sympathy and ethnic conditioning. Salim chooses the latter. Any amount of compassion for the mentally challenged boy has been superseded by an ethnic revulsion of the Other.

Sexuality is inscribed in the body and it is highly significant that the ethnic object of revulsion is a sexual organ, which is hidden, but when disclosed is judged according to its unclean uncircumcised state. Salim's ethnic gaze racialised the Chinese boy's sexual organ, a discursive instance of racialised sexuality and sexualised ethnicity. This is a performance of ethnicity in the domain of sexuality, a marker of identity.

This chapter will examine ethnic performativity in Malay sexuality as a marker of Malay identity, not to judge ethnic attitudes but to show how sexual images, fears and desires shape identity, not to essentialise but to problematise the confrontation between the ethnic and sexual selves.

Why choose the site of Malay sexuality to prove Malay identity? First, Malay identity is highly premised on ethnicity and is defined with great confidence as comprising the use of Malay language, the practice of Malay customs and traditions and the embrace of Islam.

By Constitutional and legal definition, a Malay is and must be a Muslim. For the Malays, to abandon Islam would be a renunciation of their way of life and loss of all legal and political rights accorded them 'on the basis of their claim of being indigenous people. Islam gives the Malay bonds of communal identity as strong as those developed by social and political institutions. For the Malays, the sense of community is inextricably bound up with the community of true believers. In practice, it appears that most Malays have a strong sense of racial identity, reinforced by Islamic attitudes towards the infidels.'[3] The Malays speak Bahasa Melayu ... At the same time, Malays practise Malay customs, culture and belief. Thus, constitutionally, the Malay is a person who speaks Bahasa, practices Islam and follows Malay customs. There are Muslim Indians and Chinese but they are not regarded as Malay.[4]

In Singapore, the term Malay may include non-Malay Muslims 'who for reasons of adoption, religious conversion or intermarriage intend to identify as 'Malay', but there are also Malay Muslims who do not want to be identified as Malay.[5]

In general, though, one can say with confidence that Malay ethnicity is strong and hegemonic because of clear cut bases of belonging that have solidified a core identity and have created a recognisable Malay self.

But there is relative silence on the invisible aspects such as sexuality. To begin with, sexuality has a confidential, secret nature that keeps it invisible. This invisibility is usually personal in nature. In traditional Malay societies, it is a topic generally avoided, elided, or often dismissed as a non-issue. Regarded as a taboo subject, or a necessary evil at best, sexuality seems to be regarded as a discomfiting, do-we-have-to-talk-about-it topic meant for hushed whispers or immediate dismissals.

Except for Nor Faridah Abdul Manaf's 'Sexuality in Post Independence Anglophone Writing by Three Malaysian Muslim Women's Writers', there is hardly any significant critical work on sexuality issues in Malaysian literature. There seems to be among Malay writers a hesitation, refusal or inability to express the sexual self. I can only conjecture explanations for the silence. Perhaps it is because of Islamic sanctions against the use of the human body for aesthetic purposes. Or perhaps Malay traditions impose strict cultural control on the sexual self. Whatever the reason, Malay sexuality may be invisible not only in the personal sense but also in the ethnic sense. The reticence creates a hushed air around this identity site, implying the hidden, buried nature of the Malay sexual self.

I approach the subject therefore not from the perspective of an informed scholar, but from that of an outsider-novice who dares to enter where angels fear to tread. This chapter explores the hidden terrain of Malay sexuality, hopefully to provide a discursive path toward an understanding of Malay identity. The texts to be examined are written in English, their Malay authors usually educated in a Western institution. This may be seen as a limitation in terms of representation. This may also seem to compromise the authenticity of Malay ethnicity. Nevertheless, I also see the advantage of these authors straddling cultures with different attitudes to sexuality. They may provide the small opening that will allow us a glimpse of the Malay sexual self. Zawiah Yahya asserts:

Malay women suffer from underexposure as much as in fiction as in reality ... When they do appear on the scene, they are merely on the sidelines of the action, playing their insignificant roles as prostitutes, midwives, abortionists, 'mak andams' and servants.[6]

Even in the 1990s, the portrayal of Malay women in Malaysian fiction is not without its stereotypes. Fadillah Merican cites:

> the Datin, besotted with rank, appearance and Queen Anne tableware; the neglected/victimized wives of philandering husbands; sexually-frustrated not-so-young women; the femme fatale and/or beauties from Kelantan; the mistresses/second wives with chequered pasts.[7]

In his study of Singaporean television shows, Kenneth Paul Tan observes that 'Malay females tend to be passive, objectified, and instrumental to the purposes of others ... In fact, they are portrayed as clerks, secretaries and sales assistants'.[8]

These portrayals clearly show that Malay female identity is closely linked not only to the maternal or servile, but also to functions of the body that are in the purview of sexuality. As prostitutes, midwives, abortionists, victimised wives, favoured mistresses and so forth. Malay female identity is sexually defined. Also, except for the femme fatale, the women in these portrayals are disempowered, something that Malay women share with other women in communities ruled by patriarchy. But is there something in the Malay woman's ethnicity that confines her to disempowered sexual roles? When does ethnicity shape sexuality and vice versa?

Ellina binti Abdul Majid's novel, *Khairunissa: A Good Woman*, is a repository of examples of traditional/stereotypical character types who are defined by their ethnicity.[9] Nor Faridah Abdul Manaf cites the earlier novel, *Perhaps in Paradise*, as containing more contentious sexuality issues, but for purposes of more visible ethnic markers, the second novel seems richer.[10] *Khairunissa* is about interracial marriage but halfway through, the reader tends to forget the British female character. Instead we are caught up in the intricacies of Malay life. There are four women in the novel that may be seen as providing various representations of sexuality within ethnicity. The Datin stereotype is obvious in Mak, the mother-in-law who has to pay dearly for the wealthy lifestyle she enjoys. Her husband, an influential government official, cavorts with housemaids and starlets; his position is an excuse for his indiscretions. Then there is Yati, Mak's daughter-in-law, whose husband acquires a second wife without her approval. Both are rejected sexualities by virtue of husband's desire for other women. Yet, these are 'good' sexualities because they transcend the rejection by conforming to Malay traditional values; Mak decides to let pass the indiscretions to preserve family harmony and social appearances while Yati, unable to object to something sanctioned by Islam, focuses her energies on her children.

> 'It's hurtful when someone you love betrays you'. Yati laughed and replied,
>
> 'That depends. Men are weak, oversexed creatures, only good for procreating children'.
>
> 'What matters to me are Nini and Nana; so long as they are amply provided for, why else should I care?'[11]

Yati's pronouncement can be construed as strength, but it can also be read as a form of emotional death.

The novel includes stereotypical 'negative' women sexualities. One is a starlet aptly named Little Star. She gives in to Ayah, the influential public official, thinking this is her card to a bright future.

When he put his hand on her knee and proceeded to run it up and down her thigh during dessert, she was a little ashamed but then she reminded herself, 'he is a V.V.I.P so this is an honour for me.'[12]

Lacking Little Star's naivete is the 'bad woman' of the novel, Hanni. Manipulative and vulgar, she gets Yati's husband to marry her but does not stay faithful to him. She is again judged according to her 'unclean' sexuality and is condemned by direct references to her body as a reflection of her corrupt soul:

There was something generally unclean about her; most likely it was the zits on her back and the fact that she couldn't always be bothered to change her panties everyday.[13]

Little Star and Hanni are negative sexualities because they are desired but forbidden women. Little Star will destroy the reputation of the Datuk's family. Hanni co-opts the practices of religion to legitimize what is obviously a sexual and commercial relationship.

All four women perform ethnicity by adjusting their sexual selves to the demands of being Malay. The Datin preserves the Malay family by accepting her rejected sexuality; Little Star threatens it by asserting her desirability. Yati bows to Islamic law also by accepting her rejected sexuality; Hanni uses Islamic law to her advantage to seal her desired status. All four women seem to have utilitarian reasons for being rejected and desired. Mak and Yati maintain their social positions, Little Star and Hanni use their bodies to survive. The Malay female sexual self, as seen in the novel, seems to hinge on the male presence that will either give or deprive.

Malay female sexuality, however, is more complex than *Khairunissa* suggests. In the novel, the women were the objects of desire of husbands and lovers. But does a Malay woman feel desire? In a culture that discourages blatant expressions of desire, what happens when desire conflicts with tradition and morality?

In Karim Raslan's 'Sara and the Wedding', Sara is desired and enjoys it, even if the man is hardly desirable himself. She allows herself to be taken by someone she does not love because 'years of denial and lack of interest prevented her' from saying no. Dina Zaman's 'Kacang Puteh and Assam Lady' feels the pull of physical desire even while she is selling food: 'her beneath will tug and tug and tug. Her wet comes out. Her nipples, flat from lack of attention become hard and erect.'[14] The fat woman in the story of the same title uses her body as a site of pleasure: 'When they (her breasts) were twenty years old, they were firm. *All the boys came out to play with them everyday.*'[15] Or of how she was bestowed with the name 'Virgin Killer'—she took all the boys in the neighborhood to her room and slept with them. Her legs would curl themselves up the boys' buntut while they finished whatever they had to do. They left their boy in her woman and left her as men.[16]

These excerpts show the presence of Malay female desire articulated in the invisible space of the body and mind. Yes, the Malay woman feels desire. The closures of the stories, however, are instructive as to how the Malay female characters feel about themselves as desiring subjectivities. Sara decides she just wants the power she can wield from being desired. She feels the elation of being desired, the pleasure of giving in to desire, but she also feels a need for moral and social reconstruction in the aftermath. Thus, after the act, she cries rape. The *kacang puteh* woman escapes into fantasy, suppressing the call of the flesh and fleeing her sordid real world by imagining she is a chaste princess. The fat woman who enjoyed her body when young, becomes fat and lonely in her maturity. One cannot help thinking of the punitive implications of her physical state since it transfers her from being desired to being rejected.

These closures imply the strong moral component attached to Malay female sexuality. Sexuality, especially female sexuality, seems to be a nemesis of morality. Those who have sexual pleasure are punished, those who feel the onslaught of desire are overwhelmed by guilt.

One cannot expect therefore to find *jouissance* in the Malay expression of female desire. None of the works cited here sees female sexuality as redemptive or fulfilling; it is utilitarian at best. The firm discursive structures of tradition and religion will not allow sexuality to be a site for self-discovery or personal fulfilment for the Malay woman.

But here is an interesting twist. If there is a Malay symbol for womanly goodness and virtue, it will be the *tudung*. Maznah Mohammad describes the *tudung* as a symbol of the veiled, modest, maternal Malay Muslim woman but it also represents a hyper-ethnicised feminine identity that took pre-eminence over other identities. It creates an ethnic nation of Malay woman that is separate from the women of other races. Maznah continues:

> robed Muslim men would not bat an eyelid if a scantily clad Chinese woman were to cross their path but a modestly-dressed but unveiled Malay woman in their way would strike their greater ire.[17]

But the *tudung* has recently and inadvertently acquired the secret and hidden scent of female sexuality. While it conceals the hair, a most erotic part, it also advertises what is concealed and therefore tantalizes. Alfian Sa'at's 'Bugis' illustrates a girl's display of her sexuality, not by revealing her hair but by concealing it. Ironically, Salmah's hypocritical wearing of the tudung gives her a respectability that allows her to practise her sexuality more freely. Khairunissa's Little Star, the starlet, begins to wear the *tudung* the moment she becomes pregnant. According to her, people treat an unwed pregnant girl better if she is wearing a tudung. Clearly, there is chafing against this ethnic construction of Malay female morality. How far it will go, only time will tell.

While there is also considerable silence on male sexuality, it is the de facto privileged sexuality. The male is also subject to strict moral standards and performs moral leadership in a family, but Islam gives him certain freedoms not available to a Malay female such as multiple marriage. It is easier therefore to regard the Malay male as a sexual being. It is his privilege to desire. But can he relocate himself from the space of desiring to that of desired? Can an ordinary Malay male be an object of desire? Apparently yes. Dina Zaman's two stories, 'The Passenger' and 'Night and day' use two Malay male characters as the objects of female desire. One is a taxi driver named Dasimon Salleh. He is described as riddled with acne, having thick hair which sticks out stubbornly at a certain angle and a face only a simple woman could love. And yet the woman passenger imagines erotic moments with her driver. She describes to the reader her fantasies of wild sexual encounters with him. Meanwhile the driver is passive and clueless.

The other male character is a male prostitute who is equally plain. What a plain face he had. Bulbous nose and creamed coffee skin on rather aboriginal features. A face one saw and would later forget, so insignificant, not even repulsive enough to seduce a woman.[18]

The female customer has a strange request. She wants him to hurt her. The night becomes erotically violent for the pair of them.

In both stories, the transgressive nature of female desire and the unthinkable sexual appeal of the Malay male (this is not to say that the Malay male has no sex appeal but that he is not generally thought of in that way) converge to create a different sexual representation of the Malay male. In the first story he is the passive object of desire, innocent and unaware, a role usually reserved for the female. In the second, he is the purchased body, meant to give pleasure. Again, this is a role generally assigned to the female.

Dina Zaman's feminization of the two male characters is inversely proportional to the empowerment of the woman characters. The taxi passenger dictates the sexual play in her fantasy and pleasures herself at the man's expense and without his consent. Meanwhile, the female procurer of the male body uses the male body in an extreme sense as the site of sexual play. She says: 'Tonight I will be a man and have a bit of rough myself'.[19] Wielder and receiver of violence, the woman appropriates the man for her sexual fantasies, easily conflating the pain and tenderness of the sado-masochist dream.

Interestingly, the female characters are of unknown ethnicity; this leaves us with awareness only of the ethnicity of the male characters. I cannot say if this is deliberate on Dina Zaman's part, but I read this as her avoidance of compromising the ethnicity of the women characters and her willingness to compromise that of the men. That both male characters are physically repulsive and yet sexually desirable gives Malay male sexuality an otherness and a liminal desirability that can be found in male attitudes towards women in the literature of patriarchy. By feminizing her Malay male characters not only by relocating them in passive gender roles, but also by emphasizing their otherness, thus relegating them to the margins of power, Dina Zaman writes back to the patriarchy.

Salleh Ben Joned, the 'bad boy' of Malaysian literature, picks up the cudgels for Malay male sexuality. He has written that pleasure has long been missing in Malay life and so he celebrates Malay male sexuality through his poem, 'A Hymn to My Sarong'. He refers to the feeling of 'easy sensuality' in wearing a sarong, describing 'golden mangoes dangling loose' while his 'feet are on the horizon and his rump on the earth'. He mentions the 'rubbing against the jugular/two stringy bodies/looped together', and finally, 'gushing fountains/of solitary delights/ drenching the diaphanous sky'.[20] The poem connects sexuality with objects of nature, emphasizing the naturalness of bodily pleasures. The fecundity of the earth is the fecundity of men. Wind, sun, earth and their free flow in a saronged body provide the persona with a vitality and energy to create a conjugal hymn to natural inclinations, a hymn that sings of human pleasure mingling with that of the natural world.

There is much celebration of male sexuality and solo sex in this poem which contrasts with the rather grim portrayals of male sexuality in Dina Zaman's stories. But what is significant here is the use of the sarong as main metaphor, a definite visible marker of Malay ethnicity. Salleh Ben Joned uses the sarong as a marker of sexuality in much the same way as the *tudung* has been used as a marker of Malay female sexuality. But there is no pretense in the donning of the sarong, only a freedom and pleasure not available to men who wear trousers.

The conflation of ethnicity and sexuality in the sarong is effectively delineated in Salleh Ben Joned's poem. The persona asserts a virile active sexuality within the ethnicity of a sarong, which here assumes freedom rather than containment. The sarong suggests that practice of such unabashed sexuality is possible within ethnic Malay space.

Salleh Ben Joned has lamented the relative absence of the erotic in modern Malay literature. He finds it in the traditional literary forms such as the *Hikayat Hang Tuah* and the *pantuns*.

I think it is undeniable that modern Malay literature is not notable for its achievements in the evocation of the raw pleasures of the senses—particularly the erotic experience. There have not been many attempts anyway, and of the few, the ones that could be considered memorable are less than the number of fingers of one hand. But if you move away from modern literature and venture into the imaginative world of older times, you will find some remarkable moments of unashamed sensuality and eroticism.[21]

Jouissance, it seems, is only evident in the writings of the past, not in the present. The poem 'A Hymn to My Sarong' therefore operates a retrieval of that long lost male pleasure.

Interestingly, except for one, my group of maverick writers are silent in regard to Malay alternative sexualities. Dina Zaman writes of a one night stand between a male tourist and a taxi driver, but the former is Caucasian, the latter Chinese. Alfian Sa'at writes of an aging homosexual falling in love with a young boy, but the former is Chinese and the latter of unknown ethnicity. He also writes of two young lesbians making out in public toilets, but both are Chinese.

Karim Raslan is the exception, depicting the doubly forbidden, doubly transgressive sexualities. His story, 'Neighbors', which revolves around a handsome, wealthy, gay Malay male, is much anthologised and read. But another story demonstrates the dynamics between sexuality and ethnicity more clearly and with more complexity.

The story 'Go East!' narrates the life of Mahmud, a young planter in Sabah who becomes fascinated by the wild East. Originally from the capital Kuala Lumpur, Mahmud sees in Sabah a Malaysia that is different, not only because it is geographically and culturally far from Kuala Lumpur, but also because the restrictions and certainties of the capital do not seem to apply. Here, farmers' wives and daughters are raped by pirates, the life of a man is worth 10 ringgit, and prostitutes can be had for a song. It is a Malaysia transformed and transmogrified. For Mahmud, it is also a place where one can be oneself:

> I like Sabah. I liked it from the day I arrived. I knew it was going to be different and it was. It was noisy, dirty, rough and un-Malay ... you're not expected to be one thing or another. You don't have to attend endless bloody kenduris of relatives you hardly know. There's something nice about not having too many Melayu about; they're always so disapproving—all tak boleh, tak halus, tak manis—it makes me sick.
>
> We're not an Istana anymore and we carry on as if we're all courtiers or something.[22]

Mahmud's chafing against his ethnicity brings him out of his certainty about where he belongs; this makes him both frightened and exhilarated. The town of Lahad Datu, Sabah has brought him a freedom he has never experienced.

Karim uses the trope of sexuality to intrude into acceptable notions of ethnicity. Mahmud's romantic alliance with his Malay girlfriend in Kuala Lumpur follows conventions. The couple are initially circumspect, mindful of the dictates of tradition and religion. In one impulsive moment, they spend the weekend together. Strangely, Mahmud cannot perform sexually.

The incident is repeated when Mahmud, now back in Sabah, comes home drunk and tries to have sex with his willing Indonesian maid. Again he does not perform. Is it because the women are both Muslim and sex with them is prohibited? As it turns out, Mahmud's object of desire is Anton, his Filipino servant. Neither a Malay Muslim nor a woman, Anton is the locus of a sexuality that violates the ethnic definition of a Malay man. Anton is an unofficial ethnicity, possibly an illegal. He also suggests an escape from rigid ethnic containments.

Mahmud fights the unfamiliar urges, almost succumbing. In a desperate move to resolve the question of his manhood, he seeks the services of a 13-year-old Filipina prostitute. He finally performs sexually, to his great relief, but only after furiously fantasizing about Anton during the sex act. Interestingly, he remembers only the heterosexuality of the act, not the paedophilia, prostitution, homosexual fantasy and non-Malayness that laced his sexual performance or how this act is inimical to his Malay selfhood. He creates a secret self outside Malay ethnic and cultural expectations, an identity that is not acknowledged yet because of its strangeness and its power to destabilize or erase the self he knows.

In another light, Mahmud's sexual performance can also be seen as a performative gesture allowing him to disengage from conventions that limit self-construction. With his groin and his mind, he embraces the hybridizing space created by sexual indeterminacy. While a definite racial Malayness and masculine gender defined him in the past, he now has opportunity to explore non-Malay ingredients in the formation of self, which may include a new sexuality. This he can do only in a neutral space such as Sabah where the ethnic hegemony of peninsular Malaysia loses its containing power due to the presence of other ethnicities and consequently causes the loosening of internal boundaries.

The works discussed above open the window slightly into the space of sexuality that defines ethnicity. The acceptable notion of sex in Malay culture is that it must be conjugal, procreative and heterosexual. We see that through the window, but through the same window, we also see sex that is celebratory, pleasure and fantasy oriented, regendered and non-heterosexual. Malay writers in English are sometimes resented because the sexualities they depict are not within the parameters of the prescribed and also because they disturb the formulated notions of ethnicity with their problematic sexualities.

In the end, the writers just want to tell us that our sexual selves are as essential as our public ethnic selves. We perform ethnicity to fulfil our need to belong; we perform sexuality to fulfil our need to be human.

Notes

1 Alfian Sa'at, 'Project', *Corridor: 12 Short Stories* (Singapore: Raffles, SNP Editions, 1999) 3.

2 Anne-Marie Fortier, 'Outside/In? Notes on Sexuality, Ethnicity and the Didactics of Identification'. Department of Sociology, Lancaster University. Accessed 1999. <http://www.lancs.ac.uk/sociology/papers/Fortier-Outside/In> 2.

3 Gordon Means, *Malaysian Politics* (New York: New York Univ. Press, 1970) 19.

4 Ibrahim Saad, *Competing Identities in a Plural Society* (Singapore: Institute of Southeast Asian Studies, c.1981) 15–16.

5 Cheu Hong Tong and Teoh Boon Seng, 'Malay Studies in Language, Literature, Culture and Society', ed. Chua Beng Huat, *Singapore Studies II* (Singapore: Singapore University Press for Faculty of Arts and Social Sciences, National University of Singapore, 1999) 132.

6 Quoted in Fadillah Merican, 'Malay Women in Malaysian Fiction in English in the 1990s: Seen and Heard', *Native Texts and Contexts: Essays with Post Colonial*

Perspective (Bangi: Fakulti Pengajian Bahasa, Universiti Kebangsaan Malaysia, 2001) 85.

7 Fadillah Merican, 'Malay Women in Malaysian Fiction in English' 96.

8 Kenneth Paul Tan, 'Ethnic Representation on Singapore Film and Television', ed. Lai Ah Eng, *Beyond Rituals and Riots. Ethnic Pluralism and Social Cohesion in Singapore* (Singapore: Marshall Cavendish International, 2004) 304.

9 Ellina Abdul Majid, *Khairunissa: A Good Woman* (Kuala Lumpur: The Written Word, 1998).

10 Ellina Abdul Majid, *Perhaps in Paradise* (Kuala Lumpur: The Written Word, 1997).

11 Ellina, *Khairunissa* 167.

12 Ellina, *Khairunissa* 130.

13 Ellina, *Khairunissa* 168.

14 Dina Zaman, 'Kacang Puteh and Assam Lady', *night and day* (Petaling Jaya: Rhino Press, 1997) 12.

15 Dina, 'Kacang Puteh' 56.

16 Dina, 'Kacang Puteh' 57.

17 Maznah Mohammad, 'Women in the UMNO and PAS Labyrinth', eds. Maznah Mohamad and Wong Soak Koon, *Risking Malaysia. Culture, Politics and Identity* (Bangi, Malaysia: Penerbit Universiti Kebangsaan Malaysia, 2001) 116.

18 Dina, *night and day* 46–7.

19 Dina, *night and day* 45.

20 Salleh Ben Joned, 'A Hymn to My Sarong', *Tenggara: A Journal of Southeast Asian Literature* (1989) 36–37.

21 Salleh Ben Joned, 'Malay Lay of Life, Love and Laughter', *As I Please: Selected Writings 1975–1994* (London: Skoob Books, 1994) 154.

22 Karim Raslan, 'Go East!' *Heroes and Other Stories* (Singapore & Kuala Lumpur: Times Books International, 1996) 104-05.

Works cited

Alfian Sa'at. *Corridor: 12 Short Stories*. Singapore: Raffles, SNP Editions, 1999.

Cheu Hong Tong and Teoh Boon Seng. 'Malay Studies in Language, Literature, Culture and Society' *Singapore Studies II*, ed. Chua Beng Huat. Singapore: Singapore University Press for Faculty of Arts and Social Sciences, National University of Singapore, 1999.

Dina Zaman. *night and day*. Petaling Jaya: Rhino Press, 1997.

Ellina Abdul Majid. *Khairunissa: A Good Woman*. Kuala Lumpur: The Written Word, 1998.

Ellina Abdul Majid. *Perhaps in Paradise* Kuala Lumpur: The Written Word, 1997

Fadillah Merican. 'Malay Women in Malaysian Fiction in English in the 1990s: Seen and Heard'. *Native Texts and Contexts: Essays with Post Colonial Perspective*. Bangi: Fakulti Pengajian Bahasa, Universiti Kebangsaan Malaysia, 2001.

Fortier, Anne-Marie. 'Outside/In? Notes on Sexuality, Ethnicity and the Didactics of Identification'. Department of Sociology, Lancaster University. Accessed 1999. <http://www.lancs.ac.uk/sociology/papers/Fortier-Outside/In>

Fortier, Anne-Marie. 'New Intimacies and un/marked(hetero)sexuality: Intersections of ethnicity and sexuality in new multiculturalist Britain'. Department of Sociology, Lancaster University. Accessed 2001 http://www.lancs.ac.uk/sociology /papers/Fortier-New Intimacies

Ibrahim Saad. *Competing Identities in a Plural Society.* Singapore: Institute of Southeast Asian Studies, c.1981.

Maznah Mohamad. 'Women in the UMNO and PAS Labyrinth. *Risking Malaysia. Culture, Politics and Identity,* eds Maznah Mohamad and Wong Soak Koon. Bangi, Malaysia: Penerbit Universiti Kebangsaan Malaysia, 2001.

Means, Gordon. *Malaysian Politics.* New York: New York Univ. Press, 1970.

Nor Faridah Abdul Manaf. 'Sexuality in Post Independence Anglophone Writing by Three Malaysian Muslim Women Writers'. *Malaysian Literature in English,* eds Mohammad Quayum and Peter Wicks. Petaling Jaya: Pearson Education Malaysia, 2001: 144–53.

Raslan, Karim. *Heroes and Other Stories.* Singapore & Kuala Lumpur: Times Books International, 1996.

Salleh Ben Joned. 'A Hymn to My Sarong' *Tenggara: A Journal of Southeast Asian Literature* (1989).

Salleh Ben Joned. 'Malay Lay of Life, Love and Laughter'. *As I Please: Selected Writings 1975–1994.* London: Skoob Books, 1994.

Tan, Kenneth Paul. 'Ethnic Representation on Singapore Film and Television'. *Beyond Rituals and Riots. Ethnic Pluralism and Social Cohesion in Singapore,* ed. Lai Ah Eng. Singapore: Marshall Cavendish International, 2004.

A Minority Within a Minority? Analysis of Short fiction by Che Husna Azhari and Ghulam-Sarwar Yousof

GAIK CHENG KHOO

AUSTRALIAN NATIONAL UNIVERSITY, CANBERRA

In the last thirty years or so Malaysian writings in English have been relegated by Malay language and literature critics to minority status in the public discourse around what constitutes 'Malaysian' literature or 'national' literature. Resisting the dictates of the National Cultural Policy (1971), this chapter makes the basic assumption that the content of such literature, rather than its linguistic medium, is the key to defining national literature in Malaysia. Therefore, if the subject matter reflects the Malaysian socius and sensibility, then it is 'national'. However, the task of writing in English in Malaysia, to a limited audience, creates minority writers. The two writers whose work I propose to discuss not only write in English, but write about specific regional minority identities or communities they are familiar with. This makes them doubly minor.

Ghulam-Sarwar majored in English Literature at the University of Malaya and then completed his PhD in Asian Theatre at the University of Hawaii. Better known as an academic and pioneer of Malay traditional theatre and head of the Asian Centre for the Arts at USM (Universiti Sains Malaysia) since 1970, he has written poetry (the collection *Perfumed Memories*), several plays (*Halfway Road, Penang* or *Jalan Sekerat, Pulau Pinang*; other unpublished plays considered 'sensitive' such as *The Trial of Hang Tuah the Great*, *Suvarna Padma* or *Golden Lotus*), and short stories, some of which appear in a new collection *Mirror of a Hundred Hues.*

Che Husna Azhari (b. circa 1955) is a self-identified Kelantanese Malay woman writer from a middle-class background who studied Engineering in the United Kingdom and now teaches that subject at Universiti Kebangsaan Malaysia (UKM). She has published three books, *Kelantanese Tales*, *Melor in Perspective* and *The Rambutan Orchard* and her other short stories appear in journals like *Tenggara.* Che Husna is very conscious of the dichotomous relationship between nation and region: politically, between Kuala Lumpur and Kota Bahru, Kelantan, and culturally, between Melaka and the more marginalised Pattani.

Works by Che Husna, which focus on Kelantanese society, and Ghulam-Sarwar Yousof on the Penang Indian Muslim community, can be categorised as belonging to 'a minority within a minority' in the growing body of literature in English by Malaysian writers. To illustrate this point, in relation to Ghulam-Sarwar Yousof, the Indian Muslim is in a unique position. She or he can be considered a minority within the majority of Malaysian Muslims who are ethnically Malay. But s/he is also a minority within a minority Indian ethnic group in Malaysia, since Indians are generally believed to be Hindu by religious persuasion.

I do not wish to impose an essentialised framework around the work of these two writers by categorising them as being 'a minority within a minority'. After all, a writer like K.S. Maniam often focuses on a specific ethnic community in Malaysia and so far, no one has ventured to call him a double minority writer. This begs the question, why not? What makes a writer's work categorically 'national' or 'regional'? How can we claim Che Husna and Ghulam-Sarwar's works as both national and regional? As minority work within English-language Malaysian literature? Perhaps the broader problem here is with categorising and labelling writers and their works.

Firstly, there is a point to categorising. Creating new categories or putting certain hitherto unheard-of voices into existing categories means broadening the canon and making it more inclusive. It also means destabilising the present centre by pointing out the missing, the excised, or marginalised. It provides counterpoints and multiple perspectives which may be disjunctive amongst themselves or contradictory of the norms and which therefore deconstruct what 'national literature' is. After all, who defines what Malaysian literature is? Who decides who writes it, who is able to produce it (in terms of being educated, literate, having funding while writing), who is privileged to get published, and to qualify for national literary awards. While I make the case in this chapter that these two writers fit in the category of 'double minority', in terms of class, education and opportunity, they cannot be considered 'minority'. In fact, both are educated in English, both have studied abroad in the West and are now academics teaching at local universities.

However, Indian Muslim Malaysians have an ambiguous relationship with the culturally dominant Malay majority. They are strategically used by politicians playing the Muslim card as well as the ethnic Indian card. The Indian Muslim is often called 'Mamak'—a slightly derogatory term used to connote impurity for those Malays who may have Indian ancestry, or regarded as business-minded, or in the Nasi Kandar restaurant sector.[1] Their credentials as Muslims do not seem as legitimate in the eyes of state religious officials who have confiscated pictures of Arabic verses from their restaurant and accused them of giving the 'false' impression that they sell 'halal' (permitted by Islam) food.[2] This is because in Malaysia, race or ethnicity is still the definitive factor of one's identity, and Indian Muslims are regarded as Indians first, and Muslim second. Moreover, the stereotypical linkages between ethnicity and religion still prevail in public discourse: Malay-Muslim, Chinese-Buddhist/Taoist, Indian-Hindu or Chinese and Indian Christian. Malay ethno-nationalists assume sole entitlement over Islam to mark ethnic and religious boundaries between themselves and non-Malays.

References to 'mamak restaurants' in Ghulam-Sarwar's story 'Lottery Ticket' acknowledge the ubiquitous presence and contribution of Indian Muslims to everyday space and life in urban Malaysia. Ghulam-Sarwar's colourful descriptions of the characters' surroundings ground his fiction in a very physical Georgetown. In the short story, "Lottery Ticket," he describes the banking district whose signage harkens to its colonial past: 'Right across from where he was standing at the corner of Beach Street and Union Street near Barkath Stores stood the old grey building of the Chartered Bank'.[3] The fact that these street names remain in English and Standard Chartered Bank is known by its older name situates the story in the early 1980s or earlier. 'This is not to say that Ghulam-Sarwar's work, compared to Maniam's, does not have universal appeal or lacks metaphysical or philosophical ideas. In fact, much of his poetry touches on universal themes such as the miniscule place of human beings in the time and space continuum. Moreover, his plays and other short stories deal with his academic interests in Hindu mythology and Malay *wayang kulit* (shadow puppetry). Perhaps what makes his short stories a little more unique is that his main characters are from 'outside the range of normal Malaysian characters'.[4] As he himself states, 'I try to deal with the north Indian communities, such as the Punjabis and the Mamak'.[5] Moreover, unlike Maniam, Ghulam-Sarwar being an Indian Muslim and an expert on Malay traditional arts (recently honoured with the Tokoh Ma'al Hijrah award for his contribution to Malay culture), dares to approach the subject of Islam in his work without so much fear of recrimination and criticism from certain groups of Malays.

Despite the idea that the author is dead and the text can be read apart from authorial intention, possibly yielding interpretations to a reader determined to read against the grain, I am also of the opinion that the author is an ideological subject of his and her environment, 'hailed' (as Louis Althusser would put it) by the ideologies of ethnicity, religion, class, gender and culture. Thus, the text reveals quite a lot about the writer—whether it is the fact that she or he has an active imagination, or, s/he has certain ideas about Malays and Indian Muslims, specifically their attitudes towards Islamic authority and their general understanding and practice of Islam. Or, if it is not specifically their personal views, at least the writers provide a discussion or forum on these issues in their creative work.

I will begin with Che Husna, who takes an anti-colonial position in introducing her stories in the second part of *Melor in Perspective*:

> I am dispensing with romance, neo-colonial remnants of a writing genre with generous descriptions of torpitude, torrid weather, languid memsahibs and white Tuans dispensing egalitarian and universal truths to ineffectual natives. I am also dispensing with crusading counter-studies of nationalistic-Malay fervour. I am starting on the Kelantanese's own premises, peculiar to their own culture and perceived history, innate in their psyche ... who are these Kelantanese? Are we really different from the rest of the peninsular Malays?[6]

She adds, 'We despair that historians of Malay history collectively group our history with the Malacca-centric one of Malay culture', and asks the question:

> If the Malacca Sultanate personifies the zenith of Malay culture, was it a culture of learning, of intellect, or was it a culture given to pomp, pageantry and costumed splendour? Which of these do we wish to portray and identify with?[7]

As a contrast, she explains that the Kelantanese Malays 'have their own rich, established history, identifying strongly with the civilisation of the Malay Pattani Kingdoms of Southern Thailand and of the Champas'.[8] Che Husna's stories centering around Kelantan society demonstrate her proud identification with her regional roots, as does the following statement. She writes:

> The Kelantanese are a migrating people but they will always be Kelantanese ... the new migrant generation's strong and insistent identification with their culture is not born of a parochial and chauvinistic sentiment, but of an awareness of the deep tradition of scholarship and enterprise associated with the Kelantanese.[9]

Here she is referring to the Islamic education of the madrasahs, the fact that Kelantanese women run the businesses in the markets and the flowering of Kelantanese culture through the writings of various famous ulamas.

The issues raised by both writers are many and varied but for the purposes of this chapter, I shall consider themes or issues that they both share that belie their thoughts concerning Muslim identity in Malaysia. At the same time, questions about what makes the text national or regional and what the regional perception of the national is are equally central.

Attitudes towards Islam and polygamy

In this section I shall focus on Ghulam-Sarwar's short stories 'Lottery Ticket' and 'Birthday' and Che Husna's portrayal of the Imam in 'Mariah' and 'The Mascot'. In 'The Lottery Ticket' Ghulam-Sarwar's Indian Muslim character, Aboo Bakar Maraicar, is described in the opening paragraph as 'just an ordinary Muslim, neither pious nor yet completely ignorant of Islamic tenet.[10] He is familiar with some of the Hadith and the stories of the prophets; he knows a few verses from the Holy Quran but, even he has to admit to himself, not quite enough to get him through prayers'.[11] The phrase 'just an ordinary Muslim' hints that Ghulam-Sarwar is not speaking only about Indian Muslims but is making a more general statement that pertains to his perception of ordinary Muslims in Malaysia. In fact, Ghulam-Sarwar reinforces this notion that he is including the national and not just the regional Muslim populace in his second paragraph:

> *Like most Muslims* he ritually omitted the five obligatory prayers every day, but he made sure he went to the Kapitan Keling mosque on Fridays for the Jumaat communal prayers and for the two Eid prayers every year [italics mine].[12]

The writer calls into question what being a Muslim is all about by drawing a character like Aboo Bakar who 'did not speak or understand Arabic, and so the prayers and the Quranic verses were no more than pleasant sounding words with an aura of the sacred' and for whom 'the longer *doa* and passages from the Holy Quran meant very little'.[13] I am applying this critique of Ghulam-Sarwar's about the superficial understanding of Islam to the general Muslim populace in contemporary Malaysia only, but perhaps Ghulam-Sarwar intends to make a comment about Muslims in India as well, if not globally, for he informs the reader that this has been the pattern of Aboo Bakar's religious life since he first started going to the mosque with his father more than thirty-five years ago in his village outside Nagapattinam in India. The point that Mulims have a superficial understanding of Islam, merely going through the rituals without much thought or inquiry as to why, is prevalent throughout the story of a man preoccupied with the thought of cashing in his winning lottery ticket and contemplating what to do with the winnings while at the Friday afternoon prayers.

We see in Aboo Bakar Maraicar a simple man who acknowledges his ignorance:

> He sometimes wondered ... where ... his near-complete lack of understanding of the ritual texts was to lead him, especially when it came to Hari Qiamat, the Day of Resurrection and Judgement.[14]

Yet, just as he resolves to try harder to become familiar with the prayers 'in content and method of performance', he suddenly realises 'that his ankles hurt with his whole weight placed on them' and he 'wished the [interminable] sermon would end'.[15] So here we have a man with good intentions but who is too (spiritually) weak to carry them through. A harsher criticism would be to say that Aboo Bakar is hypocritical. After all, this is a man who thinks nothing of bribing the Customs officers at Madras and calling it an 'investment'—for by giving gifts, he could escape paying duty.[16]

When we are told that the day's sermon is on 'avarice, and the need for good Muslims to avoid greed for it [leads] to behaviour contrary to Islamic teachings', this is a premonition of bad things to come.[17] First, Aboo Bakar wonders if buying lottery tickets makes him a greedy person, then he becomes arrogant (which he genuinely regrets) and then he tells a lie. When Nagore Maideen asks him why he is in a hurry, he replies saying, he has to go home and write some letters. Actually, he is on his way to the bank to cash his lottery ticket. Moreover, he rationalises that the lie is necessary in the present circumstance and he is sure God would understand.[18] When he is finally at the bank and has to produce his lottery ticket, he cannot find it and breaks down, 'sobbing like a child'.[19] This is not the unhappy denouement; on the next page the reader discovers that Aboo Bakar has ended up in the hospital and cannot even remember how he got there.

I am reluctant to make the claim that Ghulam-Sarwar is critiquing the moral hypocrisy of Muslims through the portrait of Aboo Bakar. The characterisation works at a more complex level than simply as a morality tale or the retelling of a common Malay folktale (like the Lebai Malang tale of counting one's chickens before they are hatched). This is because Aboo Bakar is also portrayed as an industrious, self-sacrificing family man who 'never allowed himself any luxuries' and regularly remitted his salary home to his family in India.[20] Can a poor, frugal migrant worker scraping to make a decent living in Malaysia, separated from his family, be denied such fantasies of finally enjoying good *nasi beriani* every day? Is it such a sin to 'imagin[e] the most lucrative manner in which his money could be utilised' or 'make some profit [from] selling [in Madras] items he did not need', bought back from Malaysia?[21] These questions cast an ambivalent or non-judgmental light on black-and-white moral values. Indeed, the notion of ambivalence is important and I shall return to it in my conclusion.

Islam is relatively new in the region compared to the centuries of animism and Hinduism in Southeast Asia's rich history. Moreover, cultural syncretism occurred when religio-cultural borders blended and merged and layers overlapped through time. Something that verged upon ambivalence or perhaps tolerance allowed for and perhaps even fostered hybridity/syncretism. Set in an ethnically diverse location such as Georgetown with its history of various migrations from Aceh, Java, and different parts of India and China, unsurprisingly the short story contains Chinese, Punjabi, Indian Muslim, Tamil Hindu and Malay characters. Aboo Bakar's distrust and essentialism of the Chinese reflects Malaysian pluralism, unlike many other writings in English and in Bahasa Malaysia which usually reflect a more racially homogeneous Malaysia. However, it is also reflective of a racialisation whereby members of ethnic groups 'know' each other only through the discourse of racial stereotypes: 'the efficiency of the Chinese'[22] or Tamil Indians 'who as a race were addicted to gossip'[23]. Despite the mingling of various ethnicities living side by side, there is a need driven by the discourse of racialisation to continuously fit identity into bounded and neat ethnic categories: for example, Aboo Bakar wondered whether Roslina, the young female bank clerk who is serving him, is Malay, Chinese or Eurasian.[24] This 'confusion' is healthy and regarded as a positive gesture towards hybridity, when the need for purity is foiled and previously preserved barriers are broken down. (It is also possible to read it as a deconstruction of Malay identity.) In another short story entitled 'Birthday', this mixture of religious beliefs is observed by the protagonist Pak Dollah, a schoolteacher and a Muslim who has consulted a Sikh palmist and a Siamese *bomoh* (medicine-man or witch doctor) without any qualms about such actions contradicting Islamic teachings or being considered unIslamic. In Che Husna's short stories about Kelantanese Malay culture, this syncretism is evident as well, and beliefs in Islam are not seen as compromised by elements of the supernatural and the practice of magic. For example, it is believed that Mek Teh, the Mak Andam (bridal attendant) of Kampung Melor died due to *pelesit* (spirit) consumption, a condition that completely mystifies doctors ('Mek Teh, Mother Andam') and when the first wife of the Imam consents to his marrying a second wife, the male villagers 'wondered what Quranic ayats the Imam blew on Cik Yam's face to subdue her' ('Mariah').[25]

Hybridity in this case becomes what is actually being practised every day; it becomes what postcolonial scholar Homi Bhabha terms 'the perplexity of the living as it interrupts the representation of the fullness of life', or, it is the performative which confounds the pedagogical, the state's ideological meaning of nation (in this case, the national religion, Islam, as narrowly defined by official religious purists).[26] The short story 'Birthday' precisely demonstrates this hybridity or syncretism, showing that Malays still believe in *ilmu jahat* (black magic) and love charms ('such things were known to actually transpire') while simultaneously undergoing Muslim rites like conducting the Haj to Mecca, having a *doa selamat* (blessings) for birthdays, and lastly, having a fatalistic attitude towards life.[27]

This fatalism is reflected in Pak Dollah's feelings that 'life and death were in the hand of God'.[28] Yet, one cannot help but wonder how much of it is acceptance of Fate/Providence/God's Will, when he only reflects upon this after he takes a second wife seemingly without any resistance from his first wife. Would Pak Dollah have so easily accepted his fate if the women did not agree? It is all too easy to accept the status quo when one has been dealt a good set of cards in life. His elder brother, Pak Kadir, whose example he follows, had earlier affirmed that Pak Kadir's marrying a second time to a woman much younger to him was 'the will of God, and if Allah willed that he should marry a third, or even a fourth wife, then he would do so, InshaAllah'.[29] As if to reinforce the strength of this belief, following this statement, it is immediately mentioned that even Pak Kadir's 'two wives concurred with him. Nothing could come in the way of God's Will'.[30]

The married Imam in Che Husna's short story 'Mariah' also believes it is fate that explains his attraction for Mariah, the *nasi* (rice) seller. He had had his heart broken by a Sheikh's daughter in his youth, one whom Mariah resembles, and being a fairly happily-married man now, he first tries to deny his feelings, spending the nights in supplication, asking God for succour. He even sees it as a test, and one which he admittedly fails: 'Forgive me, oh God, for men are weak', he supplicates while silently eating Mariah's *nasi belauk* at her stall instead of his wife's at home.[31] Eventually he changes his attitude towards this failure, re-rationalising his overwhelming passion and elation by believing that the chance meeting with Mariah 'was fated, a part of a grand design by God to heal his heart'.[32] He then proceeds with a rather abbreviated form of rationalising this:

> [C]an a beautiful alluring woman be a part of a healing process? It seems so profane to the Imam. But why should a woman be more profane than a man? Did not the Prophet himself say that three things are pleasing to him, prayers, women and perfume? There you are! Proof, exoneration for the Imam.[33]

In this line of self-questioning that deals with gender discrimination, the Imam has cleverly sidestepped the issue of his own profane selfishness and betrayal of his wife's love. For the sake of argument, one could carry his line of questioning further and ask what the consequences would be if the Imam had found a beautiful alluring *man* to be part of his healing process. Would this be considered more profane or less profane?

The Imam resolves to ask Mariah to be his second wife. Mariah agrees, after all, an Imam, being 'a man of religion', has status and respectability in a Kelantanese village.[34] But Cik Yam, the Imam's loving, devoted housewife for fifteen years, does not immediately give her consent. She breaks down in despair when he asks her permission to marry a second wife. When he tries to hold her, she pushes him away. Nevertheless, the Imam manages to placate her with promises of his love and continuing devotion even to the point of kissing her feet (the writer calls this 'a final act of submission'[35]) and by the next morning, she grants his request but on condition of equality.[36]

In this polygamous arrangement we should ask who benefits. Obviously by the end of the narrative, the Imam has fulfilled his dream on his wedding night: the suggestive line ' … before Mariah's perfume completely enveloped him and his senses', in fact concludes the short story.[37] In the privacy of their bridal chamber, Mariah too gains something from this alliance as she begins to notice how physically attractive her new husband is: 'tall, well-built and with measured movement'.[38] As for Cik Yam, the first wife, we have no further insight into her own thoughts after the night where the Imam *seduces* her into compliance and consent. Che Husna shows her discretion by omitting further description of the seduction after he kisses Cik Yam's feet. The subsequent sentence modestly jumps to the next morning:

> 'I love you and will always love you, Yam. Nothing can change that. I will alway be your husband. I will care for you, Yam' … said in between kisses on Cik Yam's forehead, hands and … feet. Thus the night passed and in the morning with the first rays of sunlight, Cik Yam said "Yes" to the Imam's request, on condition of equality.'[39]

Did the seduction continue because the Imam proved not only in words but also in kind deed how he would continue to be her husband and give her what she desires? Or did Cik Yam spend the night tossing and turning, trying to decide what to do? The gossipy narrator re-enters the scene the next morning to reveal that: 'The Imam had breakfast at home with Cik Yam and he himself spooned the *nasi belauk* into Cik Yam's mouth'.[40] This gesture, symbolising nurturance, love and support, is significant as it is usually performed between newly weds on the bridal dais during the Malay *bersanding* ceremony. However, this gesture does not necessarily confirm whether the Imam is motivated by sheer happiness and gratitude or by true love, such as he has professed the night before. We can only guess, basing our speculation on unreliable village gossip and rumour, that perhaps the added respect Cik Yam has earned from this arrangement (respect for her fortitude, her 'virtue and steadfastness') could only benefit her while on this earthly realm.[41] As for the next world, all the *kampung* folk agree that on the Day of Judgement she 'would certainly be found sheltering in the shade of the Umbrella of Siti Fatimah (the Prophet's daughter)'.[42] In short, Che Husna illustrates some initial resistance on the part of the first wife toward her husband's polygamy, but this resistance is quickly overcome, whether because Cik Yam believes the Imam to be sincere about continuing to love her or whether she feels she has no choice when it comes to matters of the unwilling heart. Although she consents on condition of equality, she is nonetheless working within a framework of limited choices. By the end of the story, it is difficult to conclude whether or not Che Husna condemns the notion of polygamy. In the eyes of the villagers who are not cognizant of the facts about the Imam's past unrequited love for the Sheikh's daughter, the Imam marries a second wife who can give him a child, since Cik Yam could not. Nevertheless, the writer reveals her own views on this subject early in the story through the caustic tone in which this reason for male polygamy is disputed:

> Like all men of his generation, it never occurred to [the Imam] he could be the culprit in his wife's supposed inability to bear children. As far as he was concerned, bearing children was a woman's job, and if she didn't there was something wrong with her. Fertility had nothing to do with men.[43]

While both the Imam and Mariah regard the second marriage as an act of Allah, no such acknowledgement of God's will is forthcoming from Cik Yam's mouth or thoughts. Thus, a certain ambivalence can be surmised on Che Husna's part on the issue of polygamy.

Perhaps Che Husna's 'The Mascot' encapsulates regional versus national tension most clearly in the form of the clash between civil law (the police) and moral law, wielded by the Imam. The catalyst of this battle between tradition and modernity, between religious morality as all-governing and the imposition of civil law (a corollary product of Western nationalism and nationhood), is the appearance of a troupe of *wayang* (theatre) performers. The Imam deeply disapproves of their presence as he regards their lifestyle as morally corrupt. Because the performers worked only at night and rested during the day, as is the normal practice of all wayang folk, 'Even this simple fact was enough to damn them forever, thought the Imam'. After all, he thinks to himself, 'Allah made the day for working and the night for resting and prayer'.[44] Moreover, dressing up the troupe master's pet monkey in human clothes contradicts the Imam's sense of social and moral decorum and is, as the policeman Cik Poleh rightly surmises, 'akin to icon worship' in the eyes of the Imam.[45] When the animal is caught by surprise by a little girl one day, it bites her. The Imam then becomes more determined to remove not just the monkey but also the whole troupe. Aided by a local gangster, he forces the *wayang* master to kill his pet with a gun. It is clear to the *wayang* performers at the end that their poor mascot is a metaphor and his public death could so very easily be their own. Sacrificing the mascot means getting rid of frivolity and playful creativity. It signals the triumph of moral austerity over civil law.

Here in this particular short story, the writer, herself a Kelantanese Malay, critiques the moral rigidity of the Imam (who perhaps symbolises the theology of the *Kaum Tua*, or Old School) through the perspectives of the more temperate, secular, petit bourgeois village committee (the teachers, Cik Gu Roni and Cik Gu Deraman, and headmaster, Master Hussein) and the *orang luar* or outsider, the policeman Cik Poleh. At the same time, Che Husna is also careful to portray the mindset of the proud and persistent Imam, who feels besieged and made 'impotent' by interference from the secularist federal government in the form of 'civil law' signified by Cik Poleh.[46] The Imam considers the policeman 'unlettered' (he means unlettered in Arabic and religious knowledge) and therefore unqualified in 'taking matters of moral import into his own hands'.[47] At the same time the policeman, after being blackmailed and threatened by the Imam who says he will dispose of the mascot and shoo off the troupe, feels that 'the Kelantanese [are] absolutely lawless'.[48] He defines lawlessness as 'having men apt to beat up people who disagreed with your way of life'.[49] Cik Poleh 'did not think that in a civil sense they had a right to prevent the *wayang* performers from earning their [decent] living, 'the women singing and acting and the men, play-acting on stage seems harmless enough.[50] This comment from Cik Poleh makes the Imam look petty and repressed, backward even.

Ultimately, this short story reflects the surge of neo-Islamicisation in Malaysia where those age-old elements of religio-cultural hybridity and syncretism, deemed unIslamic, are being eradicated (the *wayang* contains elements of Hinduism). It is also a condemnation of the weak opposition put up by the more moderate villagers and may be read to parallel the un-progressive concession that the federal government under the Alliance (Barisan National) made to combat the strength of the Islamic opposition, PAS.[51]

Ambivalence, rather than neutrality or objectivity, seems to be the attitude both Che Husna and Ghulam-Sarwar have towards their subjects' views on Islam and Muslim identity. In Che Husna's short stories this ambivalence manifests as sharp criticism of the many views on the issue of identity: the ineffectual outsider policeman, the cowardly moderates within the village elite and finally, the rigid brand of Islam personified by the Imam. Even though Che Husna's position on Islam seems to be a liberal, tolerant one, she still attempts to portray the Imam's views, productively creating a space for discussion and debate among the characters holding various positions in the text.

The title for this chapter contains a question mark, signalling my awareness of the need for further debate on the question of whether Ghulam-Sarwar and Che Husna's writings belong in the category of 'minority-within-a-minority'. It is clear that someone like Che Husna is intent on recording Kelantanese social history. Her bibliography in *Melor in Perspective* displays a variety of sources: from Malay writers writing in Malay, Muslim writings from other parts of the world, to the work of Western anthropologists and historians as well as a series of oral interviews she conducts herself. Her postcolonial, third world feminist analysis of gender relations in Kelantan society and its history (mythological and otherwise) is conveyed through the medium of English. Throughout the stories, she acts as a native informant, giving cultural asides, footnotes, translations and glossaries to the English-language reader who has no knowledge of Bahasa Malaysia or Malay culture in general. In that sense, her projected audience and readership also belongs to that broader world of English beyond the Malaysian border.

Perhaps this social, oral and historical documentation written down for posterity in a globally portable language, English, makes it harder to describe the work of Che Husna and Ghulam-Sarwar as 'a minority within a minority'. For Che Husna, writing in English situates her in a more neutral position so that she is spared from taking sides between the ideology and politics of the secular nation-state and that of the Islamic party, PAS, in Kelantan. Not only that, her use of different modes of discourse—the academic essay on Kelantanese history and culture that contains a detailed map of her hometown Melor 'drawn from memory', its theoretical postcolonial analyses of gender and nationalism in Kelantan—function collectively with the short stories that contain the distinct intrusive voice of the story-teller who narrates as well as provide poetry, incantations and other forms of discourse. These include, for example, drawing a family tree and budget sheets ('Of Bunga Telur and Bally Shoes') and establishing oral genealogy (or, as Dr Wong Soak Koon says of the tale 'Ustazah Inayah', pointing out how genealogies are constructed). In short, Che Husna's writings in English function as an ethnography that would appeal to various broad constituencies: not just the Malays in general but also Third World feminists, anthropologists and historians, tourists and literature lovers from all over the world. Ghulam-Sarwar is also interested in recovering and recording local chronotopes[52]—in the face of censorship—in his creative and academic work.

To choose to write in English is a political gesture. This ensures greater exposure for the work of Malay writers and means that they are not limited to the Malay language ethnos. Moreover, English, while only having a limited reception in Malaysia, is fast becoming the language of the middle class and it is in English that discussion and debates are occurring.[53] In fact, it might be harder to broach the topic of Malaysian religious syncretism in Malay-language mainstream discourse, since that would be subject to majority Muslim Malay scrutiny, being a 'sensitive' subject. This of course does not discount the existence of pockets of resistance in Malay-language discourse stemming from the cultural underground.

Finally, one wonders what the impact of becoming mainstream would do to literature previously considered minority. Would it not submit the more radical questions and topics being broached in English-language writing (and theatre) to a climate of pedagogical surveillance, not to mention commercialism and self-censorship? Edward Said warned us in *Orientalism* that putative 'objective' knowledge about the 'Orient' in the past was used to colonise and control the natives better. Postcolonial researchers in the growing field of Malaysian English literature might want to consider these troubling problems. We need to ask what strings come with funding and how research will not only contribute to the enrichment of a truly Malaysian culture, but also how potential consequences or backlash might affect the flowering of 'minority' artistic expression.

Notes

1 'Nasi kandar' is a style of cuisine including rice with a numerous array of curries. The Malay name stems from the rice (nasi) in baskets balanced on the two ends of a pole slung (kandar) over the seller's shoulder, a common sight during the colonial period.

2 On 26 June 2007, a raid was led and carried out by the Islamic Department of the Federal Territories on 2 restaurants: one Indian and another, Mamak. See Lim Kit Siang's blog archive, 'Jawi raid on Indian restaurant for public display of Hindu deities – PM should stop the "Little Napoleons".'

3 Yousof Ghulam-Sarwar, 'Lottery Ticket', *Mirror of a Hundred Hues* (Penang, Malaysia: The Asian Centre, 2001) 60.

4 Ghulam-Sarwar, 'An Interview with Ghulam-Sarwar', *Mirror of a Hundred Hues* 149.

5 Ghulam-Sarwar, *Mirror of a Hundred Hues* 149.

6 Che Husna Azhari, *Melor in Perspective* (Bangi, Selangor, Malaysia: Furada, 1993) 61.

7 Husna Azhari, *Melor in Perspective* 62–63.

8 Husna Azhari, *Melor in Perspective* 63.

9 Husna Azhari, *Melor in Perspective* 63.

10 Aboo Bakar is the Prophet 's father-in-law, and father of Aisha, the Prophet's favourite wife. On the other hand, Aboo Bakar is also a common Indian Muslim male name. The fact that the writer has chosen a reverential name to set up our expectations and then dashes them soon after reinforces my point that Ghulam-Sarwar is exposing the superficial understanding of most contemporary Muslims about their religion.

11 Ghulam-Sarwar, 'Lottery Ticket, *Mirror of a Hundred Hues* 49.

12 Ghulam-Sarwar, 'Lottery Ticket, *Mirror of a Hundred Hues* 49.

13 Ghulam-Sarwar, 'Lottery Ticket, *Mirror of a Hundred Hues* 49.

14 Ghulam-Sarwar, 'Lottery Ticket, *Mirror of a Hundred Hues* 50.
15 Ghulam-Sarwar, 'Lottery Ticket, *Mirror of a Hundred Hues* 50.
16 Ghulam-Sarwar, 'Lottery Ticket, *Mirror of a Hundred Hues* 52.
17 Ghulam-Sarwar, 'Lottery Ticket, *Mirror of a Hundred Hues* 51.
18 Ghulam-Sarwar, 'Lottery Ticket, *Mirror of a Hundred Hues* 59.
19 Ghulam-Sarwar, 'Lottery Ticket, *Mirror of a Hundred Hues* 66.
20 Ghulam-Sarwar, 'Lottery Ticket, *Mirror of a Hundred Hues* 51.
21 Ghulam-Sarwar, 'Lottery Ticket, *Mirror of a Hundred Hues* 54, 52.
22 Ghulam-Sarwar, 'Lottery Ticket, *Mirror of a Hundred Hues* 64.
23 Ghulam-Sarwar, 'Lottery Ticket, *Mirror of a Hundred Hues* 60.
24 Ghulam-Sarwar, 'Lottery Ticket, *Mirror of a Hundred Hues* 62.
25 Husna Azhari, 'Mek Teh, Mother Andam', *Melor in Perspective* 113; Husna Azhari, 'Mariah', *Melor in Perspective* 82.
26 Homi Bhabha, 'DissemiNation: Time, Narrative and the Margins of the Modern Nation', Ed. Homi Bhabha, *Nation and Narration* (London: Routledge, 1994) 314. Bhabha puts forth his theory of the pedagogical versus the performative in his essay 'DissemiNation' which can be found in his collection of essays *Location of Culture* and in his earlier edited book of essays on nationalism, *Nation and Narration*. Briefly and very reductively one might think of the pedagogical as theory, and the performative as practice, with the second never quite fulfilling the ideal or mandate of the first. To clarify, the pedagogical religious purists I refer to here are not represented by the Islamic fundamentalist position of wanting to govern Malaysia under Muslim law. Instead, it refers to the Muslim clerical perpective that the federal moderate Islamic, secular and Malay chauvinist government depends on to win Malay votes.
27 Ghulam-Sarwar, 'Birthday', *Mirror of a Hundred Hues* 75.
28 Ghulam-Sarwar, 'Birthday', *Mirror of a Hundred Hues* 80.
29 Ghulam-Sarwar, 'Birthday', *Mirror of a Hundred Hues* 71.
30 Ghulam-Sarwar, 'Birthday', *Mirror of a Hundred Hues* 71.This is in contrast to reports of the Prophet's wife's response when he announces the decision on polygamy as a directive from God himself. His wife Aisha was reported to have said that God seems to always support Muhammad when it comes to things like that (Nawal El Saadawi, 'Arab Women and Politics', in *The Nawal El Saadawi Reader* (London: Zed Books, 1997), 247.
31 Husna Azhari, 'Mariah', *Melor in Perspective* 79.
32 Husna Azhari, 'Mariah', *Melor in Perspective* 80.
33 Husna Azhari, 'Mariah', *Melor in Perspective* 80.
34 Husna Azhari, 'Mariah', *Melor in Perspective* 82.
35 Husna Azhari, 'Mariah', *Melor in Perspective 81*.
36 Equal treatment of all the wives is the condition in the Quran (Sura 4: 1-3 An-Nisaa). However, scholars have debated over whether this condition suggests that the Prophet is for or against polygamy. Aside from the ability to distribute equal property among the wives, the condition also acknowledges the human difficulty in having equal affection for each wife. In fact, Muslim feminists have pointed out the Prophet's acknowledged favouritism for his last wife, Ayesha.

37 Husna Azhari, 'Mariah', *Melor in Perspective* 83.
38 Husna Azhari, 'Mariah', *Melor in Perspective* 83.
39 Husna Azhari, 'Mariah', *Melor in Perspective* 81.
40 Husna Azhari, 'Mariah', *Melor in Perspective* 81.
41 Husna Azhari, 'Mariah', *Melor in Perspective* 82.
42 Husna Azhari, 'Mariah', *Melor in Perspective* 82. Dr. Noritah also pointed out the ironic tension between the name of Siti Fatimah which means 'a willing heart to sacrifice', and the perhaps not quite so willing, silent heart of Cik Yam.
43 Husna Azhari, 'Mariah', *Melor in Perspective* 75.
44 Che Husna Azhari, 'The Mascot', *The Rambutan Orchard* Bangi, Selangor, Malaysia: Furada, 1993) 40.
45 Husna Azhari, 'The Mascot', *The Rambutan Orchard* 59.
46 Husna Azhari, 'The Mascot', *The Rambutan Orchard* 38.
47 Husna Azhari, 'The Mascot', *The Rambutan Orchard* 58.
48 Husna Azhari, 'The Mascot', *The Rambutan Orchard* 57.
49 Husna Azhari, 'The Mascot', *The Rambutan Orchard* 57.
50 Husna Azhari, 'The Mascot', *The Rambutan Orchard* 57.
51 'While denying that an increasing number of Muslims are becoming apostates, the Government is exploring the possibility of introducing an Islamic Faith Rehabilitation Bill' ('Government May Table Laws to Curb Apostasy', *The Star,* 26 July 2001, 6). Critics read this move on the part of the UMNO government as a form of countering radical Islam by becoming even more Islamic to win back the Malay heartland since the 1999 election scare for UMNO (see Maznah Mohamad, Karim Raslan). Again to emphasise the currently existing 'performative' of syncretism, the same paper features a report about a religious leader from the Ma'unah movement, Mohamad Amin, who 'used his inner Amazing Feats, Court Told', (*The Star,* 26 July 2001, 16).
52 Bakhtin, Mikhail, 'Forms of Time and of the Chronotope in the Novel' in *The Dialogic Imagination.* Trans. Caryl Emerson and Michael Holquist (Austin: University of Texas Press, 1981), 250.
53 The experimental play *Lebih Kecoh*! playing at the Actors Studio from 19th-29th July, 2001, is an example of how potentially subversive forms of dialectical discussion about the construction of our history and about muted possibilities are being allowed forms of expression in English-language theatre. What makes *Lebih Kecoh!* all the more interesting is its bilingualism (the actors speak English, Manglish and Malay) and its embracing of Malaysian diversity and cultural syncretism not to mention its earnest tackling of class, gender and racial identity in contemporary Malaysia.

Works cited

Bhabha, Homi. 'DissemiNation: Time, Narrative and the Margins of the Modern Nation'. *Nation and Narration.* Ed. Homi Bhabha. London: Routledge, 1994.

El Saadawi, Nawal. *The Nawal El Saadawi Reader.* London: Zed Books, 1997.

Ghulam-Sarwar Yousof. *Mirror of a Hundred Hues*. Penang, Malaysia: The Asian Centre, 2001.

Husna Azhari, Che. 'Mariah', 'Of Bunga Telur and Bally Shoe' and 'Mek Teh, Mother Andam'. *Melor in Perspective*. Bangi, Selangor, Malaysia: Furada, 1993.

Husna Azhari, Che. 'The Mascot'. *The Rambutan Orchard*. Bangi, Selangor, Malaysia: Furada, 1993.

Karim Raslan. 'From Command Politics to Civil Society?' Seminar. University of British Columbia, 14 November, 2000.

Maniam, K.S. 'Haunting the Tiger'. *Haunting the Tiger Contemporary Stories from Malaysia*. London: Skoob Books, 1990.

Maniam, K.S. *In A Far Country*. London: Skoob Books, 1993.

Maznah Mohamad. 'UMNO and Its Partners In the New Malaysia'. *Aliran Monthly* Dec. 1999: 2–7.

Wong, Raphael. 'Mohd. Amin Can Perform Amazing Feats, Court Told'. *The Star* 26 July 2001: 16.

Islam and State Ideology: Shaping Singapore Malay Citizenship and Identity

NORITAH OMAR
UNIVERSITI PUTRA MALAYSIA

The State is represented by the establishment of its Constitution. A country's Constitution is read as a document that outlines the legal principles that govern the social, cultural, and economic structures of its citizens. The citizens of a country would believe that the Constitution is established to protect their legal rights without prejudice of their religion, race, gender, or economic background. The Singapore Government is not excluded in ensuring the welfare of its nation through its Constitution. For example, Article 152 in the Singapore Constitution states that 'it shall be the responsibility of the Government constantly to care for the interests of the racial and religious minorities in Singapore'.[1] Such a universal right informs outsiders that freedom to practise one's religion is valued in the nation, hence marking Singapore as a democratic nation. It can also be read as a mechanism for Singaporean minorities to find a resolution or to channel any racial or religious conflict that they may face in their lives. In terms of religion, Article 152 in the Singapore Constitution reflects the United Nations General Assembly's Article 18 in the Universal Declaration of Human Rights which states that:

> [e]veryone has the right to freedom of thought, conscience and religion; this right includes freedom to change his religion or belief, and freedom, either alone or in community with others and in public or private, to manifest his religion or belief in teaching, practice, worship and observance. [2]

Article 152 converges both racial and religious categories indiscriminately. I believe it can be argued that without careful interpretation of racial and religious boundaries, there may be detrimental consequences, such as divisive judgments of governmental policies which are supposed to safeguard the rights of its citizens.[3] In demonstrating this complex racial religious equation, the action taken by Singapore to ban some Malay schoolgirls from wearing headscarves (*tudung*) to school invited criticisms from outsiders, particularly Muslims beyond Singapore's shores about the status of this Muslim right.[4] The Islamic Human Rights Commission of the United Kingdom states that:

> in Singaporean society, ethnicity and religion are synonymous. Non-Muslims in Singapore effectively view Islam as a Malay affair. Views towards Muslims are indistinguishable from those held about ethnic Malays and 'Muslim' and 'Malay' are interchangeable terms.[5]

With the above premise, the issue regarding religion, in the case of Singaporean Malays, may be considered as an ethnic matter and the Singapore government may be seen to be violating not only the rights of a religious group but also a racial group which is reflected in Article 152 affirming the government's responsibility toward the rights of the Malays as a minority.[6] Further, the issue touches on Article 16, Rights in Respect of Education of Singapore Constitution, which states that '[w]ithout prejudice to the generality of Article 12, there shall be no discrimination against any citizens of Singapore on the grounds only of religion, race, descent or place of birth.'[7] Lily Zubaidah Rahim, in problematising issues relating to Islamic identities, acknowledges the various ways these identities are constructed and that Singaporean and Malaysian Islamic identities relate to issues of ethnicity.[8] I argue that in order to understand the shaping of the Malays as Singaporean citizens, it is imperative that we analyse how matters of race and religion are constructed within the National ideology. References made earlier to the Singapore Constitution highlight the significance defining Malay identity and the rights of the Malays in terms of their race and religion.

Defining Malayness in Singapore

Lily Zubaidah points out the problematics of Singaporean Malay–Muslim identity in relation to the various socio-cultural and political definitions of Malayness. Referring to several sources of interpreting the definition of Malay, Lily Zubaidah argues the instability of 'Malay' as a racial/ethnic category.[9] The most significant of her observations which is relevant to this discussion relates to her finding of an interview conducted by a local newspaper, *The Straits Times,* in 1987 with an unnamed community leader:

> ... the GRC's [Group Representative Constituencies] definition of a Malay, which excluded Islam, may be related to Article 152 of the Singapore Constitution which bestows Malay privileges such as free education. The government in excluding Islam, appears to be careful in not extending this privilege to Indian and Arabs.[10]

Therefore, the possible definition of the Singaporean Malay may not necessarily adhere to the formal definition of Malayness which applies to Malaysia and Singapore as stipulated in the Federation of Malay Agreement in 1948 and the official definition states that 'to be formally considered a Malay ... one *must be a Muslim* [my emphasis], speak Malay, and observe the traditions of the Malay culture'.[11] Ibrahim Bajunid in reviewing Timothy Bernard's *Contesting Malayness: Malay Identity Across Boundaries*, points out that the definition of Malay has been 'typically constructed from the perspective of "authority-defined" social reality, which is interpreted or imposed, or "everyday-defined" social reality which is lived and experienced'.[12] The two types of definitions of Malay are influenced by the social position and interpretation of the observers and by the people who experience the social reality.[13] These two definitions create two different types of social realities which may lead to some political and economic hardships to the Malays. Most importantly, these realities are controlled by the 'social power' prevalent in the majority-minority discourse of a nation.[14] The majority-minority discourse is inherent in the colonial ways of defining ethnicity. In the case of Singapore, the 'authority-defined' Malay as minority in the Constitution may lead to racial inferiority that can be made complicated by the religious association with Islam. Edward Said, for example, argues that Islam is perceived to be inferior since the Orient 'has uniformly been considered inferior'.[15]

The social reality of the Singaporean Malay identity may be perceived to be in a 'double-inferiority' state when considered with regard to culture and religion. If 'authority-defined' Malay is used in relation to Singaporean majority-minority discourse, the government which holds power in the Constitution and National Ideology has the 'social power' to determine the security and well-being of Singapore citizens. In the case of the perceived civil disobedience read the *tudung* (headscarf) issue, David O'Shea in his report points out that the Singapore Ministry of Education stood by the interpretation that

> [t]he schools represent a precious common space, where all young Singaporeans wear school uniforms, as a daily reminder of the need to stand together as citizens, regardless of race, religion and social status.
>
> The standard government line is that allowing the girls to wear their tudung would threaten *Singapore's racial harmony* [my emphasis].[16]

Ironically, despite the exclusion of Islam as part of religious identity (according to the GRC), the argument that the banning of the *tudung* might help protect Malay social privileges and can ensure Singapore racial harmony, the Singapore Government can be seen to highlight the significance of morality in the school curriculum by including Religious Knowledge which allows students to study one of the major religions, including Islam.[17] According to Lily Zubaidah, the introduction of Religious Knowledge in the curriculum was considered as a political strategy in order to gain more power and further enhance the image of Singapore as a country which upholds morality.[18] However, the failure of this Religious Knowledge subject in the school curriculum led to further control of what the government identified as religious 'extremism'.[19] This necessitated the government's 'secular moral education' which promoted 'Asian values' based on Confucianist orientation.[20]

National Ideology and Confucianism

Louis Althusser, in defining the structure and functioning of ideology, postulates two opposing theses: the first representing the negative—that is, 'ideology represents the imaginary relationship of individuals to their real conditions of existence'—and the second representing the positive; that is, 'ideology has a material existence'.[21] I will only focus on Althusser's first idea. He recognises that when we locate ideology as imaginary, we can only assume that the reality is embedded in the 'illusion/allusion' which can only be unravelled through the imaginary transposition which leads to the real condition of human existence.[22] This leads to the understanding that '[w]hat is represented in ideology is therefore not the system of the real relations which govern the existence of individuals, but the imaginary relation of those individuals to the real relations in which they live'.[23]

The Singaporean National Ideology which was established in 1991 consists of the Shared Values (first introduced in October 1988) in the hope of strengthening Singaporean identity. The nature of the Shared Values is specifically to form an 'ideology of pragmatism' that recognises mostly the economic success of the nation.[24] The Shared Values or the National Ideology is said to put together the multiracial nation in giving their commitment to the state—'nation before community and society above self, family as the basic unit of society, regard and community support for the individual, consensus instead of contention, and racial and religious harmony'.[25] The ideology creates an illusion of the harmony of the different cultures of Singapore and when it is transposed, the reality is read as a state strategy to control the people. John Clammer, in his discussion of the significance of Singaporean 'Shared Values,' states that the national ideology, which promotes 'statism rather than nationalism', has a political agenda to instil social change that highlights conservatism and Confucianism.[26] The role of the National Ideology which hides the Confucianist Ideology targets the economic progress of the nation and, most importantly, aims to cultivate 'cultural nationalism rather than state nationalism'.[27]

In *Lost Soul: 'Confucianism' in Contemporary Chinese Academic Discourse,* John Makeham, a researcher at the Harvard Yenching Institute, traces academic discourse on *ruxue*.[28] One of the significant arguments put by Makeham on the formation of cultural nationalism within the Chinese identity is the new form of Confucianism which influences Singapore National Ideology. This 'New Confucianism is a neo-conservative philosophical movement, with religious overtones'.[29] His study highlights the intellectual discourse of academics in China and Taiwan and has promoted an intellectual enterprise that forms a cultural nationalism in 'cultural China' or Chinese identity.[30] According to Makeham, 'the Chinese identity expresses a type of consciousness known as culturalism: the conviction that cultural identity "trumps" or is more primordial than political or even ethnic identity'.[31] Makeham reports Singapore's abortive experiment with Confucian Ethics through the failure of Religious Knowledge as a subject among Secondary 3 students. The Confucian Ethics option in the Religious Knowledge subject had to compete with institutionalised religions such as Christianity, Buddhism, and Islam. Ironically, the Religious Knowledge subject caused an increase in religious revivalism in Singapore.[32] The emphasis on Chinese identity or culturalism in Singapore has led to religious awareness of communities in terms of the significance of their own cultural identity within the Singaporean cosmopolitan lifestyle.

Islam and Issues of Citizenship and Identity

Abdullahi Ahmed An-Na'im, a Professor of Law at Emory University, in discussing the issues regarding constitutionalism, human rights and citizenship, asserts that the dichotomies between Western and Islamic concepts should be de-emphasised in order to allow the commonalities among Muslim and Non-Muslim citizens to become apparent. These commonalities are identified as the human rights of these citizens.[33] An-Na'im further redefines and extends the notion of public reason with his own term: 'civic reason'.[34] In commenting on John Rawl's definition of public reason which is based on democratic constitutional order, An-Na'im asserts that:

> Rawl's view of public reason presumes a well-developed constitutional democracy supported by the rule of law. Citizens have the right to ground their views in what he calls 'comprehensive doctrines' or broad worldviews like religion, morality, or philosophy but such doctrines should not be presented as public reason ... The exclusive view [of the comprehensive doctrine] should be upheld in a 'more or less well ordered society,' where justice and basic rights are secure, so that political values allow for the expression of public reason without reference to any comprehensive doctrine ... for example, between different groups on the issue of government

> support for religious education. In such a situation, an explanation in the public forum of 'how one's comprehensive doctrine affirms the political values' can help affirm and further legitimize the notion of public reason itself.[35]

An-Na'im further argues that in reference to Habermas, Rawl's argument 'treats the political value-sphere, which is distinguished in modern societies from other cultural value-sphere, as something given'.[36] Thus An-Na'im supports what he identifies as civic reason based on public reason as 'the requirement that the rationale and purpose of public policy or legislation be based on the sort of reasoning that most citizens can accept or reject or use to make counterproposals through public debate without reference to religious belief as such'.[37]

As an example of the impact of comprehensive doctrine within the public reason, I refer to the conflict which is present in the Malay-Muslim Singaporean social reality—faith as being an integral part of their Muslim identity. A mother whose daughter was banned from going to school stated that '[her] daughter's education is as important as [her] faith, [her] religion. Education [is something] that [she] cannot separate from faith'.[38] However, the spokesperson for the Ministry of Education in attending to the *tudung* issue asserted that '[t]he schools represent a precious common space, where all young Singaporeans wear school uniforms, as a daily reminder of the need to stand together as citizens, regardless of race, religion and social status'.[39] The headscarf is part of an Islamic culture and can be considered as one of the major determining aspects of Malay Singaporean identity and citizenship; while it can be argued within public reason that supports the government's policy to ban the headscarf, on the other hand, within civic reason, it deemphasises dichotomies of Western or Islamic institutions that highlight the commonalities of members of societies. It is further commented by the Ministry's spokesperson that:

> [a]llowing exceptions to this rule [Muslim students must not wear headscarves] would fragment our community ... our society, because it would fragment the common space that we have in school and invite competing demands from other communities to assert their own identities.[40]

The *tudung* affair may not only offer a reason for both citizens and non-citizens of Singapore to politicise the racial status of Malay as well as other ethnic groups; it may also create a space for analysing and contesting how Islam lives in the Malay culture within the nation-state of Singapore. The interchangeable terms between Muslim and Malay blur Singaporean religious and cultural identities.

Alfian Sa'at found that the images of Malay Muslims in the eyes of a Singaporean cosmopolite are culturally unbalanced:

> a 'My Singapore' music video which showed images of corporate-looking Chinese women walking through the CBD and Malay women in factory uniforms walking through a bus interchange. Tanya Chua's 'Where I Belong' shows three instances of Malay people populating the landscape: a husband and wife riding a scooter; a father and son on a bicycle, the son carrying a box one presumes is filled with curry puffs or goreng pisang, and a group of Malay youths playing soccer in a housing estate ghetto so run down, it looks like an opposition ward being denied of upgrading, or one of those satellite towns built when Jurong swamps were still being filled.
>
> But perhaps this is an improvement over other images: the satay man, the songbird owner, the mee rebus Makcik, the Malay bride and groom getting married in gold-embroidered finery.[41]

In the above remarks, Alfian is aware of the 'cultural identity' that limits Malay identity as unprogressive. This is actually against the National Ideology which states that:

> its aim was to sculpt a Singaporean identity by incorporating the relevant parts of our various cultural heritages as well as the attitudes and values which have helped us survive as a nation. It would also help safeguard against undesirable values permeating from more developed countries which may be detrimental to our social fabric.[42]

In comparison to Alfian Sa'at's images, Haresh Sharma (thinking in the context of social imagination) asserts that

> [t]he Malays are a charming, courteous and easy-going people. A common phrase among them is 'tid'apa'—nothing, really matters very much. Sir Hugh Clifford, a former governor wrote to them that they are indolent, pleasure-loving, improvident, fond of bright clothing, of comfort, of ease, and dislike toil exceedingly.[43]

The negotiated and emerging nature of Islamic culture in Singapore through Malay-Muslim images can be analysed in Alfian Sa'at's and Haresh Sharma's texts which are written in English. Alfian Sa'at and Haresh Sharma have created a space for Malay-Muslims to ponder important issues relating to Islamic culture and to the National Ideology. In Alfian Sa'at's short story 'Bugis', the issue of the *tudung* is raised. Alfian is fully aware of the cultural images created by the practice of wearing the *tudung* which centres on critical issues relating to how Muslims try to maintain Islamic standards and cope with social modernity, thus forcing them to confront a dilemma. These issues are embedded in clear-cut and not so clear-cut descriptions and symbolism. Alfian captures the Malay-Muslim dilemma as follows:

> I see a schoolgirl from a madrasah wearing a *tudung* on the MRT and she is filling in the pictures in her colouring book. There are many choices among her colour pencils which she can use for skin, but she will use orange, and colour lightly, not brown or black. I have seen her schoolmates before, eyeing branded schoolbags at pasar malams, wearing branded sports shoes, like every other kid. I want to go up to her and hug her, and tell her how her *tudung* is not just a symbol of modesty, but a symbol of inscrutability. That layer of cloth makes her suspicious to others, it can be used to smuggle in a grenade or an agenda, so she will never get a frontline desk job, she will be expected to hang around with other *tudung*-wearing women in the university. I think about the fathers who sent their daughters to schools in *tudung* and reflect on how the media has framed them as shit-stirrers rather than citizens who practise their right to civil disobedience ...[44]

The *tudung* has been an issue in Singaporean Malay 'cultural identity' when it is positioned in the Singaporean cosmopolitan culture, and when it is no longer understood as an identification of one's religiosity. In this personal commentary Alfian may be seen as cynical about Muslims as captured in the media with respect to the *tudung* affair. The act of protesting by a Muslim is not considered as a serious act of civil disobedience contesting the Singaporean Government's democratic constitutional order.

Another literary work relevant in this discussion is by a Singaporean playwright, Haresh Sharma. The play *Rosnah* centres on a character playing different roles in the context of social imagination and may also be seen as representing the dilemmas faced by a Singaporean Malay-Muslim. *Rosnah highlights* several critical issues in relation to the Malay-Muslims: the character Rosnah/Actress, a Malay/Muslim, describes her relationship with a non-Muslim man named Stephen. The character Rosnah represents the material sense of Singaporean Malay identity, one who faces social and economic challenges of being a Malay Singaporean. Issues such as opportunity for education and struggles with their own religious and cultural expectations, for example, are represented in a dialogue between Rosnah and her friend Muslinda (when she confesses to being raped):

> MUSLINDA: ... It's no big deal. Anyway, I'm graduating ... this is my home now. Why don't you spend the night? I've got some grass and—
>
> ROSNAH: You have no moral. You have no duty. Tak malu. Takda maruah. Tak ingat tuhan! Dah lupa ugama! Dah sesat! What to do now? What can anyone do? I told you. I told you right? I told you! Don't anyway blame this country or that country. Don't be a coward. Look at yourself.[45]

The above statement by Rosnah describes Muslinda as lost, and one who does not believe in God, has no religion, and who is also being irresponsible and immoral, with no sense of dignity and self-worth. Her loss of identity should not be blamed on the state. Rosnah may be seen as a modern educated Malay who is aware of her Islamic identity when her friend/Muslinda's misconduct is judged from a socio-religious angle. The separation between state and religion is captured in Rosnah's conversation. The assertion is that Muslinda's loss of Islamic identity can never be attributed to the state but rather to her lack of self-reflexivity. The Actress character is made as the conscience, spiritual and intellectual components of the identity. In commenting on the Malay-Muslim dilemma, the Actress says:

> ACTRESS: When Rosnah went home, she told Stephen. He was quiet. When she asked him why, he said after marriage, he didn't want to become Muslim. He is agnostic. He said he doesn't believe in the concept of God. But he believes in something beyond. Rosnah said no, you must become Muslim. If you want to marry me, you must become Muslim. No Muslim, no marriage. Stephen said why? What has institutionalised religion got to do with morality? Look at Muslinda. Rosnah became angry. Rational or not rational, I don't care. You must become Muslim. Stephen said okay, I will. Just for the sake of the marriage. But I won't believe in it and I won't practise it. Rosnah told Stephen to leave. Stephen left. Rosnah cried.[46]

This passage raises pertinent issues which become the centre of Malay identity such as the their belief in God, the necessary conversion to Islam by the non Muslim if s/he wants to marry a Muslim, and the promotion of morality through institutionalised religion such as Islam. This promotion of morality is further captured by Alfian in the story 'Bugis', where the degradation of morality is seen through the *tudung*-wearing girl who laughs at the expense of her friend who is being teased by the transvestite. The narrator positions the paradox of a religious *tudung* girl as someone who is immoral compared to the one who does not wear the *tudung*. Alfian Sa'at in another story, 'Video', problematises Malay habits in their Islamic practice such as giving significance to *tasbih* (rosary beads), encouraging children to drink water which has had Quranic verses recited over it (or known in Malay as *air penerang hati*-literally water which clears the heart), in order to enable them to study or remember better (to have clear heart or *terang hati*), polygamy, piety shown through appropriate discourse like giving salaam, going for Haj where Mekah is a place to seek God's help for your material well-being (such as children for the childless), displays of Islam on walls such as names of Allah and Mohammad.

The unprogressive nature of the Malay stereotype is represented in this story through Maimon the protagonist who says that 'we know that in Mekah, if you pray and your heart is pure your prayers are answered'.[47]

With the adoption of the Shared Values, the Malay Muslims' cultural and social identities may not seem to oppose their very own Islamic values. If such values are seen to promote Singapore as a conservative society, it is appropriate to consider that Malay-Muslims of Singapore model their identity within the conservatism of state ideology. At the same time, this National Ideology blueprint is recognised to be incongruent with 'the best tradition of Catholic and Western social thought'.[48] The framework for the National Ideology persists in integrating basic human values of different religions and cultural backgrounds. With the inclusion of such conventional or universal principles, it may be difficult to see any violation of Islamic values in the state ideology. Further evaluation of Singapore's conservatism may be illustrated in the banning of '[not only] English-language publications consist[ing of] primarily sexually oriented materials, but also includ[ing] some religious and political publications'.[49] Theoretically, Singapore state ideology in relation to the five shared values may seem surprising within the state's modernity and cosmopolitanism.

The social reality of the Malay Muslims of Singapore lies between the negotiated boundaries of national ideology that upholds conservatism as well as promotes modernity in the nation's cultural practices. The negotiated space at times can be perceived as one of polemics, with Malays safeguarding themselves within statism and Islamicism. An Islamic identity of Singaporean Malays, perhaps, can be defined from

> *Shari'a*, the Islamic term which is commonly rendered in English by 'Law', is rather 'the whole duty of man', moral and pastoral theology and ethics, high spiritual aspirations and the detailed ritualistic and formal observance which to some minds is a vehicle for such aspirations and to others a substitute for it, all aspects of law: public and private hygiene and even courtesy and good manners are all part and parcel of the *Shari'a*.[50]

Represented by Islamic Law, Islam can be perceived to be rigid and non-negotiable and a religion that homogenises cultures. On the other hand, Islam as a part of culture can be interpreted and adapted by Muslims to fit in with their cultural identity. This allows for a picture of Islam as a negotiable framework and one that allows individuals to make Islam work. When Islam is seen as a negotiable framework, it leads to the modernising/modernisation of tradition. Alfian Sa'at's personal observations of the Malay culture and his story 'Bugis', which focuses on the *tudung* girl, demonstrates the modernising of tradition and that Islam, framed by modern Muslims, is to a certain extent, being superficial.[51] The issue of *tudung* when negotiated opens the possibility for women to fit in cultural tradition and Islamic values in their mode of dress. In the case of the

Singaporean *tudung* affair, the Muslim parents believed that there should be no room for negotiating or not accepting the headscarf, according to Islamic law, if you are a Muslim woman. The interpretation of Islam fitting in or being negotiated with culture is seldom seen as a way through which Islam promotes the expression of individuality.

Conclusion

Islam in a secular state like Singapore may be considered as a comprehensive doctrine for the Malays. When the State Ideology is made to be the comprehensive doctrine of the Singaporean Malays, it may have recuperated the religious awareness of the Singaporean Malays and strengthened their cultural identity. The *tudung* affair and literature which focuses on the *tudung* and Malay-Muslims have affected Islamic discourse within English literature studies in Singapore. This Islamic discourse concurrently highlights the cultural-religious identity of Singaporean Malays. The negative image of Muslims globally has influenced the construction of Singapore Malay citizens as a minority group in which perceived racial weaknesses have been a concern of the Singapore Government. The negotiated Malay self, living in a cosmopolitan nationhood, is fractured both materially and spiritually.

Kirpal Singh, in explaining the 'Malay dilemma' of not writing in English, states that 'a possible explanation could lie in the culture itself—a culture nourished essentially by the soil and therefore not very comfortable in a highly technological, urban setting where the cerebrum predominates'.[52] Kirpal Singh's explanation suggests that Malay-Muslim culture is not compatible with cosmopolitan Singapore and that the incompatibility of Malay culture with material progress of Singapore may also be seen to highlight the backwardness of the Singaporean Malays. The 'Malay dilemma' of the Singaporean Malays, in the words of Syed Hussien Al-Attas in his response in 1988 to the establishment of Malaysia as an Islamic state, is that 'You can be as good a Muslim as you want in any state. That (maintaining Islamic values) can be without having an Islamic state'.[53]

Notes

1 Constitution of The Republic of Singapore. Accessed 30 January 2007. <http://statutes.agc.gov.sg/non_version/cgi-bin/...&date=latest&method=part>

2 Accessed 30 January 2007. <http://www.unesco.org/most/rr4udhr.htm> paragraph 2.

3 The argument about the inseparability between race and religion can be studied though the unique case of Malaysian notion of 'Bumiputera' which refers to

Malay. This inseparable relation has invited review of Malaysian governmental policies such as educational and economic policies. Dr Azly Rahman who is *Adjunct Professor Foundations of Civilizations, Education & Politics assertion that states '"Bumiputera"* ... [a] word that conveniently equates race and religion as inseparable. To say that a Malay is generally a Muslim and hence a "bumiputera" and therefore have special rights and privileges is an imprecise way of explaining a concept. It is an old-school approach to defining that word." http://blog.limkitsiang.com/2007/02/28/neo-bumiputeraism-clarification/.

4 Accessed 27 July 2008. <http://www.ihrc.org.uk/show.php?id=776> (paragraph 7).

5 Accessed 27 July 2008. <http://www.ihrc.org.uk/show.php?id=776> (paragraph 9).

6 'Article 152 Minorities and Special Position of Malays: (2) The Government shall exercise its functions in such manner as to recognize the special position of the Malays, who are the indigenous people of Singapore, and accordingly it shall be the responsibility of the Government to protect, safeguard, support, foster and promote their political, educational, religious, economic, social and cultural interests and the Malay language.' <http://www.unesco.org/most/rr3sing.htm>.

7 Refers to equal protection of the Law. <http://www.unesco.org/most/rr3sing.htm>.

8 Lily Zubaidah Rahim, *The Singapore Dilemma: The Political and Educational Marginality of the Malay Community* (Oxford: Oxford University Press, 1998).

9 See endnotes 8–16 for various aspects of the definition of Malay in Lily Zubaidah Rahim *The Singapore Dilemma* 25–27.

10 Endnote no. 21 in Lily Zubaidah Rahim *The Singapore Dilemma:* 'The GRC Bill was introduced in 1987. Voters would have to choose among a team of MPs in the GRC constituencies. At least one member of the GRC team has to be an ethnic minority' 45–46.

11 Lily Zubaidah Rahim, *The Singapore Dilemma* 17.

12 This is referring to Shamsul A.B. observation based on Anthony Reid's work. Ibrahim Bajunid, Book Review of *Contesting Malayness: Malay Identity Across Boundaries.* JMBRAS VOL.78 Part 2 (2005): 115.

13 Shamsul A.B. 'A History of the Identity, and the Identity of a History: The Idea and Practice of Malayness in Malaysia Reconsidered' in Timothy Bernard, *Contesting Malayness: Malay Identity Across Boundaries* (Singapore: Singapore University Press, 2005) 148.

14 The 'social power' refers to 'a nationalist, literary, and professional groups, scholars administrators, academicians, and so on', Shamsul A.B. 'A History of the Identity 148.

15 One of the Images of Malay as indolent is explained in Syed Hussien Al-Attas's book *The Myth of the Lazy Native* (London: Frank & Cass, 1977) 70–82; Edward Said 'Islam Through Western Eyes' *The Nation,* April 26 (1980) (Reprinted January 1 1998). Accessed 31 July 2007. <http://www.thenation.com/doc/19800426/19800426said>.

16 Retrieved 20 July 2007. <http://www.singapore-window.org/sw02/020327sb.htm> paragraphs 6 and 7.

17 See endnote 7 in Lily Zubaidah's *The Singapore Dilemma* 181, 161.

18 See endnote 7 in Lily Zubaidah, *The Singapore Dilemma* 162.
19 In interpreting the fear of the government of religious extremism, 'Lee Kwan Yew (in his capacity as honorary chairman of the Beijing based International Confucian Organisation) related that the government had decided to phase out the Religious Knowledge course because it had created an upsurge of interest in Christianity, Buddhism, and Islam', in John Makeham, *Lost Soul: 'Confucianism' in Contemporary Chinese Academic Discourse* (Harvard: Harvard University Press, 2008).
20 Lily Zubaidah Rahim, *The Singapore Dilemma* 162.
21 Louis Althusser, 'Ideology and Ideological State Apparatuses' (1968). From *Lenin and Philosophy and Other Essays* (1972), translated from the French by Ben Brewster. Accessed 30 July 2008. <http://www.colorado.edu/English/courses/engl2010/Readings/AlthIdeol.htm> paragraph 2
22 Althusser, 'Ideology and Ideological State Apparatuses' paragraph 3 and 4.
23 Althusser, 'Ideology and Ideological State Apparatuses' paragraph 9.
24 <http://members.tripod.com/marklsll/Writings/values.htm>.
25 <http://www.freerepublic.com/focus/news/771081/posts#comment>.
26 'John Clammer cited in Makeham's *Lost Soul* 7
27 Makeham, *Lost Soul* 7.
28 *ruxue* is associated to the the term ru which has been expended over time and the use of this term is to explain 'methods of cultivating and practice,explanatory accounts of particular moral principles, glosses of sayings attributed to Pre-Qin *ru,* and critiques of various scholarly interpretations', in Makeham, *Lost Soul* 5.
29 Makeham, *Lost Soul* 2.
30 Makeham, *Lost Soul* 9.
31 Makeham, *Lost Soul* 11.
32 Makeham, *Lost Soul* 24–25.
33 Abdullahi Ahmed An-Na'im, *Islam and the Secular State: Negotiating the Future of Shar*i'a (Cambridge: Harvard University Press, 2008).
34 Abdullahi Ahmed An-Na'im, *Islam and the Secular State* 98–101.
35 Abdullahi Ahmed An-Na'im, *Islam and the Secular State* 99.
36 Abdullahi Ahmed An-Na'im, *Islam and the Secular State* 100.
37 Abdullahi Ahmed An-Na'im, *Islam and the Secular State* 100.
38 http://www.singapore-window.org/sw02/020327sb.htm
39 http://www.singapore-window.org/sw02/020327sb.htm
40 http://www.singapore-window.org/sw02/020327sb.htm
41 http://alfian.diaryland.com/tudung.html
42 http://www.freerepublic.com/focus/news/771081/posts#comment
43 Haresh Sharma, 'Rosnah: A Monodrama', In *This Cord and Others: A Collection of Plays* (London: Minerva, 1999) 185.
44 http://alfian.dairyland.com/tudung.html
45 Haresh Sharma, 'Rosnah: A Monodrama', 187–188.
46 Haresh Sharma, 'Rosnah: A Monodrama' 188–189.
47 Alfiat Sa'at 'Video' *Corridor: 12 Short Stories* (Singapore: SNP Editions, 1999) 7-21.
48 <http://www.freerepublic.com/focus/news/771081/posts#comment>.

49 Country Reports on Human Rights Practices – 2001. Released by the Bureau of Democracy, Human Rights, and Labor March 4, 2002. Accessed November 2, 2008. <http://www.state.gov/g/drl/rls/hrrpt/2001/eap/8375.htm> paragraph 45.
50 Al-Ghazali cited in Fatima Mernissi translated by Mary Jo Lakeland *The Forgotten Queens of Islam*, Minnesota, University of Minessota Press, 1993.21.
51 http://alfian.dairyland.com/tudung.html
52 Kirpal Singh 'An Approach to Singapore Writing in English' in Mohammad A. Quayum & Peter Wicks, *Singapore Literature in English: A Critical Reader.* (Serdang: Universiti Putra Malaysia Press. 2002)
53 Abdul Rahman Haji Abdullah, *Pemikiran Islam di Malaysia: Sejarah dan Aliran* (Penang & Kuala Lumpur: Universiti Sains Malaysia & Dewan Bahasa dan Pustaka, 1998).

Works cited

Abdul Rahman, Haji Abdullah. *Pemikiran Islam di Malaysia: Sejarah dan Aliran.* Penang & Kuala Lumpur: Universiti Sains Malaysia & Dewan Bahasa dan Pustaka, 1998.

Al-Attas, Syed Hussien. *The Myth of the Lazy Native.* London: Frank & Cass, 1977.

An-Na'im, Abdullahi Ahmed. *Islam and the Secular State: Negotiating the Future of Sha*ri'a. Cambridge: Harvard University Press, 2008.

Althusser, Louis. 'Ideology and Ideological State Apparatuses' (1968). From *Lenin and Philosophy and Other Essays* (1972), translated from the French by Ben Brewster.

Bajunid, Ibrahim. Book Review of '*Contesting Malayness: Malay Identity Across Boundaries*'. *JMBRAS*, 78: 2 (2005) 115.

Makeham, John. *Lost Soul: 'Confucianism' in Contemporary Chinese Academic Discourse.* Harvard: Harvard University Press, 2008.

Mernissi, Fatima. *Beyond the Veil: Male-Female Dynamics in a Modern Muslim Society.* Bloomington: Indiana University Press. 1987.

Rahim, Lily Zubaidah. The Singapore Dilemma: The Political and Educational Marginality of the Malay Community. Oxford: Oxford University Press, 1998.

Sa'at, Alfian. *Corridor: 12 Short Stories.* Singapore: Raffles, SNP Editions, 1999.

Said, Edward. 'Islam Through Western Eyes' *The Nation,* 26 April 1980 (Reprinted 1 January 1998).

Shamsul, A.B. 'A History of the Identity, an the Identity of a History: The Idea and Practice of Malayness in Malaysia Reconsidered' in Timothy Bernard, *Contesting Malayness: Malay Identity Across Boundaries.* Singapore: Singapore University Press, 2005.

Sharma, Haresh. 'Rosnah: A Monodrama', In *This Cord and Others: A Collection of Plays.* London: Minerva, 1999.

Colonial Description of Malays and Malay Culture

SITI ROHAINI KASSIM
UNIVERSITY OF MALAYA

One of the definitions of Orientalism, as defined by Edward Said in Orientalism, is explained as 'the corporate institution for dealing with the Orient—dealing with it by making statements about it, authorising views of it, describing it, by teaching it, settling it, ruling over it: in short, Orientalism is a Western style, for dominating, restructuring, and having authority over the Orient'.[1] Briefly, it reflects an attitude of describing and explaining the East and Far East as the 'opposite' of the West, in all aspects—social, political, economy etc.

This is the general tone in which the Malay is portrayed by officers of the British government in Malaya. Prejudice in the presentation of Malay character is both overtly and covertly revealed in the stories and anecdotes of colonial officers such as Winstedt, Swettenham and Clifford who served in the Malay world during British colonial rule in Malaya, and who chose to record and publish their experiences. However, from accounts and anecdotes written by these officers, one also gets glimpses of an 'other' that is seen in a more sympathetic light: one that is not necessarily uncivilized, irrational, or different, going by Occidental criteria. The question is how sincere are these apparently sympathetic portrayals, considering the probable 'default' attitude with which the writers began their service with the British colonial government in Malaya?

This chapter considers aspects of representation of a people and its culture, as portrayed in selected writings by Sir Frank Swettenham and Sir Hugh Clifford, and reflects upon the validity and reliability of those representations. Time constraints permit references to only the two pieces of writing, the discussion of which aims at developing a 'picture' of the Malay and Malay culture as seen by both officers.[2] The description of the Malay person in Swettenham's *A Nocturne and Other Malayan Stories and Sketches* and Clifford's *In Court & Kampong: being tales & sketches of native life in the Malay Peninsula* is generally negative. In fact,

Clifford paints the Malay people of the East coast in an excessively negative light. It is obvious that everything Malay is set subconsciously against a 'civilised' white colonial standard, and consequently found wanting.

Malaysian history has had the influence of at least three colonizing powers in its making, going by a very broad definition of colonisation. The Arab and Gujerat merchants of the pre Portuguese period, the Portuguese (although very much confined) and (putting aside the very short effort of the Japanese) the British in the period of their colonial rule in Malaya up to 1957, have all left indelible marks in varying degrees. In the Malaysian experience, colonial rule may not compare equally with the harsh colonisation of the Americas by Spain, or even with Dutch rule in Indonesia. Nevertheless, the effect on the nation has been tremendous and long-lasting.

To Said, knowledge and dominance go hand in hand; to know something is to have power over it and conversely, to have power is to know the world in your own terms. British colonial rule in Malaya may have started with such an aim:

The reasons for direct British intervention in the internal affairs of the western Malay states in the preceding decade had been of several kinds: a desire to exploit the economic resources of the hinterland of the Straits Settlements; a desire to secure the peninsula as a British sphere of influence against possible intrusion by other European powers; and changing attitudes in London about the value and function of colonial possessions.[3]

Seen in a positive light through the accounts and stories of colonial officers Sir Hugh Clifford and Sir Frank Swettenham, British colonial rule in Malaya can also be said to have provided the much needed catalyst for the process of Malaya's modernisation.[4] As Sir Hugh Clifford, in his autobiographical preface to *In Court and Kampong* (1927) acknowledged:

> ... no-one who has seen the horrors of native rule, and the misery to which the people living under it are oft times reduced, can find room to doubt that, its many drawbacks not withstanding, the only salvation for the Malays lies in the increase of British influence in the Peninsula, and in the consequent spread of modern ideas, progress, and civilization.[5]

The glorified purpose of the British presence, as seen by both Clifford and Swettenham, is to understand so as to be able to assist, rather than to acquire knowledge in order to dominate. Nevertheless, the phrase 'the only salvation for the Malays' reflects the attitude that natives, without the benefits of civilisation, are in dire need of salvation, and that it is the duty of the British government to provide this. In other words, it is presumed that without British help, the Malays would probably have remained under the 'horrors of native rule', and be economically and socio-culturally backward. The apparent call of duty is the prime justification behind which all colonial empires hide their empire building objectives.

Of the two writers considered here, Sir Frank Swettenham, in my opinion, could be considered the more successful 'intermediator' between the British government and the 'Malay natives'. In his collection of stories, *A Nocturne and Other Malayan Stories and Sketches* (1993), he outlines a strategy for getting to understand the Malay and, by extension, Malay culture. This underscores his positive and sympathetic approach:

> To begin to understand the Malay you must live in his country, speak his language, respect his faith, be interested in his interests, humour his prejudices, sympathise with and help him in trouble, and share his pleasures and possibly his risks. Only thus can you hope to win his confidence. Only through that confidence can you hope to understand the inner man, and this knowledge can therefore only come to those who have the opportunity and use it.[6]

Clearly, Swettenham has set himself the task of winning the confidence of the Malay, so as to understand the 'inner man'. His collection of stories reflects this effort on his part and he treads carefully among the Malays.

In a somewhat different vein, in the autobiographical preface to his *In Court and Kampong*, Sir Hugh Clifford has this to say about the Malays in announcing his reason for writing the book:

> ... to give some idea of the lives lived by ... those Malays who, being yet untouched by contact with white men, are still in a state of original sin...[7]

Clearly Clifford has a different attitude. Whereas Swettenham makes no mention of an uncivilised or 'degenerate' state of the Malay people, Clifford strongly believes that it is the responsibility of white men to change the lot of the Malays, because so long as they 'are still untouched' by the white men, the Malays will never experience modern life.

Judging by the stories in the cited anthologies, it is probably safe to assume that Swettenham and Clifford do not always subscribe to the prejudices in attitude or approach that JWW Birch, to his own great misfortune, seemed to have adopted.[8] While both Swettenham and Clifford present the 'natives' as generally being different and 'less civilised', as set against European standards, they also acknowledge some positive traits in the character and attitude of the Malays.

Physically, the Malays of Swettenham's time were probably much different from the modern, urbanised, Westernised Malays, considering improvements in diet and intermarriages that have obviously influenced the physique and attitudes of contemporary Malays. The Malay, according to Swettenham, is physically 'short, thick-set, well built, with straight hair, dark brown complexion, thick nose and lips and bright intelligent eyes'.[9] The Malay youth seems to him more beautiful than the Malay girl:

> [T]he Malay boy is often beautiful ... a thing of wonderful eyes, eyelashes, and eyebrows, with a far-away expression of sadness and solemnity, as though he had left some better place for a compulsory exile on earth ... The Malay girl-child is not usually so attractive in appearance as the boy, and less consideration is shown to her. She runs wild till the time comes for investing her in garment, that is to say when she is about five years old.[10]

In Hugh Clifford's account of Malays known to him, physical make-up is not given much attention. Where they do exist, physical descriptions are very brief, or merely a means to distinguish one Malay group from another:

> In appearance, the Trengganu Malay is somewhat larger boned, broader featured, and more clumsily put together than is the Pahang Malay ... [The Pahang Malay] ... is more gracefully built than are most other natives on the east Coast...'[11]

These physical descriptions cannot be assumed to typify the East Coast Malay. Whereas Swettenham's description above is almost Romantic in essence, Clifford's many descriptions of the Malays, in my opinion, border on the Gothic. There is an almost vengeful tone in his description of the Kelantan man as a 'huge mass of fleshy brown humanity' who is 'plain of face, fat, ugly and ungainly of body, huge as to the hands and feet ...'[12]

A crucial point to remember is that the essence of any race is not just in the physical. It is also in the character, beliefs and attitudes of that race. Both Clifford and Swettenham have painted quite clearly the personal as well as the cultural aspects of the Malays they knew directly or from accounts provided by locals.

The Malay man, in Swettenham's eyes is generally 'kindly', 'polite and easy, never cringing', and is reserved with strangers. [13] He is courageous, trustworthy, has a strong sense of humour and loves a good joke. His Malay women, 'especially those of gentle birth',[14] are intelligent, witty and have a good sense of humour. However, Clifford feels that because of the Malay's low tolerance level for insults or slights, the Malay sense of humour will remain intact only as long as jokes do not hit at the Malay himself, or at his kith and kin. The strong clan spirit of the Malay is observed in relation to another trait—patriotism. Both Swettenham and Clifford see the Malay as being proud of his country and people, organising his life around ancient customs and traditions alongside the laws of his Islamic religion. The Malay is represented as courteous and expecting courtesy in return.

Something that would have been of great advantage to Swettenham and Clifford in performing their duties as representatives of the British government is that the Malay in that colonial era was typically a person with due respect for constituted authority. This is evident in the strong loyalty of the Malays to their chiefs and sultans, who held authority in the local government. With careful management, the British officers developed their roles and personalities so that they were also accepted as the 'authority' from the government, and so loyalty was transferred to them.

Despite his respect for authority, the Malay is also represented by Clifford and Swettenham as being extravagant, 'fond of borrowing money' (while taking his time paying money back), a great gossip, fond of gambling and, in Clifford's opinion, always 'spoiling for a fight'.[15] Probably one of the greatest hurdles in the path of the smooth running of a colonial government administration was the fact that 'above all things, [the Malay] is conservative to a degree ... does not like innovations and will resist their sudden introduction'.[16] In other words, he is always suspicious of anything new and introducing the various British government administrative laws and regulations would have required very careful planning. Swettenham portrays the Malay of the West coast as lazy, disorganised and 'know[ing] no regularity even in the hours of his meals, and considers time as of no importance'.[17] Clifford is less polite:

> [the Malay] never works if can help it, and often will not suffer himself to be induced or tempted into doing so by offers of the most extravagant wages.[18]

In his excessively negative portrayal of the people of the East Coast, Hugh Clifford groups Malays in three basically similar yet distinct categories. To him, the Pahang Malay 'in his unregenerate state, thinks chiefly of deeds of arms, illicit love intrigues, and the sports which his religion holds to be sinful'.[19] Clifford sees the Pahang Malay as self-centred, 'irreligious, ignorant and unintellectual'. Clifford also describes him as arrogant and 'hopelessly improvident'.[20] However, in Clifford's opinion, these traits are only skin deep. The Pahang Malay, Clifford asserts, is also known to be 'manly and reckless', a great sportsman and 'extraordinarily loyal'.[21] Nothing, Clifford suggests, would make the Malay move a muscle to do an honest day's work, but when the word *krah* was whispered into his ears, he could put his whole energy into work without stopping until the task was completed, and only 'on a handful of boiled rice'.[22] This labour of love, however, would only be the privilege 'of one they know, whom they regard as their Chief and in whose sight they would be ashamed to murmur at the severity of the work...'[23]

Clifford describes the Trengganu Malays as 'first and foremost, men of peace'.

They are, he considers, hardworking and good in trade:

> From his earliest infancy he grows up in an atmosphere of books, and money and trade, and manufactures, and bargainings, and hagglings. He knows how to praise the goods he is selling, and how to depreciate the wares he is buying, almost as soon as he can speak ... [24]

According to Clifford the Trengganu Malay is more interested in study than in fighting, and before reaching his teens, the Trengganu child will have read the Quran several times over and be able to read and write in his own language. It is explained that because of this difference in focus in life, these Malays are not adept at using weapons. From this Clifford extrapolates that 'the people of Trengganu generally grow up cowards'.[25] They are unlikely to be called upon to volunteer to fight for any cause deemed important by their chiefs or sultan, since fighting is not their strong point. Their strength, according to Clifford's account, is in their skills:

The best products of their looms, the brass and nickel utensils, some of the weapons, and most of the woodwork fashioned in Trengganu, are the best native wares, of their kind, in the peninsula ... [26]

Clifford's opinion of the Kelantan Malay, based on his account of the people of the East Coast, is by far the most negative. Not only is this 'huge mass of fleshy brown humanity' deemed utterly uncouth in his social behaviour, he is also attributed with the unenviable reputation of being a 'thief among thieves'.[27] Despite being relatively more even-tempered, good-natured and stolid than the Malays of Trengganu and Pahang, the Kelantan Malay is still looked upon as the rogue of the East Coast society. Although he is seen as possessing brute strength and power of endurance ('he can lift great weights, walk long distances, pole or paddle a boat for many hours at a stretch, and can, and does, work more than any other Malay'),[28] nothing will make the other East Coast Malays change this opinion of him.

Swettenham's description of the character of the Malay is probably less offensive to Malays because of the writer's careful choice of words. For example, in revealing the Malay as an inveterate gossip, he describes him as taking 'an interest in his neighbours'.[29] He sees and records the positive aspects of the Malay character almost as much as the negative, expressing them with a touch of humour:

> [T]he Malay is an Islam by profession, and would suffer crucifixion sooner than deny his faith ... he is not a bigot; indeed his tolerance compares favourably with that of the professing Christian ... from sixteen to twenty-five, [the Malay youth] ... takes his pleasure, sows his wild oats like youths of a higher civilisation, is extravagant,

> open-handed, gambles, gets into debts, runs away with his neighbour's wife and generally asserts himself ... from the age of forty [the Malay youth] probably develops into an intelligent man of miserly and rather grasping habits with some one little pet indulgence of no very expensive kind ... [30]

In fact, Swettenham even contradicts a general opinion.

> 'The Malay has often been called treacherous. I question whether he deserves the reproach more than other men.'[31]

Clifford implies that location affects the lifestyles and attitudes of the Malays of the East coast. The country folks, he suggests, 'live more chastely ... work harder, age sooner...' and are generally more attached to family than are the people in the capital, whose added interest in life is, according to Clifford, due to the 'gossip of the Court, the tales of brave deeds, the learned discussions, or the rough sports,' none of which were readily available to the people of the interior.[32] On the other hand, Swettenham's general account of the 'real Malay' is more neutral in tone. If he started his service with all the prejudices of the white man, this is not strongly reflected in his writing.

Clifford's account reflects an unrelenting attitude towards any behaviour, customs, and characteristics very different from his own. Ironically though, he seems to know that he has been excessively negative in his portrayal of Malays and makes an apology for his limitations, delivered with typical ambivalence:

> [I]f I fail, it will be because I lack the skill to depict with vividness the lives of those whom I know intimately, and whom, in spite of all their faults, and foibles, and ignorance, and queer ways, I love exceedingly.[33]

To a great extent, British colonisation of Malaya has modernised the country. With modernisation, it is only logical to expect change in all respects—attitudes, lifestyles, social and economic standing, perhaps even physical appearance. A child growing up in the twentieth century, even more so in the twenty-first, may find it hard to accept representations of the Malay as described by Swettenham and Clifford. But have the Malays changed very significantly since Swettenham and Clifford were observing them?

Obviously, there are numerous sources—sociological, anthropological, geographical, economic, and so forth—contributing to representations of the Malay and they could be compared with literary representations. But there are also alternative portrayals of the modern Malay in literary works in English (and Bahasa Melayu, for that matter) that beg investigation. Although they are beyond the scope of the present chapter, it would be interesting to see whether, with modernisation, aspects of the basic character of the Malay originally highlighted by Swettenham and Clifford—the busybody, the lover of intrigue and so forth—have survived.

Notes

1 Edward Said, *Orientalism* (New York: Vintage, 1979).
2 F. Swettenham, 'The Real Malay', *A Nocturne and Other Malayan Stories and Sketches* (Kuala Lumpur: Oxford University Press, 1993); H. Clifford, 'The people of the East Coast', *In court & kampong: being tales & sketches of native life in the Malay Peninsula* (Kuala Lumpur: Federal Rubber Stamp, 1927).
3 William R. Roff (Ed.), *Stories by Sir Hugh Clifford* (Kuala Lumpur: Oxford University Press, 1966) xi.
4 Mohd Rashidi Pakri, unpublished PhD thesis.
5 Clifford, *In Court & Kampong* 53.
6 Swettenham, *A Nocturne and Other Malayan Stories* 16.
7 Clifford, *In Court & Kampong* 51.
8 J.W.W. Birch, an officer of the British government in Malaya, was murdered in Perak.
9 Swettenham, *A Nocturne and Other Malayan Stories* 11
10 Swettenham, *A Nocturne and Other Malayan Stories* 14-16

11 Clifford, *In Court & Kampong* 23.
12 Clifford, *In Court & Kampong* 24–25.
13 http://www.sabrizain.org/malaya/malays2.htm
14 http://www.sabrizain.org/malaya/malays2.htm
15 Clifford, *In Court & Kampongs* 18.
16 http://www.sabrizain.org/malaya/malays2.htm
17 http://www.sabrizain.org/malaya/malays2.htm
18 Clifford, *In Court & Kampong* 19.
19 Clifford, *In Court & Kampong* 19.
20 Clifford, *In Court & Kampong* 18.
21 Clifford, *In Court & Kampong* 18.
22 Clifford, *In Court & Kampong* 19.
23 Clifford, *In Court & Kampong* 19.
24 Clifford, *In Court & Kampong* 20–21.
25 Clifford, *In Court & Kampong* 20–21.
26 Clifford, *In Court & Kampong* 22–23.
27 Clifford, *In Court & Kampong* 24–25.
28 Clifford, *In Court & Kampong* 24–25.
29 http://www.sabrizain.org/malaya/malays2.htm
30 http://www.sabrizain.org/malaya/malays2.htm
31 http://www.sabrizain.org/malaya/malays2.htm
32 Clifford, *In Court & Kampong* 28–29.
33 Clifford, *In Court & Kampong* 29.

Works cited

Clifford, H. *In Court & Kampong: being tales & sketches of native life in the Malay Peninsula.* London: Federal Rubber Stamp, 1927.

Mohd Rashidi Pakri, unpublished PhD thesis.

Roff, William R. (Ed.). *Stories by Sir Hugh Clifford.* Kuala Lumpur: Oxford University Press, 1966.

Said, Edward. *Orientalism.* New York: Vintage, 1979.

Swettenham, F. *A Nocturne and Other Malayan Stories and Sketches.* Kuala Lumpur: Oxford University Press, 1993.

The Malay Language in the Singaporean Novel in English

ISMAIL S. TALIB
NATIONAL UNIVERSITY OF SINGAPORE

This chapter will examine the use of Malay in the Singaporean novel in English. It concentrates on fiction, and more specifically, on some novels that present interesting perspectives on the Malay language. The works of Suchen Christine Lim are prominently represented in this chapter, as she puts forward interesting viewpoints on the use of Malay in her novels, which she relates either directly or indirectly to Singapore contexts.

The reason for concentrating on the novel is that it is quite a vibrant literary genre in the English language literature of Singapore.[1] Another reason for concentrating on fiction is that some of the peculiarities of language use are best seen in fiction.[2] Although some of these peculiarities can be generalised across literary genres, it is less easy to do so with some of the others.[3] Malay is less present in recent poetry in English, for example, when compared to the novel.

The use of language in drama presents a further set of difficulties for the analyst when compared to the analysis of the language of fiction. Language use in drama is less easy to record than that of fiction, as it is closely connected to performance factors. A related difficulty is created by the fact that most Singapore plays in English have not been published in printed form, in spite of the vibrancy of the art form in the English-language literature of Singapore.[4] The relative paucity of printed plays by Singaporean writers inevitably makes an analysis of language use in Singapore drama in English more closely tied to drama as performance than to drama as written literature. An analysis of the presence of the Malay language in dramatic performances of English-language plays is of course eminently possible, in spite of the difficulties involved. However, an attempt in this direction may need a separate study, and a different methodology, as it deals with different dimensions and domains of language use in the verbal arts.

One of the chief differences between dramatic performance and written fiction has to do with the nature of mimesis. The focus of the concept of mimesis in this chapter is on the mimesis of language use, or, more specifically for our purpose, the closeness of the relationship between what languages are used in a work of literature and their corresponding use in the real world. Both drama and fiction concern themselves with the mimesis of language use, except for some experimental examples, which try to move away from, or to subvert mimesis. But while one looks at the printed page in one's response to written fiction—hence removing the reader from the immediate experience of everyday language use—one looks at 'real' people enacting the narrative on a stage in a dramatic performance, which brings the audience closer to the immediate experience of the language in use.

Accordingly, while the nature of the mimesis of language use in a dramatic performance is iconic, it is symbolic in written fiction, with the words on the page being in some ways dissimilar to, or at several levels removed from, what they try to represent. When compared to the language of drama, this semiotic feature of fiction allows its language to be more fully deflected from what the characters are supposed to be saying if they were actual people speaking or conversing in real-life situations. Thus, if a linguistic feature appears in the narrative, or if features or stretches of another language are supposed to be present in it, it is easier to deflect from them if one is writing a fictional narrative, by resorting to indirect modes of linguistic representation, or by summary generalisations of what was supposed to be spoken. In this regard, if it is understood that a character speaks in Malay, or sprinkles Malay words in his speech, it is easier to avoid the direct representation of the speech in written narrative fiction than in drama.

In written narrative fiction in a particular language, one can, of course, indicate that another language has been used, without actually using that other language. In this regard, there are, more specifically, many instances in Singapore fiction in English of the use of English to indicate that Malay has been used, without using Malay itself.

In spite of the mimetic representation of the languages used, selectivity is involved, whether it be in drama or fiction. Comparatively, however, it can be said that for technical reasons, fiction can afford to be more selective in its direct representation of language use than drama, thus further reducing the direct presence of other languages in the genre, even in instances in the narrative when their usage is assumed. One reason for this is the more direct representation of speech in the language of drama, as a contrast to the language of fiction, where, through the use of indirect speech and other means, only a selection of the use of other languages may actually be represented, which in turn can be summarised or truncated in the main language of the text.

In Singapore fiction in English, the avoidance of the actual use of another language entirely, even if the other language is supposed to be used, can be seen in Shaik Kadir's novella *A Kite in the Evening Sky*. Kadir has a self-conscious tendency to avoid the use of the Malay language in the novella.[5] This is an important aspect of his work, as some of the characters speak only Malay, and their language use could have been represented more directly than what has been achieved in the narrative. But there is a good reason for its avoidance in Kadir's novella, as the text is meant for school use. In this connection, the audience is an important general consideration in the depiction of another language in the work, a point which will be made again later in this chapter.

In spite of the technical possibility of avoiding the exact depiction of other languages in fiction, some words and clauses in Malay can still be found in some works of Singapore fiction in English. However, due partly to the fact that the novel is in English, which should therefore be the dominant language, this can only be attempted in parts in the text.

An obvious example of the use of an exact word in Malay can be found in the title of Gopal Baratham's novel *Sayang*. Clearly, there is no satisfactory English equivalent for the word 'sayang', as indicated by the first-person narrator of the novel, Joseph Samy:

> It was a truly Southeast Asian word, soft as its people and well-understood from Marang to Manila, Surabaya to Sulawesi, Kuala Lumpur to Kota Kinabalu. It describes a love bound to sadness, a tenderness trembling on the edge of tears, a passion from which pity could not be detached.[6]

According to Joseph, even the Greeks did not have an equivalent word for it: 'The Greeks with their division of love into *eros*, *Philos* and *Agape* had no such word'.

Apart from using the exact words, the Malay words may be grammaticalised in English. This may represent the indigenisation of English, where words in local languages that are frequently used in the local variety of English, are made to follow the grammar of English, including the morphological shift from one part of speech to another. There are a number of examples of the grammaticalisation or Anglicisation of Malay words in the Singapore novel in English. For example, the words 'pontenged' and 'champorisation', which can be found in Shelley's *The Shrimp People*, and 'kachaued' in Fiona Cheong's *Shadow Theatre*.[7]

As Malay cannot be used in long stretches in a fictional work in English, the use of the language is often mixed with English. This is not only a technical consideration in the avoidance of the drawn-out use of a non-English language, but to a certain extent—if not always faithfully—it is a depiction of language as it is actually used. We can see this at various points of Shelley's *The Shrimp People* and the other novels of his tetralogy. One example can be found in *The Shrimp People*, which uses the word 'champorisation' mentioned above, and which is spoken by the character Ethel in the novel: 'Black, white, what? ... Kopi susu? Chinese and Malay *champorisation*?'.

Mixing of languages, or what is better known perhaps by its technical term, *code mixing*, can also be found at various points in Suchen Christine Lim's novels. The following is an example from *Rice Bowl,* which is spoken by a bus conductor. 'You go back I not see you, I ring bell and door close susah-lah, right?'[8]

It is interesting to note the difference in motivation to code mix in Shelley's and Lim's novels. The bus conductor's language in Lim's novel does have a particular politeness effect which is not possible if only English is used. However, the example from Shelley's novel has the opposite effect from that apparently achieved in the extract from Lim's *Rice Bowl*, and is obviously meant to be taken as rather rude.

Of course, other languages are also found in Singapore fiction in English, such as Tamil and the various Chinese languages, especially Hokkien and Cantonese, as well as Mandarin Chinese, the government-imposed 'mother tongue' of the Chinese. But comparatively speaking, Malay plays quite an important role in Singapore fiction in English. One reason for this is its historical importance as a lingua franca, a language of inter-ethnic communication.

There is good evidence of the depiction of Malay as a historical lingua franca in Singaporean English-language fiction. Sister Beatrice in Suchen Christine Lim's *Rice Bowl*, for example, is a nun of Spanish origin, but she is able to speak Malay, even if she is not really proficient in the language. This is made clear in the novel, as seen, for instance, in examples of her use of Malay. Sister Beatrice's use of Malay underlines the previous status of Malay as a lingua franca in Singapore: the language is used even by foreigners in Singapore for a Christian missionary purpose, even though no members of their congregation were of Malay ethnic origin. We can see the use of Malay as a lingua franca in another context in Philip Jeyaretnam's *Abraham's Promise.*[9] When Isaac Abraham's family goes to a Chinese farm in the 1940s, they speak Malay with the farmer and his family.

However, in spite of the historical importance of Malay, its use in a literary work may create problems for the contemporary local audience, especially if the work in question is not intended for use in schools. In this regard, the general Singapore readership has become progressively less conversant in Malay, and this is a consideration for the contemporary novelist. This situation may create difficulties in the depiction of historical scenes at a time when the use of Malay was more widespread, but with an eye on contemporary Singaporean readers who are less competent in, or have no knowledge of, the language. One way out—apart from using English and claiming that Malay is actually used, as done quite extensively by Kadir in *A Kite in the Evening Sky*—is the compilation of a glossary at the end of the novel, which Shelley does in *The Shrimp People*, and which Kadir also does in his work, but for a more direct pedagogical purpose.

In addition to the historical importance of Malay as an inter-ethnic lingua franca, there are political sentiments expressed in the Singapore novel in English about the regional significance of the language. In Suchen Christine Lim's *Rice Bowl* for example, the character Ken has this to say about the contexts of the language use of another character:

> 'He thinks he's local because he can speak Mandarin but I'm more local than he is, I speak Malay. And if we want to talk of a South-East Asia we're in a Malay-speaking world aren't we?'[10]

Indeed, the regional representativeness of Malay, in contrast, for example, with the Chinese languages, is one of the more important linguistic perspectives to be found in the novels of Lim. In *A Bit of Earth*, she has the character, Chan Ah Fook advising the main character of the novel, Wong Tuck Heng, to learn Malay: 'In these parts you must speak the Malay tongue. Don't fear shame. Open your mouth more. Soon you'll be speaking like me'.[11] Although Tuck Weng and Ah Fook are located in the novel in what is now Malaysia, such a sentiment could easily be transported to Singapore, at least historically, and can still be heard today.

Malay, of course, also has an ethnic connection. However, one must be careful here in making too much of this connection, as the relationship of language to ethnicity is not a deductive given, but an empirical fact open to observation and confirmation. The relationship between language and ethnicity is brought up by the character Suwen in Lim's *Fistful of Colours*, who questions their tenuous relationship:

D'you think language defines a man the way an artist's forms and lines define him? I was born ethnically Chinese. I grow up speaking English. Am I not Chinese still? Or am I just half Chinese? Not because of a physical change but because of a language change?[12]

However, the relationship between the Malay language and ethnicity appears to be valid in Singapore today—perhaps even more valid than in the past. Increasingly, speakers of Malay in Singapore are more likely to be ethnically Malay as well, although this is less true in Malaysia today and in Singapore previously. Therefore, it can be said that comparatively speaking, the Malay language has a stronger ethnic connection in contemporary Singapore, as there are fewer Singaporean speakers of the language who are of non-Malay ethnic backgrounds when compared to Malaysia today and the situation in the past in Singapore itself.

Another historical factor which can be noted is the further complication when one considers mother-tongue speakers of Malay, a good number of whom were of Chinese peranakan decent. This fact is quite well represented in Singapore fiction in English, as seen very clearly again in the novels of Lim. Although, over the years, progressively fewer Chinese of peranakan ancestry speak Malay as fluently as was the case in the past, a peranakan Chinese-speaking Malay is not a mere historical anomaly.

In Fiona Cheong's *Shadow Theatre*, for example, which has a relatively more contemporary setting than many of the novels discussed so far, there is the Chinese peranakan character, Helena Sim, whose voice is sprinkled with a number of Malay words, such as 'betul betul' and 'bukan'.[13] Often, these words are code mixed with English, such as 'bukan' which is interestingly used as a negative tag-question indicator instead of the English equivalent, 'isn't it', which itself is a prominent feature of colloquial Singapore English.

Apart from the Straits or peranakan Chinese, the Eurasians also have a linguistic affinity with Malay, although to a lesser extent than the Straits Chinese. Kristang, the language of the Portuguese Eurasians, has some loan words from Malay,[14] and even when Eurasians speak in English, they readily infuse their language with code-mixed lexical items from Malay. This is clearly seen in Rex Shelley's tetralogy. *The Shrimp People*, the first novel in the tetralogy, has been quoted earlier. Among several other examples from this novel are words such as 'cincalok', 'gedebak-gedebuk' and of course the word 'geragok' (geragau) itself, which gives the novel its title, and which has a peculiar punch when translated into English as 'the shrimp people'.[15]

The mimetic depiction of language use in contemporary Singapore will quite naturally present a situation where the Malay language plays a less prominent role. One important reason for this is the onslaught of English, which has become the most important official language of Singapore. Of course, English became prominent because of its practical value, but other interesting perspectives on English are presented in the Singapore novel in English. There is the teacher of Latin and English, Isaac Abraham, in Jeyaretnam's *Abraham's Promise*, for example, who believes in the aesthetic value of English, especially if it is spoken and written well, as a standard language. In Lim's *A Bit of Earth*, Long Mahmud has a political reason for learning English, as he says to his son:

> Many have learned to speak our tongue and turn our words against us. My son, I would like you to learn their tongue and read their writings. So we will know for sure that what they say to us in our tongue is the same as what they write into their books in their own tongue.[16]

Malay may very well play a less important role in contemporary Singapore fiction in English. Not only is its use decreasing in contemporary Singapore, but the younger writers themselves, with the exception of those of Malay or Chinese peranakan ancestry or ethnic affiliation, are less competent or even not at all competent in it. But there is no doubt that a number of Malay words, such as 'makan', 'tidur' and 'kaki' among a number of other lexical items, have become part of Singapore colloquial English. Therefore, it is likely that words originally from Malay will continue to be found, even though it is now part of the colloquial variety of Singapore English, and not Malay per se.

Notes

1 For example, in my bibliographical surveys of Singapore literature in English for the years 2002 and 2003, published by the *Journal of Commonwealth Literature*, there were a total of twenty-four volumes of fiction, whereas poetry has seventeen volumes.

2 Genre is, unfortunately, a neglected issue in postcolonial literary criticism in general: see Peter Hitchcock, 'The Genre of Postcoloniality' *New Literary History* 34 (2003): 299–330.

3 I have discussed some of these generic considerations in postcolonial literatures in English in general in my book *The Language of Postcolonial Literatures: An Introduction* (London: Routledge, 2002).

4 In my bibliographical surveys indicated in endnote 1, there were only five printed volumes of plays, far fewer than the number for fiction and poetry.

5 Shaik Kadir, *A Kite in the Evening Sky* (Singapore: EPB Publishers, 1989).

6 Gopal Baratham, *Sayang* (Singapore: Times Books, 1991) 47.

7 'Pontenged' (from the Malay word 'ponteng'): to be absent; to play truant. 'Champorisation' (from the Malay word 'campur'): a mixture; in his novel, Shelley obviously intends the neologism to mean linguistic or racial mixture. From the Malay word 'kacau': to be disturbed; Rex Shelley, *The Shrimp People* (Singapore: Times Books, 1991); Cheong, Fiona, *Shadow Theatre* (New York: Soho, 2002).

8 'Susah-lah': 'it's going to make things difficult for me', Apart from the politeness effect discussed in the main text above, the Malay expression is also more economical. Suchen Christine Lim, *Rice Bowl* (Singapore: Times Books, 1984) 170.

9 Philip Jeyaretnam, *Abraham's Promise* (Singapore: Times Books, 1995).

10 Lim, *Rice Bowl* 206.

11 Suchen Christine Lim, *A Bit of Earth* (Singapore: Times Books, 2001) 13.

12 Lim, *Fistful of Colours* 82–3. I have also quoted this extract, in relation to a discussion of the relationship between language and ethnicity in my forthcoming review of the reader edited by Harris and Rampton.
13 'Betul betul': carefully or correctly; 'bukan': the negative marker 'not'. As indicated above, the word can also be used as a tag-question indicator.
14 See for example, Alan N. Baxter and Patrick De Silva *A Dictionary of Kristang, (Malacca Creole Portuguse)* (Canberra: Pacific Linguistics, 2005), which lists a number of Malay loan words.
15 'Cincalok': a shrimp paste; 'gedebak-gedebuk': to describe someone as being in extreme hurry and making a lot of noise in the process; 'geragok' or (in standard Malay) 'geragau': a species of shrimp from which cincalok is made. Since many of the Portuguese Eurasians used to make their living from catching 'geragau', they were themselves called 'geragau', which was then extended as a derogatory term to all Eurasians: see my discussion on this in 'Emigration as a Resistant Factor'.
16 Lim, *A Bit of Earth* 109.

Works cited

Baratham, Gopal. *Sayang.* Singapore: Times Books, 1991.

Baxter, Alan N. and Patrick De Silva *A Dictionary of Kristang, (Malacca Creole Portuguse).* Canberra: Pacific Linguistics, 2005.

Cheong, Fiona. *Shadow Theatre.* New York: Soho, 2002.

Harris, Roxy and Ben Rampton eds. *The Language, Ethnicity and Race Reader.* London: Routledge, 2003.

Hitchcock, Peter. 'The Genre of Postcoloniality'. *New Literary History* 34 (2003): 299–330.

Jeyaretnam, Philip. *Abraham's Promise.* Singapore: Times Books, 1995.

Lim, Suchen Christine. *A Bit of Earth.* Singapore: Times Books, 2001.

Lim, Suchen Christine. *A Fistful of Colours.* Singapore: EPB Publishers, 1993.

Lim, Suchen Christine. *Rice Bowl.* Singapore: Times Books, 1984.

Shaik Kadir. *A Kite in the Evening Sky.* Singapore: EPB Publishers, 1989.

Shelley, Rex. *The Shrimp People.* Singapore: Times Books, 1991.

Talib, Ismail S. 'Emigration as a Resistant Factor in the Creation of a National Literature: Rex Shelley's *The Shrimp People*' *Ideas of Home*, ed. Geoffrey Kain (East Lansing, Michigan: Michigan State UP, 1997) 101-14.

Talib, Ismail S. *The Language of Postcolonial Literatures: An Introduction.* London: Routledge, 2002.

Talib, Ismail S. Rev. of *The Language, Ethnicity and Race Reader.* Eds Roxy Harris and Ben Rampton *Language and Literature* 14.3 (2005): 317--20.

Talib, Ismail S. 'Singapore' *Journal of Commonwealth Literature* 37.3 (2002): 121–42.

Talib, Ismail S. 'Singapore' *Journal of Commonwealth Literature* 38.4 (2003): 101–24.

Exploring the Myth of the Prodigal Son in Malaysian-Singaporean Literature: The Case of Three Poets

RUZY SULIZA HASHIM
UNIVERSITI KEBANGSAAN MALAYSIA

Malaysian poets Muhammad Haji Salleh and Salleh ben Joned, as well as Singaporean poet Alfian Sa'at, have been moved to re-imagine the story of Si-Tenggang. In the Malay folktale, Si-Tenggang leaves home, makes a fortune overseas, comes back to his old village, disowns his mother and is turned into stone as a result of his filial impiety. When writers choose culturally accepted and defined figures or stories and appropriate them for different ends, they are consciously inviting new critical assessment. In 'The Travel Journals of Si Tenggang II', Muhammad Haji Salleh re-casts Si Tenggang so that he is no longer an ungrateful son but a new Malay, ready to share his wealth with his people. Salleh ben Joned, known for his philosophy of testing parameters, unflinchingly remodels his Si-Tenggang as 'Si-Tegang' in 'The Salacious Rhymes of a Self-Taut Prodigal'. Punning on the word 'taut', his Malay translation as *Tegang* has deliberate sexual innuendoes. *Tegang* refers to an erect male organ. The poem salaciously describes a sexually virile protagonist whose travels open up a new world. Although Si-Tegang completely embraces its permissiveness and liberty, he yearns for his kampung and is disillusioned when he returns to the folds of his motherland. Alfian Sa'at's 'Si-Tanggang Pura-pura' takes on a new meaning because he is no longer concerned with the breed of new Malays as envisioned by both Muhammad Haji Salleh and Salleh ben Joned, but with the separation of two nations, Malaysia and Singapore, and the issues which continue to strain their relationship.

The myth of Si Tenggang is well-known amongst the Malays. Malay mothers, mostly, are fond of telling this tale of filial impiety to their children because Tenggang's fate is a grim reminder of what may befall the ungrateful child. Filial obligation is universally demanded of every child. In the English tradition, no one can quite forget Shakespeare's version of filial impiety. King Lear's heart-rending plea, reminding his daughter Regan of her filial responsibilities towards her parents, is a timeless western expression of this relationship: 'thou better know'st/ the offices of nature, bond of childhood/effects of courtesy, dues of gratitude'.[1] In Islam, respect for parents is an absolute, with mothers being afforded the more privileged treatment, as Imam Muslim has recorded:

> Abu Hurarira reported that a man came to Allah's Messenger (pbuh) and said: 'Who among the people is most deserving of a fine treatment from my hand?' He [the Holy Prophet] said: 'Your mother'. He [the man] again said: 'Then who (is the next one)'? He [the Holy Prophet] said: 'Again your mother (who deserves the best treatment from you)'. He [the man] said: 'Then who (is the next one)'? He (the Holy Prophet) said: 'Again, your mother'. He [the man] (again) said: 'Then who?' Thereupon he [the Holy Prophet] said: 'Then your father'.[2]

This hadith shows that filial piety is important in the familial institution. Prodigality should be an alien concept in the Islamic-Malay culture, but the existence of the folktale of Si-Tenggang, and subsequent preoccupation with it among Malay writers, shows otherwise.

The story of Si-Tenggang is a heart wrenching story of a son's rejection of his old and doting mother. It is also a reminder that God listens to the prayers of parents.

Appropriation of old texts (written and oral traditions) by writers is not a new practice. William Shakespeare freely used old sources in his plays. This practice is also seen in parody. Contemporary terminology includes intertextuality and re-visioning. I prefer the term re-visioning because of its two-pronged meaning. 'Revise' suggest ways in which writers revise the old texts in their adaptations. 'Re-vision' insinuates techniques of bending, tending, stretching old texts so that they become completely new works. The practice of re-visioning is associated with post-structuralism where writers challenge and dismantle dominant readings. Re-visionary writers seek to deconstruct representations of the past by adapting and modifying them in order to give readers other alternatives, other interpretations, other 'norms' quite different from their originals.

Unlike deconstruction, re-visioning is not formalized as a theory. One of the earliest proponents of re-visioning, Adrienne Rich, an American poet and critic, highlights the politics of re-visioning:

Re-vision: an act of looking back, of seeing with fresh eyes, of entering an old text from a new critical direction, is for us more than a chapter in cultural history: it is an act of survival. Until we understand the assumption in which we are drenched, we cannot know ourselves.[3]

Another writer, Alicia Ostriker, who has done work on the re-visioning of mythical figures in contemporary American poetry, suggests that re-visionary writing is a method whereby the writer chooses a figure or story previously accepted and defined by a culture and appropriates it for altered ends that ultimately make cultural change possible.[4] From a post-colonial perspective, re-visioning involves deconstructing mediated history. As ably argued by Lily Roxas-Tope, a critic from the Philippines who studied postcolonial writers from Southeast Asia, writers appropriate the technique of re-visioning because they are aware of the partiality of any historical discourse.[5] These three perspectives from the 1980s and 1990s—Rich's, Ostriker's and Roxas-Tope's—pertain to the strategies of the poets discussed in the paper.

All three poets practise re-visioning when they enter an old text from a 'new critical direction' to highlight issues which continue to haunt the Malay race. Si-Tenggang, the ungrateful child, is given a new identity. The poets tackle this identity in different ways, attributable perhaps to personal idiosyncracies, but nevertheless providing similarities and contrasts worthy of note.

The Malaysian poets Muhammad Haji Salleh and Salleh ben Joned echo each other in their poems. Yoking these two poets together, I am perhaps being irreverent. Muhammad Haji Salleh is *Sasterawan Negara* (National Laureate), the highest literary award given to creative writers for their literary finesse and contribution to the Malay literary world. Salleh ben Joned, on the other hand, confers his own award on himself—Angkasawan Negara (National Astronaut) and '*Sura rumah tangga*' (house husband). The term *sura rumah tangga* does not exist in the Malay dictionary—the correct term for a female homemaker is '*suri rumahtangga*'. Interestingly, however, both Muhammad Haji Salleh and Salleh ben Joned identify with Si-Tenggang. Modern day Tenggang, as seen by both poets, is spurred not by ideas of material wealth but by academic knowledge. Both poets have similarly enriched educational backgrounds, Muhammad Haji Salleh being the more seasoned traveller by virtue of his academic profession, but Salleh ben Joned, too, has had his share of sojourns abroad. Both poets have been exposed to new ideas, schools of thought and lifestyles. As experienced travellers, they share the seafaring spirit of the old Tenggang.

Muhammad Haji Salleh's Tenggang poem, originally written in Malay as *Buku Perjalanan Si Tenggang II*, translated by the poet himself, is known as *Si Tenggang's Homecoming*. The indication that the poem is a second part (II) is perplexing at first because there is no Si Tenggang I (by the poet). However, the implied first part is the original Tenggang folktale, and the narrator in *Buku Perjalanan Si Tenggang II* is the modern traveller who follows the inclinations and wanderings of the old Tenggang, but one who returns to his old village as the wiser and more educated man. The English translation, *Si Tenggang's Homecoming*, now forms part of the literature section of the language syllabus (a compulsory subject) for secondary school students in Forms 4 and 5. The fact that all 16–17 year old students in Malaysia are now required to study Muhammad Haji Salleh's poem shows recognition of its literary and thematic value and perhaps also encourages Malaysian students to unlearn the axiom that Tenggang equals filial impiety.

Just like the old Tenggang, Muhammad Haji Salleh's Si-Tenggang is alienated from his people. He describes his travels as an eye-opening experience of 'one who has learnt to see'.[6] From the time he leaves home until his return, Si-Tenggang undergoes some kind of metamorphosis; he becomes more cautious and 'reflects' and 'chooses'. The inexperienced Si-Tenggang, one presumes, is naïve, easily duped, fearful. The new Si-Tenggang is:

> Broadened by land and languages
> … no longer afraid of the oceans
> Or the differences between people
> No longer easily snared
> By words or ideas [7]

The new Si-Tenggang, like the old, is misunderstood and thus, alienated. Muhammad Haji Salleh's Si-Tenggang shows us that he is troubled by this estrangement and lack of sympathy. His mother and grandmother, he explains, do not consider his predicament. We know that the old Si-Tenggang, forcibly taken from the embrace of his mother, must have needed extraordinary emotional strength to be able to succeed as an adult. The experience abroad of Muhammad Haji Salleh's Si-Tenggang is equally fraught with difficulties. Lonely and alienated, the protagonist copes by adapting to the new habitat. Taking on a (foreign?) wife, and learning the 'ways of the rude/ to hold actuality in a new logic/debate with hard and loud fact', he sees himself as a better, more learned person.[8] The rest of the kampung folks, it would seem, are still ensnared by traditions that continue to hamper their mental progress.

In the Malay/Muslim context, being assertive, especially with one's parents, is disrespectful. In trying to make his mother and grandmother understand his predicament, Muhammad Haji Salleh's protagonist 'growls' at them. In trying to make them unlearn some of the 'soils and ways' of village life, he is eager to share 'the contents of his boats' with them.[9] He insists that he is very much a Malay 'sensitive to what is good' and more sympathetic than his other Malay brothers. By having to justify that he is still a Malay, and not very different from the other kampung folks, Muhammad Haji Salleh's protagonist shows the extent to which he is at odds with them. Therefore, his return to the embrace of his motherland is more challenging than his adventures overseas.

Salleh ben Joned's blurb for the second edition of his *Poems Sacred and Profane* deliberately appropriates Muhammad Haji Salleh's comments on the first edition: 'the appearance of Salleh ben Joned's book of poems ... was the most traumatic experience for the Malay literary scene'. By placing Muhammad Haji Salleh comments on the blurb, Salleh ben Joned highlights the difference between him and the National Laureate. Salleh ben Joned's poems show his delight in cataloguing women's bodies, sexual encounters, and Malay hypocrisy, although such things are considered taboo in the Malay world. While Muhammad Haji Salleh's works also show admiration for women's bodies, relish sexual attraction between men and women, and describe distasteful aspects of Malay life, he is more 'halus' (tactful). Salleh ben Joned's language, by contrast, is earthier, bordering on vulgarity. In his after word, Salleh ben Joned writes:

> The last meaning is the origin of the term Mat Salleh meaning the Whites. Because of the values that inform my poems, and because I used to be married to two white women (fortunately not at the same time, but I could have done so because I am a Muslim, though an odd one, even an apostate, according to many of the Malay writers and critics), I am often called Mat Saleh.[10]

When a Malay is called *Mat Salleh*, the term is normally derogatory because many western values run contrary to Malay values. Salleh ben Joned chooses to dismiss the question: Is he 'still a 'Malay' or has he 'become a Mat Saleh of sorts?' Readers might find the earthiness of his language and frankness of his compositions striking and confronting. He is comfortable with terms such as 'hard-on', 'necrophilic crap' and 'boring *babi*' (boring pig)' and he is totally unperturbed when describing the hypocrisy of new Malays (bumigeois), sexual permissiveness, and the wonders of women's sexuality. In his poem 'A Hymn to My Sarong', Salleh ben Joned pays tribute to the canopy that allows air to flow around his 'shame and pride'—his golden mangoes of the sun, dangling loose in the tingling caress of the breeze'.[11] Hymns are meant for giving tribute to higher order things, not something as irreverent as admiration for one's own sexual organ. For Salleh ben Joned, very little separates the sacred from the profane; he finds pleasure in both.

By choosing to call his poem *Si Tegang's Home Coming*, Salleh ben Joned's version is a parody of Muhammad Haji Salleh's *Si Tenggang's Home coming*. Rightly salacious, the protagonist, 'Mat Salleh', describes his childhood, puberty, sojourn in a foreign country and return to his village. Just like Tenggang, Mat

Salleh leaves home, gathers wealth (not financially, but educationally) and returns to his motherland. But unlike the original Tenggang who returns by chance, his conscious choice to return proves to be a traumatic experience.

How different is Salleh ben Joned's prodigal son? To begin with, the protagonist is depicted as a precocious young boy who loves 'watching the coupling of buffaloes and amorous couples'.[12] Although he has been taught the principles of Islam by the Ustaz (Muslim religious instructor), he indulges in behaviour contrary to Islamic principles:

> Crazed by the burning sun, drunk on spicy sins,
> I turned the pondok into a hothouse of lust,
> Five times a day, twixt the azan and other din,
> I abused my body like nobody's business.
>
> Reading the Book, I'd sometimes get a hard-on;
> The scent of paradise meant sex in every nook;
> The passion of Zulaika always turned me on,
> To the amazement of the pious gooks.[13]

'Si-Tegang', as the poem is aptly called, depicts the protagonist as shamelessly revelling in sexual behaviour. His actions are an excess in nature; when his father dies young, the protagonist is not able to accept it as fate and goes into 'amuk' mode because his mind 'accepted and didn't accept/ what's said in the Book about fate and all that'.[14]

The chance to go to 'the land of the free', which the speaker attributes to his Bumi status, opens up new opportunities. The Bumi status is given to all Malays and indigenous people of Malaysia and it comes with certain privileges. In Si Tegang's case, he is given a chance to study abroad where he 'wallows in satanic fun'. If in the kampung he caresses an albino buffalo, in the 'deserts of dazzling snow' he frolics in the comfort of blondes. The protagonist truly lives the motto *carpe diem*.

But then, Si Tegang is suddenly seized by a '*rindu*' (homesickness) for his kampung and heads home. No matter how much liberty he is given overseas, he craves his mother's *sambal* (spicy prawn paste). In the original folktale, Tenggang refuses his mother food. But it is his old kampung, the *sawahs* (paddy fields) and buffaloes, Ustazs and azans that call to the protagonist to return.

Si Tegang is, however, disillusioned by what he sees on his homecoming. His idyllic kampung now houses a giant condo. The Bumis, says the speaker, have all become materialistic—'politikus, puitikus, kritikus, mistikus, kopratikus'. As

Salleh ben Joned explains in his glossary, these terms are words of:

> uncertain provenance with rumour having it that they were stolen from English, Malayanized and used to dress up the contemporary Malay writers' poverty of ideas and feelings, 'Tikus' (on its own, meaning mouse or rat) but when added to another word is very popular among Malay literary critics and academics, especially those with a dangerous smattering of English.[15]

Si Tegang returns to the folds of his motherland to be cleansed, but he is disenchanted that his people have blindly followed the imperialist dream. 'Drinking pepsi, eating KFC, following the new way' conflict with the protagonist's vision of progress.[16] Having lived in a progressive white nation, he returns home to seek some salvation of the soul. But he finds that the souls of Bumis have been exchanged for corrupt values, more sinful that the speaker's own propensity to sexual trysts.

When the two poems 'Si Tenggang's Homecoming' and 'The Salacious Rhymes of a Self-Taut Prodigal' are compared, we notice the similarity of situation experienced by the two speakers. They both feel alienated, Muhammad Haji Salleh's speaker because the people around him find him not Malay enough since he exhibits unMalay characteristics such as disrespect to elders, speaking his own mind, and assertiveness. Muhammad Haji Salleh's speaker is alienated because he cannot come to terms with the Bumis' brand of progress.

Muhammad Haji Salleh's Tenggang urges open-mindedness. He wants his fellow Malays to be wary of blind loyalty and not to accept everything at face value. Salleh ben Joned's 'self-taut' prodigal, on the other hand, implores Malay folk to be more discerning of the progress that they have embraced. In another poem *Ballad of Mat Solo*, for instance, Salleh ben Joned highlights the tragedy of Mat Solo, a young kampung man who is caught between tradition and modernity and goes berserk, amok style (like a true, wronged Malay). Sadly, he is shot by the rifles of sharp shooters—a sign of progressive Malaysia. Salleh ben Joned's Si-Tegang cautions against the alienation of the soul which leads to mental breakdown. However, because of the crudity of his language and frankness of his conviction, Salleh ben Joned's Si Tegang finds it difficult to reach average Malays who find his works shockingly truthful and therefore difficult to swallow. Both of Malaysia's prodigal sons have a lot to share with their fellow country folk; by re-visioning they show how the progress of the Malays must be more carefully considered. They suggest that Malays must take time to re-examine some of what has been lost in the quest for progress.

Alfian Sa'at, a Singaporean Malay, has appropriated the same figure of Tenggang in his poem 'Si Tanggang Pura-pura'. Much younger than either

Muhammad Haji Salleh or Salleh ben Joned, his re-vision of Tenggang suggests that this Malay tragic hero is still popular among Malay writers. In sharp contrast, however, Alfian departs from the preoccupation with Malayness. Alfian Sa'at's re-vision addresses issues arising from the separation of a son from his mother. Singapore is the estranged son of Malaysia, the motherland. Speaking from the son's point of view, the speaker shows the ways in which the separation has brought about good things:

> So we were quarantined
> From the mother soil's diseases.
>
> rom the leprous potholes
> And haemorrhages of floods
> And the climbing fevers of a people
> Tossing with the sweat of rhetoric.[17]

The overwhelming imagery of medical disorders such as leprosy, haemorrhage and climbing fevers (perhaps SARS) depicts the mother soil as diseased and contagious. Leprous potholes and haemorrhages of floods also point to inefficient government maintenance on the other side of Singapore. By listing the ills suffered in Malaysia, the speaker seems thankful that Singaporean Malays are spared those disorders. From the perspective of the prodigal son, then, the motherland seems endlessly fraught with calamities.

While the traffic between mother and son is fairly free, the relationship is marked with several hiccups which the speaker terms as 'occasional protest'.[18] The 'doctor', most probably the previous Prime Minister of Malaysia (Tun Dr Mahathir Mohamed), the agent of healing, swabs 'the festering swamps and stretched sinews'.[19] The water that separates the two nations is a great source of wealth to the prodigal son, bearing 'crests of gold' and 'bloated barges', while on the other side, the poor relative's situation remains the same, like the 'projects billboard peeled by rain'.[20]

The vast difference in progress between the two nations is the source of discontent as the son laments:

> O poor ragged mother
> Poor blind ragged mother,
> Where is your perfect eyesight? [21]

Malaysia is represented as the mother whose vision is faulty. While Muhammad Haji Salleh's Tenggang weeps for the lack of modernity of thought and Salleh ben Joned's Si Tegang laments unstructured progress and blind acceptance of imperialistic values, Alfian's Si Tenggang expresses grief over the ways in which Singapore has left Malaysia behind. It is suggested that while Singapore has moved forward in leaps and bounds, Malaysia is still struggling with basic problems of road maintenance and flash floods. Hence, the Singaporean Si-Tenggang is not able to accept his mother 'Aku tidak kenal siapa perempuan ini'.[22]

But why '*Si-Tanggang Pura-pura*' (Si-Tanggang's Pretence)? Is the Singaporean Si-Tanggang merely pretending to be contented?:

> Every evening the chilly winds
> Sweep in from the north
> The chatterings of a madwoman
> And all men gaze upwards
> Like pebbles from a well's depths
> Or peep behind the comfort of concrete
> Smiling, with epitaphs on their lips
> Sumpahan batu.[23]

The Malays in Singapore are actually trapped in their concrete jungle, never to experience the flash floods suffered by their Malay brethren. Yet, instead of looking down from their high-rise condominiums, they 'gaze' upwards, an action closely associated with the Muslim way of reciting the *doa* (prayers to God). The oxymoron of concrete 'comfort' and 'smiling' shows the incongruity of the situation. While seemingly wealthy, they are unhappy because their lips perpetually commemorate inscriptions of death 'smiling, with epitaphs on their lips'.[24] The Singaporean prodigal son, who shows aversion towards his country of birth, is actually pretending to be so. The separation of the two nations means that he can never return. The treaty that separates the two nations is a curse on the prodigal son ('*sumpahan batu*') which is not reversible.[25] In the light of this predicament, his need to make believe that his chosen land is greener is understandable.

The motives that propel the Malaysian poets, Muhammad Haji Salleh and Salleh ben Joned, to write are different from Singaporean Alfian's purpose. Both Muhammad Haji Salleh and Salleh ben Joned lament the situation that Malays have languished in while Alfian expresses grief over the separation of the two nations, caught in the image of a son being unfilial to his own mother. It would be interesting to see how Malaysian writers depict Singaporean Malays in their works. A brief look at Alfian's poem, 'A Visit to a Relative's House in Malaysia', reveals how the more affluent Singaporean relatives pity their poor Malaysian relatives. However the Malaysian relatives feel sorry for the militant lifestyles of their Singaporean kin. In another poem, 'The Johor Incident', the speaker is upset by an incident involving Malaysian relatives. He says:

> … I imagined them talking
> About me, this Singaporean boy,
> Who did not respect the twilight, the Maghrib,
> Who was deaf to the twitter of spirits in the jambu tree.
> I swung higher and higher, crying with rage,
> Wondering whose fault it was, whose error,
> That what was once a bridge is now a wall.[26]

Alfian's poems show the prickly relations between Malay Malaysians and Malay Singaporeans. Seen in the context of 'Si Tanggang Pura-pura', the speaker shows the anguish of separation. I am reminded of the term used in the issue of separation between Malaysia and Singapore. Singapore (known as Temasik in Malay) was part of Malaysia until the former's exit in 1963. Singapore's official version of the separation refers to the momentous event as an 'expulsion', showing Malaysia as the active agent wanting to sever the umbilical cord. The historian Cheah Boon Kheng observed: 'In Singapore at a televised press conference on the same day, Lee said the separation was for him "a moment of anguish". He was so "emotionally affected" that he broke down, and the conference was terminated'.[27]

In Alfian's re-vision, the anguish of the son is obvious in the final two stanzas 'Every evening the chilly winds/ … *Sumpahan batu*'. Likewise, the Malaysian poets highlight the pain of the Malaysian prodigal sons. It is heartening to see that as Malay creative writers, separated by the causeway and age, they nevertheless return to the same treasure trove of folklores, myths, legends, folktales to show connections. Although not homogeneous in emotions and emphases, their re-visions highlight the strategies of engagement with the past so that other alternatives and meanings can emerge. The Malaysian poets are more concerned with changing the worldviews of their Malay kin and with making them re-evaluate old or comfortable practices. Alfian, on the other hand, is disquieted by the Singaporean Malays' exuberance over the separation with the motherland. The convergence of the three poets' views of the Malays and their problems emphasises their commonality of ideas in making the Malay agenda important subject matter in their creative works.

Notes

1 William Shakespeare, *King Lear* (London: Methuen, 1952) 179–181.
2 *Sahih Muslim*, 4 vols, trans. Abdul Hamid Siddiqi (India: Adam Publishers & Distributors, 1996) 164.
3 Adrienne Rich, *On Lies, Secrets and Silences: Selected prose, 1966-1978* (New York: Norton, 1980) 35.
4 Alicia Ostriker, *Stealing the Language: The Emergence of Women's Poetry in America* (New York: Beacon, 1986).
5 Lily Rose Roxas-Tope, *(Un)framing Southeast Asia: Nationalism and the Post-colonial Text in English in Singapore, Malaysia and the Philippines* (University of Philippines: Office of Research Coordination, 1986).
6 Muhammad Haji Salleh, *Rowing By Two Rivers* (Bangi: Penerbit Universiti Kebangsaan Malaysia, 2000) 233.
7 Muhammad Haji Salleh, *Rowing By Two Rivers* 234.
8 Muhammad Haji Salleh, *Rowing By Two Rivers* 235.
9 Muhammad Haji Salleh, *Rowing By Two Rivers* 234.
10 Salleh ben Joned, *Poems Sacred and Profane* (Kuala Lumpur: Pustaka Cipta, 2002) 66
11 Salleh ben Joned, *Poems Sacred and Profane* 18.
12 Salleh ben Joned, *Poems Sacred and Profane* 39.
13 Salleh ben Joned, *Poems Sacred and Profane* 39.
14 Salleh ben Joned, *Poems Sacred and Profane* 40.
15 Salleh ben Joned, *Poems Sacred and Profane* 40.
16 Salleh ben Joned, *Poems Sacred and Profane* 44.
17 Salleh ben Joned, *Poems Sacred and Profane* 43.
18 Alfian Sa'at, *One Fierce Hour* (Singapore: Landmark Books, 1998) 25.
19 Alfian Sa'at, *One Fierce Hour* 25.
20 Alfian Sa'at, *One Fierce Hour* 25.
21 Alfian Sa'at, *One Fierce Hour* 26.
22 Alfian Sa'at, *One Fierce Hour* 26.
23 Alfian Sa'at, *One Fierce Hour* 26.
24 Alfian Sa'at, *One Fierce Hour* 25.
25 Alfian Sa'at, *One Fierce Hour* 26.
26 Alfian Sa'at, *One Fierce Hour* 24.
27 Cheah Boon Keng, *Malaysia: The Making of a Nation* (Singapore: Institute of Southeast Asian Studies, 2002) 101–102.

Works cited

Albert, Lau. *A Moment of Anguish: Singapore in Malaysia and the Politics of Disengagement*. Singapore: Singapore Times Academic Press, 1998.

Alfian Sa'at. *One Fierce Hour.* Singapore: Landmark Books, 1998.

Cheah Boon Keng. *Malaysia: The Making of a Nation*. Singapore: Institute of Southeast Asian Studies, 2002.

Mohammad A. Quayum & Peter Wicks. *Singaporean Literature in English: A Critical Reader.* Serdang: Universiti Putra Malaysia Press, 2002.

Muhammad Haji Salleh. *Rowing Down Two Rivers.* Bangi: Penerbit Universiti Kebangsaan Malaysia, 2000.

Ostriker, Alicia. *Stealing the Language: The Emergence of Women's Poetry in America.* New York: Beacon, 1986.

Rich, Adrienne. *On Lies, Secrets and Silences: Selected Prose, 1966-1978.* New York: Norton. 1980.

Roxas-Tope, Lily Rose. *(Un)framing Southeast Asia: Nationalism and the Post-colonial Text in English in Singapore, Malaysia and the Philippines.* University of Philippines: Office of Research Coordination, 1998.

Sahih Muslim. 4 Vols. Trans. Abdul Hamid Siddiqi. India: Adam Publishers & Distributors, 1996.

Salleh ben Joned. *Poems Sacred and Profane.* Kuala Lumpur: Pustaka Cipta, 2002.

Shakespeare, William. *King Lear.* London: Methuen, 1952.

Malay Text Worlds: Constructing the Malay in Malaysian and Singaporean Literature in English

WASHIMA CHE DAN
UNIVERSITI PUTRA MALAYSIA

The Malays as a race carry the burden of constantly being subjected to negative images of themselves. From Hikayat Abdullah, to Anthony Burgess's *Malay Trilogy*, to Mahathir Mohamad's *Malay Dilemma, stereotypes representing what are perceived to be* Malay weaknesses have been laid bare for study by both non-Malay and Malay scholars and also much politicised as the country tries to come to terms with its multicultural identity as a nation. This continuous impression of 'cultural deficiency' is also explained by Lily Zubaidah Rahim as 'the prevailing culturalist view that Malays were marginal because they were not sufficiently hardworking, motivated, industrious, and numerous other non-affirming "were not's"'.[1]

Syed Hussein Al-Attas in *The Myth of the Lazy Native* argues that 'the image of the indolent native was the product of colonial domination' made worse by '[t]he distortion of Malay character by the authors of the *Revolusi Mental*, and to some extent by Mahathir ... due to their lack of insight into the social sciences, their loose reasoning, and their unfamiliarity with Malay history'.[2]

This chapter examines the construction of Malay text worlds in creative works in English by both non-Malay and Malay writers, from Singapore and Malaysia. It begins with the premise that negative stereotypes of the Malays and Malay culture continue to be perpetuated in writings by non-Malay and Malay writers alike. In this respect, it will be argued that writers writing in English are trapped in colonialist or orientalist discourse of Malays and Malay culture because of the language that they use, thus continuing a discursive legacy left behind by the colonisers.

The theoretical framework adopted in this paper is based on Paul Werth's 'text world theory' which explains how text worlds are constructed as we read. According to Werth, writers 'build up mental constructs called **text worlds** (emphasis author's) which can be described as "conceptual scenarios containing just enough information to make sense of the particular utterance they correspond to"'.[3] He further defines the text world as:

> a deictic space, defined initially by the discourse itself, and specifically by the deictic and referential elements in it ... The deictic and referential elements are given by the discourse. The referential elements, in their turn, activate relevant areas of memory, including complex conceptual structures known as frames.[4]

Frames are then explained as whole chunks of experience and situations, codified and stored in memory as single items ... These then operate to 'flesh out' the discourse from the knowledge and imagination of the participants. This accounts for the fact that every individual will build up a slightly different text world from the same discourse input. At the same time, there are strong restrictions on this so that individual differences remain within accepted boundaries.[5]

Elena Semino focuses on text worlds in poetry and defines the text world that we infer '"behind" the text' as the 'context, scenario or type of reality that is evoked in our minds during reading and that (we conclude) is referred to by the text'.[6] In this chapter I use text world theory by looking at the cultural references used by the writers in their narration which in turn activate the 'knowledge and imagination' of the readers concerning the Malays, which leads to a construction of Malay text worlds as created or evoked by the writers in the readers' minds. In other words, what kinds of worlds/contexts/scenarios/types of realities are constructed in the readers' mind by these authors?

Analysis of text worlds goes back to studies of possible worlds adopted by logicians between the late 1950s and the early 1960s.[7] The idea of infinite possible worlds where the actual world (that we live in) is only one of the worlds has provided 'a framework within which it is possible to determine the truth-values of propositions beyond the constraints of the actual world, and particularly to define the concepts of possibility and necessity'.[8]

The question of possibility and necessity relates to notions of truth and falsity in that in contrast to a one-world model where the actual world represents the only frame of reference, and that propositions can be classified as true or false,[9] the possible world model allows that:

> possible truth applies to propositions that are true in at least one possible world, necessary truth to propositions that are true in all possible worlds, and necessary falsity to propositions that are false in all possible worlds.[10]

In understanding fictional worlds, as readers 'we use our knowledge of reality to fill any relevant gaps in the content of fictional worlds'.[11] Thus '[i]n reconstructing the content of fictional worlds, we operate with an underlying assumption that they share the same properties as the actual world unless we are explicitly told otherwise'.[12]

Fiction and literature have been used interchangeably whereby literature tends to be judged according to its fictionality or the projection of 'alternative realities beyond social and cultural norms'.[13] Such alternative models of reality in literature are created out of criteria other than practical usefulness or faithfulness to the actual world, such as 'interestingness, originality, novelty, and so on'.[14] This suggests, that even though in realistic works of fiction 'the domain that is taken as actual is governed by the same laws that apply to the world of reality', a less than accurate picture of the 'actual world' is created.[15]

In the construction of Malay text worlds, it can be argued that the representations that have been created and perpetuated of the Malays and Malay culture should be considered as belonging to the domain of alternative worlds (thus constructed) rather than reflecting the actual world. As most short stories and novels in English from Singapore and Malaysia adopt the mode of realism, mimicking the actual world, the question of how realistic such representations are can be raised.[16]

The fundamental questions addressed in this chapter within the framework of text world theory are: What kinds of text worlds are constructed in Singaporean and Malaysian literature in English by both Malay and non-Malay writers? How are these text worlds similar and how are they different? Do such text worlds perpetuate negative images of the Malays? If so, in what ways? And if not, how have the writers represented the Malays otherwise?

It is important to note at this juncture that the Malay text world constructed in my analysis is the Malay text world that is created in English, a colonial legacy, and a form of neo-colonialism. How far that has an influence in the worlds constructed is also to be considered. The Sapir-Whorf hypothesis of linguistic relativity—that the language that we speak may be a fetter to the way we see the world—can be seen to work here in relation to English, the language used by these writers in telling stories which are locally based. Further, the comparison between Malay and non-Malay writers, and at another level, Malaysian and Singaporean writers, is expected to provide different dimensions to the representations of Malay text worlds.

In order to explore the aforementioned questions, the works of writers from Singapore such as Suchen Christine Lim and Alfian Sa'at, and the works of writers from Malaysia such as Shirley Geok-lin Lim and Karim Raslan are studied. Alfian Sa'at and Karim Raslan are chosen to represent Malay writers: one from Singapore and the other from Malaysia, while Suchen Christine Lim and Shirley Geok-lin Lim are selected to represent non-Malay writers (both of Chinese origin), again one from Singapore and the other from Malaysia. The works chosen are the novels *A Bit of Earth* (2001) by Suchen Christine Lim and *Joss and Gold* (2001) by Shirley Geok-lin Lim and the short stories 'Bugis' (1999) by Alfian Sa'at and 'Neighbours' (1996) by Karim Raslan.

I begin my exploration of Malay text worlds in the selected texts with the non-Malay writers, assuming that they might provide more of an 'other' perspective in comparison with the Malay writers. Further, the two writers chose to write in the novel form which allows for character development, where the Malay characters that inhabit the text worlds of the two novels are minor characters. It will be interesting to see how these characters have been represented in view of the above problematics.

The Malay Text World of Suchen Christine Lim's *A Bit of Earth*

In the novel *A Bit of Earth*, Suchen Christine Lim combines history and fiction to tell the story of a China-born immigrant, Wong Tuck Heng, who survived and prospered in Malaya despite the change in the ruling power from Malay to British colonial government.

The narration of *A Bit of Earth* deploys an omniscient narrator who tells the story from the third person perspective, providing an ideal 'actual world' of the text from which the story is told. In approaching the representation of Malays in her works, Suchen Lim appears at first reading to promote a more positive image, resisting negative colonial discourses on the Malays by emphasising their cultural superiority.

The Malay characters of *A Bit of Earth* are, namely, Datuk Long Mahmud, the *menteri* of Bandong, his son Ibrahim, and arguably (in light of discussions of Malayness), Musa Talib the Indian Muslim trader (the Mamak).

The Malay text world created in the novel is one in which the Malays rule supreme. Suchen romanticises the Malay warrior and leader through the character of Datuk Long Mahmud, first mentioned at the beginning of Chapter 3 of the novel; he is seen as an exoticised powerful Malay chief, with a bevy of slaves and a harem to do his bidding. Datuk Long Mahmud is described as:

> [a] strikingly handsome man in his late thirties, he was aristocratic in his bearing, with a high forehead and an aquiline nose with a neat black moustache beneath it. He carried himself like a warrior prince, demanding unquestioning obedience from his followers. Like his father before him.[17]

The world constructed belongs in the past, in the days of feudal power, with the Malay character's sexuality and sensuality particularly foregrounded as being his most salient characteristics, conforming to Edward Said's take on how the orient has been presented in the West. Malay sexuality is expressed through a master-slave relationship in which the Malay lord is free to choose from among his slaves a woman who pleases him and will serve him (presumably sexually). The text world created of Datuk Long Mahmud's life is filled with subservient women and deferential men, all eager to please him.

Slaves and servants hovered about him. When he moved, their eyes followed him. When he stopped, they waited for a word or an order, their eyes anticipating his wishes. When he stopped at the foot of the steps, one of his female slaves descended in haste and knelt before him with head bowed and eyes lowered. 'Pardon, my great lord and master! Your most unworthy slave welcomes you home. Please pardon your unworthy slave for her slowness in greeting your lordship. May His Most Merciful and Bountiful shower His blessings on you!'

She removed his sandals with the reverence of one touching a sacred object. Then, using a polished coconut half-shell, she scooped water out of a stone jar and gently washed away the sand clinging to his feet. She knelt to dry them with a soft cloth, her lips brushing his feet lightly. He admired the suppleness of her body and the roundness and fullness of the breasts beneath her cotton blouse.

> 'Come and serve me tonight.'
> 'Your unworthy slave hears and obeys you.'[18]

The above depiction draws upon stereotypes of encounters with exotic colonial discourses or stories of the East. Perhaps it does not matter in this narrative that the character is Malay; the setting could quite easily be any Eastern or oriental setting.

The second Malay character introduced in the chapter is Ibrahim, Datuk Long Mahmud's son, who is described in a similar manner to the father:

> He was a tall noble-looking youth with the same proud eyes as his father. His high forehead and smooth sun-browned face belonged to his Celebes ancestors, but the dignity with which he conducted himself was his mother's, the daughter of a noble family of chief ministers.[19]

Suchen Lim is clear about who she defines as Malay in the novel; neither Indian Muslims nor the Mamak are seen as Malay. This can be explained with respect to the timeframe of the novel, which is pre-independence Malaya, before the construction of Malayness had been constitutionalised.

If we take the constitutional definition, Musa Talib, the Indian Muslim trader in the story, might be perceived as a Malay character. Nevertheless, he is depicted as one who lives on the margins of his society. His position is represented as that of an opportunistic servant who serves the Malay lords, acting as a mediator between the Chinese and the Malays. He is depicted as a most deferential subject, overly excessive in his praise and submissiveness to the Malay lord:

> His face lit up when he saw the Kedah trader. Musa Talib was kneeling at the top of the steps, reeling off a string of salaams and other words of respect.
>
> . . .
>
> 'O my lord, you honour me. Please accept my thanks and gratitude. May Allah in His most gracious and bountiful mercy continue to bless your lordship and your lordship's son!'[20]

The description of Musa Talib is almost derogatory both in his physique and in character. Whilst Musa Talib is described as being offended by the derogatory term *mamak* (a term used to refer to Indian Muslims in Malaysia and Singapore, and which differentiates them from the Malays), his description draws upon animalistic frames of reference (buffalo, young bucks), suggesting the servitude and wiliness of his character.

Musa Talib bowed low as he waited for the slave girl to fill his plate with fragrant rice. He kept his eyes on Datuk Long Mahmud's face as he scooped up a ball of white rice with the stubby fingers of his right hand and put it into his mouth. He ate delicately and sparingly despite his great bulk. He was a big-boned man with chocolate brown skin. Everything about him was broad and generous, from his wide face to his flat nose and thick brown lips. His dark eyes were watchful as he ate, his jaws masticating upon a piece of beef, like a buffalo chewing cud. He had grown together with the Datuk in those far-off days, before the Datuk's father had acquired land rights, tin mining rights, revenue collection rights and trading boats to sail up and down the coast of Perak. In those days, Musa's father, the Indian-Muslim trader, gave credit and loans to the Datuk's father. Musa and Datuk Long Mahmud were carefree young bucks then, out to have a good time together.[21]

The *mamak*'s claim to *bumiputra* status can be seen in the character's thoughts of his rights in the country and his feelings about still being treated as an outsider despite his not being taken seriously by indigenous Malays like Datuk Long Mahmud:

> But Mamak Musa would never betray that he was affronted by the derogatory name. Why should he be such a fool? Years of serving the Malay chiefs had taught him to be servile in words and wily in deeds. He was not ashamed of his own lineage. His Indian-Muslim ancestors had settled in Kedah more than three hundred years ago. But that Datuk Long Mahmud mused, was typical of Musa's hyperbolic stories.[22]

The Malay Text World of Shirley Geok-lin Lim's *Joss and Gold*

In *Joss and Gold*, Malays again are minor characters, in this instance Abdullah and Samad, Li An's university friends. Shirley Lim's depiction of the two characters seems sympathetic, empathising with the Malays' struggle to assert themselves as rightful heirs to the nation. However, her representation of Malays is coloured by a condescending perception of the Malays as a backward race, one that can only speak 'simple slow English'—unlike the Chinese characters of the novel:

> Of course, she thought, it must be just as bad for Abdullah to express himself in English instead of Malay. He must feel like the blinded six-year-old groping around in his mind for the objects of his thoughts. He must have been made mute at the university by the loss of his language.
>
> But how well he explained himself, even with his simple slow English! She felt an admiration for him.[23]

The Malay text world represented by Abdullah and Samad is one in which the Malays are seen as a backward race compared to the Chinese. This is reflected in their inability to master English, and also in their obsession with politics and nationalistic pride, which is manifest in the materialistic privileges that the Malays receive as *Bumiputras* (sons of the soil). The Chinese, on the other hand, are depicted in the novel to be more comfortable with English than with Malay, the national and official language of Malaysia.

> 'Like English,' Abdullah said. 'Don't want you to feel bad, yah, Li An, but English is a bastard language. In Malaysia we must all speak national language.'[24]
>
> Could they really do it, she wondered? What would happen if they all suddenly switched to Malay right now? How would she express herself? Like a halting six-year-old, groping for light in a darkened world? …
>
> 'For us Malays, yah, we have to speak English everywhere—in school, office. We not so good in English. But why must we speak English? That not our national language.' Abdullah's voice was gentle, he spoke in the same manner Henry did, like a teacher explaining a difficult lesson to a favorite child.[25]

Abdullah further reiterates why Malays are not good with English, in comparison with non-Malays:

> 'For the one percent, of course they must learn English. This one percent will be top government people. Everybody else like taxi driver, even teacher, why need English? Malay is good enough for this country.'[26]

Shirley Lim's discomfort with the Malays is also a part of the text world of the novel, illustrated through Li An's feelings towards the Malay characters:

At first it had made her uncomfortable that Chester and Abdullah were roommates, but then she had spoken to Abdullah on several occasions and found him funny and gentle. She liked talking to him, although his conversation was always about politics. His position was quite clear, but he argued with her subtly, like a good partner observing the patterns and courtesies of an elaborate dance. She didn't feel threatened when he explained the need for Malay special rights intelligently and elegantly; he made it seem fair and just, a readjustment to the fundamental design of the dance. She liked the idea of the Malaysian future as this gentle weaving readjustment and had asked Abdullah why his paper did not present its position in that light. He answered that it did, she was simply not reading it correctly ... [27]

Reminiscent of Suchen's concerted effort to construct the Malays in a positive light, the Malay text world that is created in Lim's work is one that does not draw from commonly accepted perceptions, which leads to the Malay characters being seen as unconvincing, unrealistic and caricatured, like stereotypes of Malays presented in earlier colonial literature. It would appear that the non-Malay writers in English from Malaysia and Singapore as represented by Shirley Lim and Suchen Lim have not really broken away from such negative perceptions of the Malays. This practice continues in other ways. Apart from the language issue, the Malays are also shown to be narrow minded when it comes to multicultural issues, wary of interracial relationships, as seen in this remark by Abdullah:

'Very difficult this interracial affair,' Abdullah said to Chester. 'Better that like stay with like. Indian and Chinese cannot mix, too many differences—food, custom, language. To be husband and wife must share same religion, same race, same history. Malay and Chinese also cannot mix, like oil and water. Malays have many adat, Islam also have shariat. All teach good action. Chinese have no adat, they eat pork, they like gamble, make money.' He stopped, then said to Li An, 'Of course Chinese also have their own religion. But they must become like Malay if they want to marry Malay.'[28]

It is clear that the Malay text world that has been constructed by Shirley Lim represents her own discomfort and uncertainty about the Malays. Malay women wearing *tudung* in the novel are described as 'walking corpses' on the streets of Kuala Lumpur:

She didn't know. After all, for nine years she had successfully avoided Kuala Lumpur, its smoky afternoon haze, the foul snorting lorries and women wrapped in black purdah like walking corpses.[29]

While Suchen Lim romanticises the Malays, Shirley Lim reverses the reality of Malaysia, representing the majority Malays as minor characters, especially in the characters of Abdullah and Samad. The contentious issue of *bumiputra*, and images of the Malays as unprogressive, corrupt and dependent on government subsidies for their success are represented in the lives of the characters Abdullah and Samad.

Such representations of the Malays in *Joss and Gold* echo the general opinion that Malays are not as comfortable with the English language compared to other races. Kirpal Singh, for example, asserts that:

> [f]or some peculiar reason very few Malays in Singapore have attempted to write in English. The bulk of poetry, prose, and drama seems to be written by Indians and Chinese. Whether this indicates that the Malay is reluctant to use a language not inherently his own, or whether this indicates a shyness or lack of confidence, is a matter for further investigation. Like the Indians and Chinese, the Malays have generally enjoyed the same kind of exposure to English as anyone else in Singapore and their competence in the language is ably demonstrated in their professional work. So it is a little difficult to fathom as to why they have not ventured to creative writing. I suspect that a possible explanation could lie in the culture itself—a culture nourished essentially by the soil and therefore not very comfortable in a highly technological, urban setting where the cerebrum predominates. Traditional Malay literature tends very much to be in the romantic mode and this, of course, does not find a ready audience in a tough-minded Singapore. A few of the attempts that I myself have seen reflect the unease of the Malay writer almost to the point of excruciation; it is hoped that this unease will diminish with the years.[30].

The Malay Text World of Alfian Sa'at's 'Bugis'

Alfian Sa'at writes about modern-day Singapore, where the Malays still struggle with their identity as members of what was once a majority group but which is now a minority. The Malays face the onslaught of modernisation in a rapidly progressive society while trying very hard to uphold their cultural traditions and religious identity.[31]

'Bugis' tells the story of a young woman who 'talks' to the reader of the changes in her life: of her friendship with her childhood best friend Salmah who has now donned the headscarf, the *tudung*; of her confusion in facing her own transition from tomboy to woman read in her own hidden desire (perhaps even to herself) to be recognised as a woman, and not a tomboy anymore.[32] When this recognition is accorded, it is not in the way she wants, by Sazalie (Salmah's boyfriend, to whom she is secretly attracted). Instead, it is by a chance meeting in the MRT (Mass Rapid Transit) with a *pondan* (transvestite, or 'a general Malay term for gay/faggot/drag queen' [www.urbandictionary.com/define.php?term=pondan. Retrieved 30 January 2009]) who tells her admiringly that she looks like the famous and sexy Malaysian songstress Ziana Zain. This recognition comes from someone who is marginal in society, deviant in the way that he presents himself, and it becomes an embarrassment instead of a source of pride for the protagonist. She struggles to contain her self-consciousness and embarrassment which culminate in her act of pulling off Salmah's *tudung.* She reveals Salmah's hair, and symbolically exposing her hypocrisy, when, despite the protagonist's protests, Salmah wants to tell Sazalie of their encounter on the MRT (thus exposing the protagonist's shame at her own desires to be recognised as a woman read by the *pondan*, and her growing attraction towards her best friend's [Salmah] boyfriend, Sazalie).

'Bugis' is a 'realistic' short story told in the voice of a young woman. It deploys a first person narrator and assumes a silent audience (the reader) located within a shared deictic environment. This is achieved by the repeated use of first person pronouns, (the 'I/we' referring to the narrator); the use of present tense, suggesting simultaneity of content and coding time (continuous throughout the narrative except for the flashback of how they met the boys of the void deck); the use of proximal space deixis (here); and the use of direct statements or asides for the audience (the repeated use of 'for those who don't know') as below:

> Suddenly I go, 'Yesterday my grandma made trouble again.'
>
> Salmah looks up from her Particle Mechanics lecture notes.
>
> 'What did she do?' she asks.
>
> 'Don't know lah.' I always go 'don't know lah' before I start off telling a long story. I'm not sure where I picked the habit up from, but it has been pointed out to me by who else, but my best friend since primary school. For those who don't know, it's Salmah.[33]

Alfian Sa'at's 'Bugis' projects a discourse situation in which the protagonist narrates her story in a confidential manner to an assumed audience of different backgrounds. The first world constructed through the story is the world seen through the eyes of the protagonist as a young woman. She faces a crisis about her identity, resisting her own transformation from her comfort zone, of being a tomboy into a woman. The second world constructed is that of the Malay Muslim seen through the eyes of the other. Sa'at problematises the identity conflict of contemporary Singaporean Malay Muslim women who struggle with the external expression of their identity by the wearing of the *tudung.* The question put forward here is how are *tudung* wearing women perceived? Practical questions like 'isn't it hot?' or 'is your hair clean in there?' and more judgemental ones such as 'are you really as good as you appear?' are part of society's (both Malay and non Malay) perceived consciousness of a section of

Malay society, (the *tudung* wearing women), given voice by Alfian through the unnamed protagonist. In doing so, Sa'at reveals the hypocrisy of the ideal that to wear the *tudung* promises nun-like chastity or modesty.

'Bugis' is a story constructed by a Malay author, which reveals a convincing Malay text world in which the confusion of the Malays in reconciling with a modern urban identity that living in Singapore demands, while at the same time still being strongly attached to their religious Islamic identity. (In Malaysia and Singapore, being Malay equates to being Muslim). At present, the most visible act of religiosity is measured in the way that women dress within the Malay world, where the *tudung* has become a common sight; among Malay women, both in Malaysia and Singapore, to wear the *tudung* is more common than not. The *tudung*, while representing the 'good' Muslim woman/girl, has been appropriated so that instead of, or rather, as well as, fulfilling its original intention of piety and modesty, it has now become a fashion item. This is captured well by Alfian in the Malay world he constructs, through the character Salmah.

It can perhaps be read that the *tudung*, 'this scarf that good Muslim girls wear', is used to show the hypocrisy of religiosity within the Malay text world.[34] Judgement of the superficiality of overt religiosity is made less harsh by the lens through which it is seen: the world constructed through an adolescent girl's perspective as she tries to make sense of her world. In the final analysis, perhaps it can be argued that the *pondan* actually represents someone who is more honest with himself than either Salmah or the protagonist.

The Malay Text World of Karim Raslan's 'Neighbours'

Karim Raslan is a Malay writer of mixed blood (English and Malay). He is known for his short stories about the urban Malay middle class, and for his prose writing reflecting on the state of his own identity as well as Malaysia's struggles as it moves towards becoming a developed nation.

In 'Neighbours', Raslan presents a Malay text world in which the third person narrator, in a gossipy tone reminiscent of Jane Austen's style of narration, tells the story of Datin Sarina, the nosy wife of Datuk Mus, typifying a new breed of nouveau rich women who spend their husbands' money and worry about whose husband is marrying which new young starlet.[35]

The story again draws from the idea of the hypocrisy of the religious in society, through the character of Encik Kassim, who appears to be the ideal neighbour and the 'epitome of Malay respectability'.[36] Malay sexuality and sensuality are the central themes of the story. The Malay text world constructed is a familiar one in which the Malays are obsessed with image, with materialism, and with other people's affairs. The story, however, shocks the reader in its depiction of deviant sexuality, which is explicitly described by Raslan in the homosexual exploits of the respectable Encik Kassim, as seen through the peeping eyes of Sarina. As Sarina is shocked at her discovery of her neighbour's secret sexual life, she is confronted with her own less than respectable lifestyle.

This chapter began with the premise that the perpetuation of negative images of Malays is a continuing tradition in literature in English from Singapore and Malaysia. As I explore the different text worlds, I find that the comparisons made between the Singaporean and Malaysian writers may not be sustainable. Suchen Lim (a Chinese writer writing from a country where the Chinese is the majority) writes from a majority voice in a language recognised as the official language of Singapore; this enables a more positive depiction of Malays and Malayness. Unfortunately, despite her obviously conscious effort to present a more positive image of the Malays, the novel (*A Bit of Earth*) still inadvertently falls into the usual stereotypical depiction of Malays with predominantly stock Malay characters who trigger the usual 'resources of memory and imagination'.[37] In contrast, Shirley Lim (a Chinese writer writing from a country where the Chinese is a minority group) writes as a minority and a diasporic writer, allowing for more of her anger and disappointment to emerge in her writings. The Malay text world of Shirley Lim is the world of her memories of how the Malays were, and how alien and different they have become to her.

For the Malay writers writing about themselves, Karim Raslan writing in English in Malaysia addresses a minority audience—fiction in English is still a minority genre in Malaysia, albeit an elitist one—while Alfian Sa'at, on the other hand, writing in Singapore, addresses a majority audience. This state of affairs leads to a representation of a minority elite by Raslan and a representation of majority voice by Alfian, despite is belonging to a minority group.

What persistently emerges in the representation of Malayness and Malay culture in literary texts in English from both countries is the conflict of identity that Malays face in reconciling their religiosity and their sexuality. However, the multicultural reality that we live in requires us to see the *us and them* divide as a continuum rather than clear-cut differences. Defining other ethnicities in multicultural settings such as Singapore and Malaysia as the 'other', rather than seeing them as an extension of 'us', means missing the point: that negative constructions of ourselves by our neighbours provide a site for self-reflexivity as much as when we write about ourselves. The Malay writers show a different view of the Malays: Karim Raslan reflects on the hypocrisy of middle class Malays, while Alfian Sa'at chooses to highlight the struggles of working class Malays in Singapore in defining their identity.

It appears that a reading of the works by the non-Malay writers selected in this chapter reveals continuing stereotyping of Malays as seen through the eyes of the other despite the purported multicultural nature of both Malaysia and Singapore. In Suchen Christine Lim's work, the Malays are exoticised, maintaining a strongly colonial depiction of the Malays as sensual or even worse, highly over-sexed despite (or perhaps because of?) their overt religiosity. In the case of the Indian Muslim trader, Mamak Musa Talib, the sense of otherness is even stronger, leading to an almost unchecked negative representation of a wily and cunning opportunist, despicably submissive and ubiquitous in ensuring favour from the indigenous Malay leader, the Datuk.

In Shirley Lim's work, similarly (and perhaps not surprisingly), the Malay characters are represented as uncouth, opportunistic individuals, with stereotypically ethnocentric tendencies bordering on racism. Their religiosity offers strangely skewed perceptions of ethnicity (to be Muslim and Malay is one and the same, as in the Malaysian constitution).

While the two non-Malay authors represent perceptions of Malayness, Suchen Christine Lim writes from the position of an ethnic majority (Chinese) in Singapore, romanticising the Malays but not including the *mamak* in her categorisation of the Malays. Shirley Lim, on the other hand, writes from the position of an ethnic minority embittered by Malaysian policy on Malay rights, which she perceives marginalising the non-Malays. This results in a general depiction of the Malays as less educated and less worldly than the main Chinese characters, perhaps underlying the belief that they are undeserving of the privileges accorded to them.

To reiterate the findings of my research questions: in the non-Malay writers' works, the Malay text worlds constructed are still, unfortunately, based on stereotypical negative images of the Malays as part of a colonial legacy, as identified by Lily Zubaidah Rahim. Their Malay characters tend to be flat or stock characters, without any attempt to deconstruct stereotypes.

The Malay writers, Alfian Sa'at and Karim Raslan, offer more self-reflexive representations of the Malays through the text worlds they construct and therefore, arguably, are more realistic in their depictions. This does not necessarily mean their work presents more positive images. Rather, as authors, they are more honest in their representation of the hypocrisy of the Malays, observed through overt displays of religiosity. In other words, while their characters may be Malay, the representation of their very human weaknesses is universal in nature, and therefore most convincing. Admittedly, such 'honest' depictions are easier coming from within (Malays writing about Malays) than from without (non-Malays writing about Malays).

Notes

1 Lily Zubaidah Rahim, *The Singapore Dilemma: The Political and Educational Marginality of the Malay Community* (New York: Oxford University Press, 1998) Preface.
2 Syed Hussien Al-Attas, *The Myth of the Lazy Native* (London: Frank & Cass, 1977) 70, 166; *Revolusi Mental* (or Mental Revolution) was published in 1971 by UMNO (United Malay National Organization), the dominant ruling party of Malaysia delineated negative traits of the Malays, thus reiterating the colonial construction of stereotypical characteristics of the Malays.
3 Paul Werth, *Text Worlds: Representing Conceptual Space in Discourse* (New York: Pearson, 1999) 7. Emphasis the author's
4 Werth, *Text Worlds* 20.
5 Werth, *Text Worlds* 20.
6 Elena Semino, *Language and World Creation in Poems and Other Texts* (London: Longman, 1997) 1.
7 Semino, *Language and World Creation* 58.
8 Semino, *Language and World Creation* 58.
9 Semino, *Language and World Creation* 58.
10 Bradley and Swartz, cited in Semino, *Language and World Creation* 58.
11 Semino, *Language and World Creation* 64.
12 Semino, *Language and World Creation* 64.
13 Widdowson, cited in Semino, *Language and World Creation* 69.
14 Semino, *Language and World Creation* 69.
15 Semino, *Language and World Creation* 71.
16 This is generally so, apart from works within the horror genre such as by Tunku Halim, although to think of it, within the context of the Malays' continuing belief in the supernatural, this may perhaps be also seen as based on Malay reality.
17 Suchen Christine Lim, *A Bit of Earth* (Singapore: Times Books International, 2001) 28.
18 Lim, A Bit of Earth, 31-32
19 Lim, *A Bit of Earth* 33.
20 Lim, *A Bit of Earth* 34.
21 Lim, *A Bit of Earth* 35.
22 Lim, *A Bit of Earth* 35.
23 Shirley Geok-lin Lim, *Joss and Gold* (Singapore: Times Books International, 2001) 70.
24 Lim, *Joss and Gold* 69.
25 Lim, *Joss and Gold* 69–70.
26 Lim, *Joss and Gold* 70.
27 Lim, *Joss and Gold* 56.
28 Lim, *Joss and Gold* 58.
29 Lim, *Joss and Gold* 198.
30 I have to thank Alfian Saat for drawing my attention to this particular quote. Kirpal Singh, 'An Approach to Singapore Writing in English', In Quayum,

M.A. & Peter Wicks (eds), *Singaporean Literature in English: A Critical Reader* (Serdang: UPM, 2002) 226–227.

31 The Malays of Singapore automatically became a minority ethnic group when Singapore separated from Malaysia in 1965.

32 Throughout the story, this line is typical of how the protagonist would begin her narration, thus a distinctive childlike 'know-it-all' voice is created by Sa'at of the main character. Alfian Sa'at, 'Bugis'. In *Corridor* (Singapore: Raffles, 1999).

33 Sa'at, 'Bugis' 2.

34 Sa'at, 'Bugis' 1.

35 Karim Raslan, 'Neighbours', in Karim Raslan, *Heroes and Other Stories* (Kuala Lumpur: Times Books International, 1996.).

36 I have discussed this story at length in another paper entitled 'Between Religiosity and Sexuality: The "Religious Malay" in Malay Text Worlds', in Tan Bee Hoon, Washima Che Dan, Mardziah Hayati Abdullah, Noritah Omar, Faiz Sathi Abdullah, & Rosli Talif (eds), *Theoretical and Practical Orientations in Language and Literature Studies* (Petaling Jaya: Pearson, 2007) 226.

37 Werth, *Text Worlds* 17.

Works cited

Al-Attas, Syed Hussien. *The Myth of Lazy Native.* London: Frank & Cass, 1977.

Alfian Sa'at. 'Bugis'. In *Corridor.* Singapore: Raffles, 1999.

Lim, Shirley Geok-lin. *Joss and Gold.* Singapore: Times Books International, 2001.

Lim, Suchen Christine. *A Bit of Earth.* Singapore: Times Books International, 2001.

Mahathir Mohamad. *The Malay Dilemma.* Singapore: Marshall Cavendish, 1970.

Quayum, M.A. & Peter Wicks (eds). *Malaysian Literature in English: A Critical Reader.* Petaling Jaya: Pearson Longman, 2001.

Quayum, M.A. & Peter Wicks (eds). *Singaporean Literature in English: A Critical Reader.* Serdang: UPM, 2002.

Rahim, Lily Zubaidah. *The Singapore Dilemma: The Political and Educational Marginality of the Malay Community.* New York: Oxford University Press, 1998.

Raslan, Karim. 'Neighbours'. In Karim Raslan. *Heroes and Other Stories.* Kuala Lumpur: Times Books International, 1996.

Semino, Elena. *Language and World Creation in Poems and Other Texts.* London: Longman, 1997.

Singh, Kirpal. 'An Approach to Singapore Writing in English.' In Quayum, M.A. & Peter Wicks (eds). *Singaporean Literature in English: A Critical Reader.* Serdang: UPM, 2002.

Washima Che Dan. 'Between Religiosity and Sexuality: The "Religious Malay" in Malay Text Worlds.' In Tan Bee Hoon, Washima Che Dan, Mardziah Hayati Abdullah, Noritah Omar, Faiz Sathi Abdullah, & Rosli Talif (eds). *Theoretical and Practical Orientations in Language and Literature Studies*. Petaling Jaya: Pearson, 2007.

Werth, Paul. *Text Worlds: Representing Conceptual Space in Discourse*. New York: Pearson, 1999.

No Less a Malay: The Bilingual Singaporean

JARIAH MOHD JAN
UNIVERSITY OF MALAYA

The Malay community in Singapore comprises about 432,500 people, in a population of nearly 3,000,000.[1] Though a minority, the Malays have moved in tandem with mainstream Singaporeans, sharing their problems as well as progress, while retaining most of their Malay heritage.

The Malay language assumed a position of importance in Singapore during early 1960s. Malay was selected as the national language when Singapore became independent in 1965. The dominance of the language in Malay homes and social networks until recently remained unrivalled. However, in recent years, the status and importance of Malay have declined. This is due to changes in the social, political and economic life of the Malays which, in turn, have brought about changes with respect to the status, functions and, to some extent, the structure of the language. The Malay community, realising the futility of efforts to reverse the trend, accepted the situation and the Malay language now assumes third position in importance in Singapore after English and Mandarin.[2]

In Singapore, English has been designated the role of official working language because it is the purported lingua franca of the multilingual society. Although it is the language of former colonial rule, the use of English has been defended as a necessity since the early years of Singapore's independence.[3] Ain Nadzimah and Rosli Talif (1997) state that 'with modernisation, international recognition, and desire for progress, the English language seems to be the logical language of choice'. The English language is chosen primarily on the basis of its 'utility and actual use in the domains of science and technology'.[4] Its value is purely instrumental as it enables a nation to participate in and to advance techno-economically, and so achieve global status and mobility.

It was the motivation to be 'higher up on the social ladder' and also to be successful in the corporate world that led parents to educate their children in

English at the expense of Malay. Mastery of English is not only viewed as a sign of intellectual development but also as a means of improving communication.

The road to techno-economic and educational advancement that Singapore has chosen requires access to important knowledge, power and status conferred by mastery of the English language. This is a point underscored in a statement presented by the first Prime Minister of Singapore, Lee Kuan Yew, in 1970 and reinforced by the present Prime Minister, Goh Chok Tong, who stipulates that Singapore can now hope to 'compete on a more equal footing with the advanced nations'.[5]

Today, English has been accepted as an important tool in the social and professional life of Singaporeans. Since English remains the dominant language of business communication, it has become an important language to be acquired by all Singaporeans.

English has become the compulsory first language and also the medium of education from primary school through to (pre)university level. Each of the other three official ethnic languages is assigned the status of *mother tongue* second language, catering to the ethno-cultural needs of the three respective ethnic communities. It is thus pre-determined that the Chinese are expected to study Mandarin, the Malays the Malay language and the Indians, Tamil. Many families in Singapore are therefore bilingual in English and one other language.

Communication between Singaporeans does not consist of a simple straightforward use of a standard language. The issue of bilingualism is very pertinent in the Singaporean context and needs particular attention.

Etymologically, the word bilingualism means two languages. It has been defined in many different ways ranging from the total, simultaneous and alternating mastery of two languages to some degree of knowledge of a second language. Sociolinguists such as Hamers and Blanc (1989) define bilinguality as the psychological state of an individual who has access to more than one linguistic code as a means of social communication, while Romaine (1994: 56) defines bilingualism as 'acquiring competence in more than one language'. In other words, language users do have access to the use of both the native language and some variety of English. Romaine further acknowledges that the bilingual individual's skill may not be the same for both languages, but can differ at the lexical, syntactic, stylistic, phonological and semantic levels. Romaine's definition is adopted for the purpose of this essay since bilingual Malays in Singapore are most likely to be proficient in one language only.

Further, bilingualism has also been said to be the equal ability to communicate in two languages but with the possibility of greater skills in one language. A bilingual person, as such, is one who has mastered two linguistic systems, and is able to switch rapidly and effortlessly from one linguistic system to another as circumstances change. According to Jariah Mohd Jan, 'Being bilingual encourages ... the ability to communicate and interact with a wide range of people and allows one to gain access to knowledge sources thus bringing social, cognitive, and economic advantages to a person.'[6]

There are a large proportion of bilingual individuals in Singapore and the social environment is such that various languages are used in daily communication. As such, the opportunity to master two or three languages has always been promoted in the education system. The immediate effect of promoting English has meant that all Singaporean Malays have had to undergo their education in English as their first language (level) while learning Malay formally at second language level, that is, as a school subject.

Most Malays use Malay more for social and cultural purposes. According to Kamsiah Abdullah (1994), the domain of the Malay language has been relegated and restricted to family, neighbourhood and religious domains only.[7] Malay parents speak Malay to their children and as such, it is the predominant language in the Malay household. However, statistics from the 1990 Census reveal that the position of the Malay language in the homes declined from 99.4% in 1957 to 94.3% in 1990 because it had been increasingly challenged by English.[8] In addition, the popularity among Malays of an English education is reflected in the Census data.

In many respects, socio-economic forces in a rapidly developing nation have had a profound effect on language maintenance and language shift in the Malay community. There is a perception that the standard of Malay spoken by the younger generation of Malays has declined. The younger generation has also ceased to see the importance of their mother tongue. Furthermore, groups of Malay elites and professionals have demonstrated their high level of proficiency in English and it is not expected that everyone should be a balanced and effectively bilingual at the highest level.

Non-English speaking Malay home environments produce children with poor proficiency in English. This in turn contributes significantly to poor performance in major public examinations which are primarily conducted in English. In contrast, children with English educated parents are more likely to speak fluent English.

The clearest indication of the future spread or rather shift in the use of English in the home is found in the 1990 Census figures indicating that Malays were beginning to realise the importance of English for job opportunities for their children, unlike the Chinese who could easily find support from Chinese businesses.

This chapter investigates the use of Malay and English by the Singaporean Malays, from two social perspectives: family and economic domains. It also examines the perception of the Singaporean Malays regarding the importance of each of these languages.

For the purpose of this study, the method of stratified sampling was used in order to gain insights representative of a particular population within a specific stratum. Since the topic under investigation is related to the Singaporean Malay community, a purposive sampling procedure was essential. As such, particular attention was given to the selection of respondents in order to obtain the most appropriate subjects for the study. The criteria for selection included ethnicity (Malays), age, education level and availability.

In keeping with the tradition of ethnographic research, a questionnaire survey was employed as the main tool of inquiry to gain the necessary data. The survey (questionnaire) was administered to a total of 66 Singaporean Malays—37.9% males (25) and 56.1% females (37). These respondents grew up in Singapore and during their early years the majority (51.5% or 34 of them) used Malay and English while 10.6% (7) used English only with their friends at home and school. As adults, however, respondents showed an increase in English usage. 56.1% of the respondents used Malay and English (37) and 25.8% (17) used English with their colleagues.

In order to achieve triangulation, a combination of qualitative and quantitative methods has been employed.[9] The Statistical Package for the Social Sciences (SPSS) was used to analyse the data. The age group of the respondents ranged from 30–50 years and the highest level of education attained was secondary level (36.4%).

Table 1. Education Level of the Respondents

Education Level	Frequency	Percent	Valid Percent	Cumulative Percent
No answer	6	9.1	9.1	9.1
Primary	3	4.5	4.5	13.6
Secondary	24	36.4	36.4	50.0
Junior College/ Pre-University	11	16.7	16.7	66.7
Polytechnic	9	13.6	13.6	80.3
University	13	19.7	19.7	100.0
Total	66	100.0	100.0	

A total of 19.7% of the respondents graduated with a degree at university level and only 16.7% completed their junior college/pre-university studies (see Table 1). The majority of the respondents were teachers (24.2%), executive/officers (12.1%) or clerical/administration (7.6%).

According to the 1980 Census, the majority of English speaking households were more likely to have an income of more than S$3,000 per month, whereas non-English speaking households tended to have income of less than S$1,500 per month.[10] A decade later, the National Census of 1990 revealed that there were disproportionately fewer Malays earning more than S$1,000 per month and more Malays earning less than S$600 per month compared to other ethnic communities.[11]

Table 2. Income Distribution of the Respondents

Income Bracket	Frequency	Percent	Valid Percent	Cumulative Percent
No answer	12	18.2	18.2	18.2
Below $1,000	5	7.6	7.6	25.8
$1,000 - $1,999	15	22.7	22.7	48.5
$2,000 - $2,999	12	18.2	18.2	66.7
$3,000 - $3,999	8	12.1	12.1	78.8
$4,000 - $4,999	5	7.6	7.6	86.4
Above $5,000	9	13.6	13.6	100.0
Total	66	100.0	100.0	

As can be seen from Table 2, the most common income bracket of the Malay respondents is less than S$1,999 (22.7%) and this is followed by those who earn less than S$2,999 (18.2%) per month. Only 13.6% of the respondents earns more than S$5,000 (see Table 2).

Most of those surveyed seemed comfortable responding in English. 53% agreed that the survey should be conducted in English while 40.9% preferred Malay.

The 1990 Population Census revealed that the most commonly used language in wealthier families whose income exceeded S$10,000 was English. There was a general tendency for the less educated Singaporeans to speak more of 'their mother tongue' rather than English at home.[12]

The responses obtained in reference to language use in this survey indicate that adults (56.1%) and children (51.5%) use both Malay and English. However, adults (25.8%), in particular, use more English than children (7.0%) while children use more Malay (19%) compared to adults (9.1%). The majority of the respondents also reported that their medium of instruction at the primary (63.6%), secondary (66.7%) and junior (45.5%) level was English.

Respondents of the survey were asked to indicate their perception of language particularly with respect to comprehending and understanding, speaking, reading and writing. Most respondents (53%) indicated that their comprehension and understanding of English was good while 45.4% reported that their comprehension and understanding of Malay was excellent. Most of the respondents felt that they could speak English (63.6%) and Malay (45.5%) well.

Most respondents (87.9%) indicated that they read more in English every day compared to 42.4% who only read Malay daily. This may be due to the fact that reading materials in English are readily available and accessible compared to those written in Malay. For instance, the survey shows that 56.1% of the respondents sometimes read Malay and English magazines, while 31.8% always read magazines in English, and only 1.5% always read Malay magazines.

The respondents also believed that they wrote more than they read in English. This may be because in the workplace they are constantly engaged in writing business correspondence, memos, notes, minutes of meetings, reports, and other related documents.

The majority of the respondents (87.9%) strongly felt that the Malay language should continue to receive institutional support from the Singaporean government. 92.4% agreed that it is important for English to be maintained in Singapore because that is the language of the workplace.

Interestingly, less than 50% of the respondents believed that those born Malay should be expected to speak Malay as much as possible. The majority of the respondents (59.1%) admitted that they spoke about the same amount in Malay and English while 21.1% claimed that they spoke much more English than Malay.

The data also showed that the respondents were more comfortable speaking in English (87.9%) and they also used English (72.7%) more effectively with those of other ethnic communities.

The survey also showed that Singaporean Malays, generally, use Malay and English at home. 57.6% of the respondents stated that they use both languages to describe an incident or to converse with family members.

When asked what language they would think in when they are *not* speaking, the majority of the respondents (28.8%) pointed out that they thought more in Malay than English, though the percentage of those who thought in English was quite high as well (24.2%). However, while speaking in Malay, 45.5% of the respondents would immediately code switch and used English if they were lost for words in Malay. In other words, the respondents seem to use Malay and English alternately in their utterances. This is a good example of alternating language practices among the Singaporean Malays in verbal interaction.

Nearly all of the respondents felt that the Malay language must be maintained and 77.3% indicated that they want their children to speak Malay. However, 92.4% of the respondents also stressed the importance of English and stipulated that it is a language that must be acquired. As such, most of the respondents (98.5%) agreed that they needed to learn English since they have to use the language daily. 80.3% also agreed that being proficient in English would definitely advance one's career.

Respondents generally felt that it was essential to be equally good in English and Malay. As bilingual Singaporeans, they believed they would have increased sensitivity to the social nuances and communicative functions of language, be it in the household environment or workplace. Respondents thought that proficiency in English and Malay was an asset, making them more marketable and giving them more earning power. According to Rosli Talif and Ain Nadzimah, 'employers from the private sector workplace see bilingualism as valuable, profitable, and necessary for securing jobs and getting promotions'.[13]

The power of the Malay language is 'the seedbed for expressing Malay identity and values'.[14] As long as there is a conscious effort to support Malay language and culture and as long as these values are transmitted across generations, the mother tongue will not face any imminent decline. In this respect, the family unit is crucial since, as this study shows, it reinforces Malay values and identity through the use of the mother tongue.

English in Singapore is vital in that it is the working language of the country. The finding that English was the predominant household language of 13.6% of the respondents represents a language shift towards the language of production. The Singaporean Malays especially are responding to demands made on them by a highly successful process of societal diglossia where different languages (English and Malay) are used for different functions and purposes.[15] Subsequently, individuals are absorbed 'into the sociocultural patterns and privileges to which that language pertain[s]'.[16]

The bilingual Singaporean Malay uses English as a tool for economic survival and advancement. The relationship between Malay and English is one related to domains of use. Each language seems to have its own separate functional domain. Using the two languages does not make the Singaporean Malay any less Malay. Promoting the use of English may not necessarily result in the loss of the Malay identity. At this juncture, it is worth noting Ismail Hussein who insists that language 'is the soul of a race. We should master English but let it not master us'.[17] In the final analysis, it must be realised that one language should not undermine another; instead the relationship should be complementary.

Notes

1 Abdullah, Kamsiah and Jan Ayyub, Bibi, 'Malay Language Issues and Trends', in S. Gopinathan, Anne Pakir, Ho Wah Kam and Vanithamani Saravanan (eds), *Language, Society and Education in Singapore: Issues and Trends* (Singapore: Singapore Times Academic Press, 2000) 179.

2 Kamsiah & Jan Ayub, 'Malay Language Issues and Trends' 180.

3 Tan Su Hwi, 'Theoretical Ideals and Ideologized Reality in Language Planning', in S. Gopinathan, Anne Pakir, Ho Wah Kam and Vanithamani Saravanan (eds.), *Language, Society and Education in Singapore: Issues and Trends* (Singapore: Singapore Times Academic Press, 2000) 46.

4 J. Fishman (ed.), *Readings in the Sociology of Language* (The Hague: Mouton de Gruyter, 1968) 46.

5 *The Straits Times*, 'PM: get ready for super league contest', 17 August, 1992.

6 Jariah Mohd Jan, 'Malaysian Talk Shows: A Study of Power and Solidarity in Inter-Gender Verbal Interaction', Unpublished Ph.D Thesis (University of Malaya, Kula Lumpur, 1999) 92.

7 Abdullah Kamsiah, 'Maintaining Cultural Values and Identity: The Case of Malay Language', in Singapore in Elwyn Thomas (ed.), *International Perspectives on Culture and Schooling: A Symposium Proceedings* (London: University of London, 1994).

8 *Census of Population* (1990), Advance Data Release. Department of Statistics, 1991. Singapore: Singapore National Printers.

9 E. Morais, 'Codeswitching in Malaysian Business and its Role in the Management of Conflict', *Working Paper No.3, in Culturally Conditioned Models of Conflict Resolutuion: The Case of Malaysia and Sweden* (University of Gothenburg, Sweden, 1990) states that triangulation is facilitated in order to cross-check, verifies and confirms perceptions, interpretations and findings as well as strengthens the researcher's observations to yield validity and reliability.

10 Lily Zubaidah Rahim, *The Singapore Dilemma: The Political and Educational Marginality of the Malay Community* (Kuala Lumpur: Oxford University Press, 1998) 140.
11 J. Jesudason, *Ethnicity and the Economy: The State Chinese Business and Multinationals in Malaysia* (Singapore: Oxford University Press, 1989); see Zubaidah Rahim, *The Singapore Dilemma.*
12 Zubaidah Rahim, *The Singapore Dilemma.*
13 Rosli Talif and Ain Nadzimah Abdullah, 'The Malaysian Bilingual Iceberg', in Chan Swee Heng, Mohammad A. Quayum, and Rosli Talif (eds.), *Diverse Voices: Readings in Languages, Literatures and Cultures* (Serdang, Selangor: UPM Press, 2000) 202.
14 Kamsiah & Jan Ayub, 'Malay Language Issues and Trends' 189.
15 C.A. Ferguson, 'Diglossia', *Word*, 15 (1959): 325–40.
16 J. Fishman, *The Sociology of Language* (Rowley, MA: Newbury House, 1972) 104.
17 *Malaysian Business*, October 1–15, 1992. Kuala Lumpur.

Works cited

Census of Population (1990). Advance Data Release. Department of Statistics, 1991. Singapore: Singapore National Printers.

Ferguson, C.A. 'Diglossia' *Word*, 15 (1959): 325–40.

Fishman, J. (ed.). *Readings in the Sociology of Language.* The Hague: Mouton de Gruyter, 1968.

Fishman, J. (1972). *The Sociology of Language.* Rowley, MA: Newbury House.

Hamers, J.F. and Blanc, M. *Bilinguality and Bilingualism.* Cambridge: Cambridge University Press, 1989).

Jariah Mohd Jan. 'Malaysian Talk Shows: A Study of Power and Solidarity in Inter-Gender Verbal Interaction'. Unpublished Ph.D Thesis. University of Malaya, Kula Lumpur, 1999).

Jesudason, J. *Ethnicity and the Economy: The State Chinese Business and Multinationals in Malaysia.* Singapore: Oxford University Press, 1989).

Kamsiah Abdullah. 'Maintaining Cultural Values and Identity: The Case of Malay Language'. Ed. Elwyn Thomas. *International Perspectives on Culture and Schooling: A Symposium Proceedings.* London: University of London, 1994).

Kamsiah, Abdullah and Jan Ayyub, Bibi. 'Malay Language Issues and Trends'. Eds S. Gopinathan, Anne Pakir, Ho Wah Kam and Vanithamani Saravanan. *Language, Society and Education in Singapore: Issues and Trends.* Singapore: Singapore Times Academic Press, 2000.

Malaysian Business, October 1-15, 1992. Kuala Lumpur.

Morais, E. 'Codeswitching in Malaysian Business and its Role in the Management of Conflict'. *Working Paper No.3, in Culturally Conditioned Models of*

Conflict Resolution: The Case of Malaysia and Sweden. University of Gothenburg, Sweden, 1990.

Romaine, S. *Language in Society: An Introduction to Sociolinguistics*. Oxford: Oxford University Press, 1994.

Rosli Talif and Ain Nadzimah Abdullah. 'The Malaysian Bilingual Iceberg'. Eds Chan Swee Heng, Mohammad A. Quayum, and Rosli Talif. *Diverse Voices: Readings in Languages, Literatures and Cultures*. Serdang, Selangor: UPM Press, 2000).

Tan Su Hwi. 'Theoretical Ideals and Ideologized Reality in Language Planning'. Eds S. Gopinathan, Anne Pakir, Ho Wah Kam and Vanithamani Saravanan. *Language, Society and Education in Singapore: Issues and Trends*. Singapore: Singapore Times Academic Press, 2000).

Zubaidah Rahim, Lily. *The Singapore Dilemma: The Political and Educational Marginality of the Malay Community*. Kuala Lumpur: Oxford University Press, 1998).

Malay Ideals Revisited: Constructing Identities

SURAIYA MOHD ALI
UNIVERSITY OF MALAYA

Our framework for understanding a group of people is often determined by our understanding of that group's cultural values, social norms and intellectual traditions. In this context, the Malays of Singapore and the Malays of Malaysia are believed to share elements of a cultural tradition, an historical association and a linguistic affinity. The image and identity of the Singapore Malay and the Malaysian Malay groups, however, cannot be assumed to be similarly based on such notions as common ethnicity or race, shared histories, language and literature, let alone on integrated world-views and religious beliefs. These days most would argue that ethnic identity is not a fixed entity; rather, ethnic identity is believed to be

> a process, a set of symbols, a matrix of significance and meaning, a concept which is relative and contingent. For there to be expressions of identity to be understood there must be shared agreement concerning what is significant.[1]

Thus the identity of the modern Singapore Malay on one hand, and that of the modern Malaysian Malay on the other, is not necessarily the same. Besides,

> [t]he formula of Islam, culture, and language in defining the ethnic boundaries in Singapore and Malaysia has conflicted with the historical Malay identity that is strongly regional rather than religious in base.[2]

Ethnic and cultural stereotyping often represents Malays in Singapore and Malaysia as lazy, stupid and unmotivated, tolerant, humble and accommodating. Negative attributes such as these are often said to have been the cause for their economic and social backwardness. This seems obvious when comparing the Malays to the Chinese in both countries; the latter are often described as more prosperous as a result of their diligence and different outlook in life. However, despite sharing a multiracial fabric, the situation in Singapore is different from that in Malaysia, in the sense that while the Malays are a minority group in Singapore, they form the majority in Malaysia. Together with the social and political effects that result from these realities, other forces have imposed and shaped the identity of the modern Singapore Malays and the modern Malaysian Malays, in particular affecting their ideals and aspirations. As Lily Zubaidah Rahim has noted of the situation in Singapore:

> I was not satisfied with the prevailing culturalist view that Malays were marginal because they were not sufficiently hardworking, motivated, industrious, and numerous other non-affirming 'were not's' ... this perspective was too simplistic, smacked of racism, and represented a truncated explanation to a complex phenomenon.[3]

After more than four decades of independence, disparate levels of integration are still lamentably evident in the various ethnic groups in modern Malaysia. Racial intolerance sometimes erupts, as noted by Dr Asrul Zamani:

> The Chinese have come to characterize the Malays as being a 'subsidy' race. They are never hurried, always casual and easygoing. They have not to work for anything because they are unfailingly spoon-fed. Everything a Malay needs can be requested from the government ... [4]

Cultural values and ideals embedded in representations of Malays in the region have been much discussed by scholars, political leaders and in the respective communities. Often such discussion poses several questions about whether there is some truth in the labels given to the Malays. Has it not been stereotyping and the resultant myths that have done so much damage to the Malay image? Are these representations acceptable to the modern Malay? Whether justified or not, these representations of Malays in the region are briefly discussed below, with reference to what is found in Dr Asrul Zamani's book, *The Malay Ideals* (2002).

Among other things, the Malays in the region are said to be simple natured, used to a relaxed way of life handed down from one generation to another. They have adapted to the art of living with little effort and work under the hot and humid conditions. This is said to have attributed to the 'malaise' mentality of the Malays, perceived by the colonists as laziness, perpetuating their notion of the stupid native. Is it mere coincidence that the pronunciation for 'malaise' is like that for 'Malays'? Again, the Malay word *malas* does seem to have a close resemblance in terms of its orthographic representation to 'malaise'. Does linguistic form not play a part in determining people's world-views—in this particular example, that of the seemingly bias perception of the colonists towards the Malays as being *malas* or having the 'malaise' mentality?

The Malays are said to be ill-prepared to meet challenges, preferring not to make changes in their life *vis-à-vis* the richer Chinese. They have resisted mixing and competing with the Chinese, and have even been willing to give up their own land in the towns to the Chinese so they could move back to their more familiar *kampong*. However, one can no longer describe the modern enterprising Malays in such simple terms; whether they live in towns, cities or villages, they are as equally competitive as the Chinese and other races. The phrase 'the towering Malay' is now often quoted by Malay politicians in Malaysia to highlight the fact that the Malays are aspiring to be people with a mission and a vision.

The Malays are so tolerant and accommodating that they are willing to change their manner of speaking Malay—their mother tongue; they even pronounce and structure the language to reflect the way in which the Chinese and Indians speak Malay. The result is denigrating to the Malay language itself. Furthermore, the modern Malays themselves can end up with a less-than-perfect command of their mother tongue, both spoken and written.

The Malays are known to be humble and unassuming as well as polite and respectful. This trait is a result of their concern for what others think of them. They are horrified when their children misbehave or are too loud or bold, and therefore they encourage shyness. The word *malu* (shy) is frequently used. Shyness that is carried into adulthood enables the perception that Malays lack confidence and are less likely to assert themselves. Shyness is the reason others often perceive the Malays as accommodating, humble and unassuming.

The Malays tend to avoid conflict and confrontation; this may be attributed to living in a tight-knit and inter-related community where is encouraged to *mengalah* (give in). Over time they have developed tolerance, courtesy and politeness. Malays avoid offending others as a result of their sensitivity and are said to prefer indirectness in their dealings with others.

Another way the Malays show respect for others is to be submissive and graceful. Malay culture may encourage the Malay to be slow—that is, not being hurried—which reinforces the stereotype of laziness. Submissiveness is said to stem from collective, communal life in the village. How far this rings true for the modern Malay remains to be seen in this survey.

Perceived by the colonists as lazy natives, the Malays were said to be people who did not like to accumulate or display wealth. In relation to this, there is a Malay proverb which describes the simple nature of the Malays: *kais pagi makan pagi kais petang makan petang* (earnings that are enough for the day). We can ask the question whether this label applies to the modern Malays, for they seem to be doing just a well as the other races in terms of accumulating wealth and displaying it.

In the past, the Malays were said to have developed protectives for their families as a result of living in hazardous surroundings and environments. What about the modern Malays? Do safer surroundings make them less protective of their families? Modernization has brought all kinds of social evils such as drug addiction and sexual promiscuity among Malay youths. There are cases of *bosia;* that is, young Malay girls who have been hired to provide sexual services to older men and are being kept as their mistresses. So where are the protective Malays?

Malays are said to be prone to sibling rivalry and jealousy because they cannot stand bragging and superiority among themselves. It is a common perception that it is more bearable for the Malays to see a non-Malay becoming successful than to see another Malay becoming more successful than themselves. However, whether this characteristic is evident in the way the Malays conduct their business today is questionable.

Malays are said to be emotional and sensitive people who, when under pressure, can behave irrationally and run *amok*. The dictionary definition of *amok* is 'a state of murderous frenzy originally observed among Malays'. This is a rare occurrence. Moreover, a person experiencing *amok* is often a deranged person and such behaviour is found among other people as well, even among Americans.

Malays are said to have become guardians of tradition as a result of their mistrust of foreigners. It is often asserted that they resisted the assimilation of western knowledge and ideology to safeguard their religion, traditions and customs, at the risk of becoming intellectually stagnant. They are said to have used Islam to justify their claims that innovation is evil. In regard to Islam, the Malays are thought to have become unquestioning and resigned to their fate. Are the modern Malays who are Muslims lacking in intellectual thinking as claimed?

Last but not least, Malays are said to be people who believe in the mystical powers of their rulers and headmen, in various spirits and ghosts, wild beasts and snakes, in charms and occults such as sea-worship (*puja pantai*) and grave-worship. This representation of a group of people or race is not exclusive to the Malays; among others, West Indians demonstrate similar traits. These beliefs, which are actually run counter to the teachings of Islam, may have been common in the thirteenth century when Islam first arrived in the Malay lands and when Islam was not fully understood yet. These beliefs are no longer common among the modern Malays who are more educated and aware of the true teachings of Islam.

In this chapter, 'modern Malay' refers to the Malays of Malaysia as well as the Malays of Singapore. In Singapore a 'Malay' is defined as a person belonging to the Malay community whether the person is of the Malay race or not. The Malays in Singapore are synonymous with Muslims, and the term 'Malay-Muslim' is increasingly used.[5] The same rationale applies to the definition of a 'Malay' in Malaysia. The Malays in Malaysia are also synonymous with Muslims and the traditional belief is that a Muslim must always be a Malay.

The study is underpinned by two assumptions. First, even though they share a cultural tradition, a historical link and a linguistic affinity, the images and identities of the Singapore Malays and the Malaysian Malays are not necessarily similar. Second, social and economic as well political realities in both countries have imposed and shaped the identity of the modern Singapore Malay and the Modern Malaysian Malay.

This chapter presents the findings of a survey examining Singapore Malays' and Malaysian Malays' responses to issues related to the Malay image and identity within a multicultural framework. The chapter compares the ethnic images upheld by the Singapore Malays and the Malaysian Malays, exploring the ways in which these two groups express and demonstrate their own identity in relation to their neighbours, especially to the Chinese and the Indians.

A questionnaire survey was administered in March 2004 to Singapore Malays and Malaysian Malays within three age groups: 30 years and under; 30 to 50 years; and over 50 years. A total of 110 respondents, 55 in each group, participated in this study. The statistical package for the Social Sciences (SPSS) has been used to compute the data gathered.

Two sub-domains of issues related to identities and values are examined in this survey. The first sub-domain examines issues in terms of the Malays' perception towards the Malay culture and identity. The second sub-domain examines issues in terms of the Malays' perception towards Malay values and ideals.

Items to be examined in the first sub-domain have been adapted with modifications from *Survey on Social Attitudes of Singaporeans* (SAS).[6] Items to be examined in the second sub-domain are adapted from the literature on Malay values and ideals, notably from Dr Asrul Zamani's *The Malay Ideals*.

Table 1 presents the demographic profile of respondents from the Singapore group of Malays. As shown in the demographic profile, 34.5% of the Singaporean respondents were below thirty years old and 45.5% were from 30–50 years while 20% were over fifty years old. The majority (40%) had a secondary level education while only 18.2% had a university education. Most of the respondents were teachers (27.3%) while 23.6% did not indicate any occupation. The majority of them (47.3%) came from the S$1,000-S$1,999 and S$2,000-S$2,999 monthly income household and 12.7% came from the average S$3,000–S$3,999 income household while only 14.5% come from higher income household (S$5,000 and above).

Table 2 presents the demographic profile of respondents from the Malaysian group of Malays. As shown in the demographic profile, 34.5% of the Malaysian respondents were below 30 years of age and 65.5% were from 30–50 years while only 7.3% were over 50 years old. The majority of them (67.3%) had a university education while 21.8% had at least a secondary education. Most of them were either lecturers (27.3%) or teachers (20.0%) while 10.9% did not indicate any occupation. The majority (40%) came from the average monthly RM2,000–RM2,999 and $3,000–$3,999 while 27.3% came from higher income brackets ($5,000 and above).

Table 1. Demographic Profile of Singaporean Respondents

Variable	Sample size (%)
Gender	
Male	40.0
Female	60.0
Total	100.0
Age	
No answer	00.0
Under 30 years	34.5
30 - 50 years	45.5
More than 50 years	20.0
Total	100.0
Education	
No answer	3.6
Primary	5.5
Secondary	40.0
Junior college/ pre-university	18.2
Polytechnic	14.5
University	18.2
	100.0

Occupation	
No answer	23.6
Executive/Officer	9.1
Pensioner	3.6
Clerical/ Administration	9.1
Salesman	3.6
Technician	7.3
Head of Department	1.8
Housewife	1.8
Teacher	27.3
Student	7.3
Business owner	3.6
Apprentice	1.8
Total	100.0
Income	
No answer	9.1
Below $1,000	9.1
S$1,000 - S$1,999	27.3
S$2,000 - S$2,999	20.0
S$3,000 - S$3,999	12.7
S$4,000 - S$4,999	7.3
Above S$5,000	14.5
Total	100.0

Note: Sample size = 55

The items examined in the survey in terms of the two sub-domains of issues are shown in Table 3 and Table 4. The terms 'Singapore' or 'Singaporean' and 'Malaysia' or 'Malaysian' are included accordingly in the respective questionnaires for each group of Malay respondents.

Table 2. Demographic Profile of Malaysian Respondents

Variable	Sample Size (%)
Gender	
Male	41.8
Female	58.2
Total	100.0
Age	
No answer	1.8
Under 30 years	25.5
30 – 50 years	65.5
More than 50 years	7.3
Total	100.0
Education	
No answer	1.8
Secondary	21.8
Junior college/ pre-university	7.3
Polytechnic	1.8
University	67.3
Total	100.0
Occupation	
No answer	10.9
Executive/officer	16.4
Clerical/ Administration	10.9
Technician	5.5
Teacher	20.0
Business owner	1.8
Lecturer	27.3
Engineer	7.3
Total	100.0
Income	
No answer	3.6
Below RM1,000	10.9
RM1,000 - RM1,999	12.7
RM2,000 - RM2,999	29.1
RM3,000 - RM3,999	10.9
RM4,000 - RM4,999	5.5
Above RM5,000	27.3
Total	100.0

Note: Sample size = 55

Table 3. Items examined in terms of Perception toward Identities

Item no.	Item
1.	I follow the traditional practices of the Malay racial and cultural heritage.
2.	I believe the special position of the Malays as provided in: article 152 of the Singapore Constitution/ the Malaysian Constitution should be retained.
3.	The special position of the Malays is symbolic rather than legal in Singapore/ Malaysia.
4.	I feel a strong sense of identity with others who have the same religion and religious beliefs as myself.
5.	I feel a strong sense of Singapore/ Malaysia as my home.
6.	I have close friends (i.e. friends whom I tell my personal problems to) who are not Malay.
7.	It is good to have people of different races living in the same neighborhood.
8.	I am satisfied with race relations in Singapore/ Malaysia.
9.	I believe relations among races in Singapore/ Malaysia will continue to improve over the next ten years.
10.	I am satisfied with the relations among the religious groups in Singapore/ Malaysia.
11.	Singaporean Malay/ Malaysian Malay males are irrational, violent and emasculated.
12.	Singaporean Malay females/ Malaysian Malay females are passive, marginalized and stereotyped.
13.	Singaporean Malays/ Malaysian Malays do not participate in business and economic activities.
14.	Singaporean Malays/ Malaysian Malays participate in cultural and social activities.

Table 4. Items examined in terms of Perception towards Values

Item no.	Item
A	used to a relaxed atmosphere and easy-going way of life reflecting the simple nature of the Malay
B	lazy
C	unable to meet challenges/ ill-prepared to face competition
D	tolerant and accommodating
E	humble and unassuming
F	apt to avoid conflict and confrontation
G	die-hard loyalists
H	indirect in their use of language
I	polite, respectful and graceful
J	materialistic,/ showing conspicuous wealth
K	superior to the other races
L	guardians of traditions – *biar mati anak jangan mati adat*
M	afraid of change or innovations
N	unquestioning – not encouraged to ask previously established truth
O	protective of family
P	prone to sibling rivalry
Q	always displaying emotional and irrational thinking
R	liking to delve in spirits and the supernatural

Findings

This section presents the findings on Singaporean Malays' and Malaysian Malays' perception of the issues examined, relating firstly to the Malay culture and identity and, secondly, to Malay values and ideals. It discusses the implications of these findings through a comparison of the ethnic images upheld by the Singapore Malays and the Malaysian Malays.

Singaporean Malays' Perception towards Malay Culture and Identity

Table 5: Results of Survey on Singaporean Malays' Perception towards Malay Culture and Identity

Items	1	2	3	4	5	6	7	8	9	10	11	12	13	14
Ratings	(%)	(%)	(%)	(%)	(%)	(%)	(%)	(%)	(%)	(%)	(%)	(%)	(%)	(%)
No answer	1.8	16.4	12.7	3.6	1.8	3.6	1.8	5.5	1.8	1.8	3.6	5.5	1.8	1.8
Strongly agree	27.3	16.4	9.1	27.3	41.8	34.5	58.2	25.5	23.6	20.0	3.6	3.6	3.6	14.5
Agree	49.1	34.5	43.6	58.2	40.0	30.9	40.0	49.1	47.3	58.2	1.8	1.8	1.8	61.8
Uncertain	9.1	30.9	25.5	5.5	9.1	16.4		12.7	21.8	16.4	14.5	18.2	18.3	14.5
Disagree	12.7	1.8	3.6	5.5	1.8	12.7		5.5	3.6	3.6	43.6	43.6	54.5	9.1
Strongly disagree			5.5		5.5	1.8		1.1	1.8		27.3	27.3	20.0	

Note: sample size = 55 (100%)

Generally, the findings indicate that Singaporean Malays have a positive attitude on a number of issues with regard to the truth about their perceptions of Malay culture and identity. The majority of Singaporean Malays have a sense of racial identity and they follow traditional practices of the Malay racial and cultural heritage while identifying with those of similar religion as themselves. However, only about half of them believe that the special position of the Malays should be retained in the Constitution and that it is actually symbolic rather than legal. Most of them also strongly regard Singapore as their home and they have friends who were not Malays, almost totally agreeing that it was good to live together with the other races.

These findings seemed to indicate that the future of race relations and religious group relations in Singapore will be good. Singaporean Malays do not seem to mind so much about the abolishment of the special position or rights of the Malays. For example, there has been little resistance among the Malays over the 2002 case of three young Muslims schoolgirls who had been suspended from school for wearing traditional Muslim headscarves. The Prime Minister, Goh Chok Tong, said that the ban was aimed at promoting racial harmony in Singapore.[7]

There is a high level of disagreement to the proposition that Singaporean Malay males are irrational, violent and emasculated and that Singaporean Malay females are passive, marginalized and stereotyped; this testifies to the fact that these perceptions are widely challenged. That Singaporean Malays do not participate in business and economic activities is also shown to be a false perception, since the majority of the respondents indicated disagreement.

Singaporean Malays' Perception towards Malay Values and Ideals

Table 6: Results of Survey on Singaporean Malays' Perception towards Malay Values and Ideals

Items	a	b	c	d	e	f	g	h	i	j	k	l	m	n	o	p	q	r
Ratings	%	%	%	%	%	%	%	%	%	%	%	%	%	%	%	%	%	%
No answer	1.8	1.8	3.6	1.8	5.5	7.3	3.6	3.6	3.6	1.8	1.8	3.6	3.6	3.6	1.8	5.5	3.6	3.6
Strongly agree	9.1		1.8	14.5	14.5	9.1	3.6	7.3	27.3	5.5	1.8	14.5	3.6	1.8	38.2	3.6	5.5	3.6
Agree	41.8	10.9	14.5	56.4	56.4	61.1	41.8	41.8	50.9	14.5	16.4	56.4	12.7	18.2	47.3	12.7	7.3	23.3
Uncertain	9.1	16.4	16.5	18.2	18.2	12.7	25.5	27.3	14.5	36.4	45.5	16.4	25.5	29.1	12.7	30.9	27.3	29.1
Disagree	30.9	45.5	45.5	7.3	3.6	7.3	23.6	16.4	3.6	34.5	30.5	7.3	41.8	34.5		36.4	41.8	21.8
Strongly Disagree		25.5	18.2	1.8	1.8	1.8	1.8	3.6		7.3	3.6	1.8	12.7	12.7		10.9	14.5	18.2

Note: sample size = 55 (100%)

Table 6 shows the findings of Singaporean Malays' perception towards Malay values and ideals. Generally the pattern of results indicates Singaporean Malays' positive association with positive values and negative association with negative values. As for positive values, the majority agreed that they are relaxed and easy-going, tolerant and accommodating, humble and unassuming, apt to avoid conflict and confrontations, polite and respectful, guardians of tradition and protective of their families.

Meanwhile, when associated with negative values, the majority disagree that they are lazy, ill-prepared to face competition, uninnovative, and always display emotional and irrational thinking. These findings indicate that negative values associated with Singaporean Malays are misplaced. One can speculate that Singaporean Malays are changing in terms of their values and identity. A case in point is the headscarf issue; it shows that Singaporean Malays are indeed tolerant and accommodating, apt to avoid conflict and not prone to display emotional and irrational thinking even when they are being denied of their special position in the constitution as well as their religious rights.

Malaysian Malays' Perception towards Malay Culture and Identity

Table 7: Results of Survey on Malaysian Malays' Perception towards Malay Culture and Identity

Items	1	2	3	4	5	6	7	8	9	10	11	12	13	14
Ratings	(%)	(%)	(%)	(%)	(%)	(%)	(%)	(%)	(%)	(%)	(%)	(%)	(%)	(%)
No answer	5.5	3.6	3.6	5.5	3.6	7.3	3.6	3.6	5.5	5.5	7.3	5.5	3.6	3.6
Strongly agree	29.1	54.5	20.0	38.2	78.2	20.0	38.2	27.3	21.8	16.4	10.9	7.3	5.5	20.0
Agree	50.9	29.1	47.3	47.3	16.4	34.5	50.9	54.5	49.1	52.7	16.4	14.5	7.3	63.6
Uncertain	5.5	7.3	7.3	5.5		12.7	3.6	5.5	20.0	12.7	14.5	14.5	12.7	9.1
Disagree	9.1	3.6	20.0	3.6		25.5	3.6	9.1	3.6	10.9	32.7	41.8	52.2	1.8
Strongly disagree		1.8	1.8							1.8	18.2	16.4	18.2	1.8

Note: sample size = 55 (100%)

Generally, the findings indicated that Malaysian Malays have a positive attitude on a number of issues with regard to the truth about their perceptions of Malay culture and identity. The majority of Malaysian Malays feel a sense of racial identity: that is, they follow traditional practices of the Malay racial and cultural heritage. A large majority also identify with those of similar religion as themselves. Similarly, a large majority of the respondents believe that the special position of the Malays should be retained in the Constitution and that it is actually symbolic rather than legal. Most of them also strongly regard Malaysia as their home and they have friends who were not Malays. A large majority agree that it is good to live together with the other races. These findings seemed to indicate that the future of race relations and religious group relations in Malaysia will be good.

There was a high proportion of disagreement with the proposition that Malaysian Malay males are irrational, violent and emasculated and that Malaysian Malay females are passive, marginalized and stereotyped. This shows that these perceptions can be challenged and are seen as false. A majority of the respondents also did not agree that Malaysian Malays do not participate in business and economic activities which clearly shows that this is a false perception.

Malaysian Malays' Perception towards Malay Values and Ideals

Table 8: Results of Survey on Malaysian Malays' Perception towards Malay Values and Ideals

Items	a	b	c	d	e	f	g	h	i	j	k	l	m	n	o	p	q	r
Ratings	%	%	%	%	%	%	%	%	%	%	%	%	%	%	%	%	%	%
No answer	9.1	3.6	5.5	3.6	3.6	3.6	5.5	5.5	5.5	5.5	3.6	3.6	7.3	5.5	5.5	7.3	5.5	7.3
Strongly agree	20.0	5.5	1.8	21.8	20.0	7..3	18.2	12.7	32.7	3.6	7.3	5.5	7.3	1.8	9.1	3.6	23.6	1.8
Agree	49.1	16.4	29.1	65.5	49.1	40.0	25.5	54.5	54.5	16.4	32.7	30.9	27.3	21.8	60.0	27.3		34.5
Uncertain	3.6	5.5	9.1	7.3	14.5	18.2	25.5	10.9	3.6	25.5	20.0	29.1	16.4	12.7	18.2	23.6	14.5	21.8
Disagree	10.9	41.8	34.5		10.9	27.3	23.6	16.4	3.6	40.0	25.5	23.6	34.5	45.5	7.3	34.5	49.1	30.9
Strongly Disagree	7.3	27.3	20.0	1.8	1.8	3.6	1.8			9.1	10.9	7.3	7.3	12.7		3.6	7.3	3.6

Note: sample size = 55 (100%)

Table 8 shows the findings of Malaysian Malays' perception towards Malay values and ideals. Generally the pattern of results indicates Malaysian Malays' positive association with positive values and negative association with negative values. As for positive values, the majority agree that they are relaxed and easy-going, tolerant and accommodating, humble and unassuming, apt to avoid conflict and confrontations, polite and respectful, guardians of tradition and protective of their families. The majority also indicate agreement about being better than the other races.

Meanwhile, when associated with negative values, the majority disagree that they are lazy, ill-prepared to face competition, unquestioning, uninnovative, and always display emotional and irrational thinking. Most of them also indicate that they do not like to display their wealth. These findings indicate that negative values associated with Malaysian Malays are misplaced.

A Comparison of Perception towards Malay Culture and Identity

The findings on the two groups of Malays in terms of their perception towards Malay identity seem to suggest many similarities and an overall positive attitude. However, detailed analyses show differences between Singapore Malays and Malaysian Malays in their perceptions of some of the issues.

Interestingly, only about half of Singaporean Malays (50.9%) believe in the special position of the Malays, while a lower percentage (30.9%) show uncertainty about the issue. On the other hand, a large majority (83.6%) of Malaysian Malays clearly believe in the special position of the Malays. These findings seem to indicate that Malaysian Malays are more certain and confident of their identity and position in relation to the other races than Singaporean Malays.

Another interesting evidence of differences is seen in the very low proportion of Singaporean Malays (5.4%) who perceived Malay males as being irrational, violent and emasculated as compared to a bigger proportion of Malaysian Malays (27.3%). While the majority in each group disagree that Malay males are irrational, violent and emasculated, Singaporean Malays showed a higher percentage of disagreement than Malaysian Malays. Almost similar patterns of result are observed on the perception on females being passive, marginalized and stereotyped with a higher percentage of disagreement shown by Singaporean Malays (70.9%) than by Malaysian Malays (58.2%).

What these findings suggest is that Singaporean Malays tend to disassociate themselves more with markers of a negative Malay identity. Demographic differences between the two nations may have contributed to this difference. That is, the relatively smaller Malay population in Singapore may provide fewer opportunities for Singaporean Malays to observe themselves as having negative attributes. In Malaysia, the possibility for Malays to observe themselves as having negative attributes may be more because of a much larger Malay population.

A Comparison of Perception towards Malay Values and Ideals

The findings about the two groups of Malays in terms of their perception towards Malay values and ideals seem to suggest many similarities and an overall positive attitude. However, detailed analyses show differences in terms of proportions of agreement and disagreement in each group towards some of the Malay values and ideals.

A bigger majority of Malaysian Malays (69.9%) responded to the stereotype of being relaxed and easy going, compared with only 50.9% of Singaporean Malays. This suggests that Singaporean Malays perceive themselves as being more hardworking, which is supported by their indication of a higher proportion of disagreement (71.0%) to being lazy.

Another interesting insight into the differences in perceptions between the two groups is seen in the higher proportion of Singaporean Malays (70.9%) who agree that they are apt to avoid conflict and confrontation, while only 47.3% of Malaysian Malays think so.

It is interesting to note that the proportions disagreeing that they are superior to other races were about the same in each group. The majority of Malaysian Malays (40%), however, agree that they are superior to the other races while only 18.2% of Singaporean think so.

Singaporean Malays show a much higher percentage of agreement (70.9%) about being guardians of traditions, compared with Malaysian Malays (36.4%). A higher percentage Singaporean Malays (54.5%) reveal that they are not afraid of change or innovations, compared with Malaysian Malays (41.8%). A much larger majority of Singaporean Malays agree (85.5%) that they are protective of their families, compared with only 69.1% of Malaysian Malays.

General Implications

Although both Singaporean Malays and Malaysian Malays have a strong sense of racial and religious identity as well as the sense of a shared cultural heritage, it is interesting to find that not many Singaporean Malays believe in the constitutional special position of the Malays, nor in that special position being symbolic rather than legal as compared to the large majority of Malaysian Malays who hold such views. Singaporean Malays belong to a minority group who, perhaps, do not see that this special position benefits them in any way. On the other hand, Malaysian Malays do enjoy the rights that come with the special position of being Malay.

Whether they live in Singapore or Malaysia, Malays feel proud to regard their respective countries as home. They also have a strong sense of integration with the other races. The findings reveal that the large majority of both Singaporean Malays and Malaysian Malays are optimistic about the future of race relations and about living together with other races. However, the results show that Malaysian Malays are less satisfied with relations with other religious groups; a small proportion, albeit higher than that of Singaporean Malays, indicates that it is not at all satisfied. One reason may be that Malaysians, irrespective of any religious affiliation, tend to be too preoccupied with their own religious group activities that they do not have any regard for those who do not share their beliefs. Nevertheless, Malaysians generally respect and tolerate each other's religious beliefs. The Malaysian respondents in this survey are mostly Malaysian Malays of the middle and higher income brackets. Their expectations for more religious group interaction could be higher due to the kind of education and exposure that they have in a multi-racial country. On the other hand, the Singaporean respondents are mostly a minority group from low and middle income brackets; presumably they are content with being left alone to mind their own business and to leave others to mind theirs.

On Malay males being irrational, violent and emasculated, the majority of Singaporean Malays and Malaysian Malays disagree, but Singaporean Malays show a much higher degree of disagreement. The findings reveal similar pattern of perception on Malay females; that is, Malay women being seen as passive, marginalised and stereotyped. Malaysian Malays are more likely to perceive

Malay men and women in these ways because the Malaysian respondents come from high and middle income brackets and are better educated. Therefore, owing to some paradigm shifts in their thinking of what males and females should be like, their expectations of them are higher.

On not participating in business and economic activities, the majority of Singaporean Malays and Malaysian Malays disagree. However, the small percentage agreement among Malaysian Malays may be due to the fact that, despite having seen many Malays participating in business and economic activities, their performance and output is not on a par with that of the other races. Nonetheless, the findings show both groups concurring that they participate in cultural and social activities which is very much expected.

The findings reveal an overall positive attitude by both Singaporean Malays and Malaysian Malays on their perceptions of Malay values and ideals. Generally, the majority of Singaporean Malays as well as Malaysian Malays perceive themselves as relaxed and easy-going, whereas it is interesting to find that Singaporean Malays are less likely to think of themselves as relaxed and easy-going. Perhaps, being a minority group, Singaporean Malays cannot afford to be relaxed and easy going like Malaysian Malays and, therefore, do not perceive themselves as such. The majority of both Singaporean Malays and Malaysian Malays, however, do not perceive themselves as lazy, except that a higher percentage agreement is seen among Malaysian Malays. In fact, Malaysian Malays are easily perceived as relatively lazy when compared to the other races. Even a previous Prime Minister of Malaysia has lamented the fact that Malays are lazy and unable to meet challenges. Nevertheless, on being labelled as a race that is unable to meet challenges, the majority of both groups concur on disagreeing. The survey results, however, show that Malaysian Malays are seen as more likely to perceive themselves as being unable to meet challenges which justifies the grave concern of our previous Premier.

On being tolerant and accommodating, as well as being humble and unassuming, the survey results show the large majority of both Singaporean Malays as well as Malaysian Malays agreeing. These two values are perhaps perceived as the ideal Malay makeup by both groups. On being apt to avoid conflict and confrontation, Singaporean Malays are way ahead in agreement as compared to Malaysian Malays. Again, this may be because Singaporean Malays are a minority group. As for being die-hard loyalist, the majority of both agree although the percentage in each group is less than half.

Less than half of Singaporean Malays perceive themselves as being indirect in their use of language as compared a larger majority of Malaysian Malays. This may reflect the reality that rather less Malay and more English is spoken by the Malays in Singapore and, therefore, there is less need to be indirect in their language use. These findings seem to tally with the findings on them being polite, respectful and grateful. Malaysian Malays are more likely to perceive themselves as being polite and respectful because they use more Malay, a language that has indirectness as a mechanism for showing politeness and respect to others.

On being materialistic and showing conspicuous wealth, the findings show that the majority of both groups disagree although the percentage is less than half. A small but substantial proportion of both groups, however, agree to being materialistic which may prove that Malay values are changing in Singapore as well as in Malaysia. The survey results also notably reveal that the majority of Malaysian Malays agree that they are superior to the other races although the percentage is less than half. This again reveals that times have changed, and the Malays in Malaysia now accept that they can be just as good if not better than the other races. The fact they are politically, if not economically, dominant may have also contributed to this perception of themselves as being superior to the other races. On the other hand, while both groups show a similar proportion of disagreement, the bigger majority of Singaporean Malays are not sure whether they are superior to the other races. This may be attributed to the fact that they are not a dominant group in Singapore. The findings also reveal that Singaporean Malays are more likely to favour themselves as guardians of traditions as compared to Malaysian Malays. The need to maintain and safeguard traditions for fear of extinction must be strongly felt by Singaporean Malays because they are not dominant.

However, it is interesting to note that Singaporean Malays are less likely to be afraid of change and innovation compared with Malaysian Malays. Any minority group that does not want to be left behind and forgotten will surely perceive change and innovation positively. The results show about the same pattern of perception by both groups with regard to them being unquestioning; the majority disagree in each group. However, Malaysian Malays are more likely to disagree that they are unquestioning because most of the Malaysian respondents have a higher level of education and therefore they do not take things for granted.

Although the majority of both groups are protective of their families, Singaporean Malays seem to be much more protective. This tallies with the findings that Singaporean Malays are less likely to be prone to sibling rivalry as compared with Malaysian Malays. The protectiveness and close-knit family life among Singaporean Malays perhaps bring some kind of solace to the realities of belonging to a minority group.

The findings reveal that the majority of both groups do not agree to always displaying emotional and irrational thinking. Malaysian Malays are, however, more likely to agree than Singaporean Malays on this matter, because the possibility of 'amok' related incidents is more likely to be observed in predominantly Malay-populated Malaysia than in Singapore. Lastly the results of the survey show that the majority of both groups also do not agree about an interest in spirits and the supernatural, although the proportions are less than half. This is expected because times have changed, and the Malays in both countries are more educated and enlightened about spiritual and religious matters, deterring them from delving in the supernatural.

Overall, the findings have confirmed the assumptions of this study, that despite some fundamental similarities in terms of their attitudes and perceptions, both groups show evidence of not concurring on some of the important issues. Social and economic as well as political realities have been cited has reasons for these differences between the two groups of Malays.

It would be interesting in the future to survey a bigger population of Malays of similar educational and income background in both countries to compare with the findings of the current survey. A bigger survey which keeps variables such as educational and income background constant may provide more convincing findings in the sense that one can look at other factors that will explain respondents' attitudinal and perceptual tendencies towards certain values and ideals. It would also be more enlightening if a more in depth study of the differences in perceptions between the two Malay groups concerning their attitudes towards certain values and ideals found in this survey could be undertaken in subsequent surveys.

Notes

1 M. Hitchcock and V.T. King, V.T., eds., *Images of Malay-Indonesian Identity* (Kuala Lumpur: Oxford University Press, 1997: 6-7)

2 Lily Zubaidah Rahim, *The Singapore Dilemma*: The Political and Educational Marginality of the Malay Community (New York: Oxford University Press, 1998: 25)

3 Lily Zubaidah Rahim, *The Singapore Dilemma*: The Political and Educational Marginality of the Malay Community (New York: Oxford University Press, 1998: preface)

4 Asrul Zamani, *The Malay Ideals* (Kuala Lumpur: Golden Books Centre Sdn. Bhd., 2002:7)

5 Chua Beng Huat (ed.), *Singapore Studies II: Critical Surveys of the Humanities and Social Sciences* (National University of Singapore: Singapore University Press, 1999).

6 Chan, D. 'Attitudes on Race and Religion: Survey on Social Attitudes of Singaporeans (SAS) 2001', Monograph commissioned by Ministry of Community Development and Sports, 2002.
7 http:/news.bbc.co.uk/1/talking_point/south_/1803073.stm

Works cited

Chan, D. 'Attitudes on Race and Religion: Survey on Social Attitudes of Singaporeans (SAS) 2001'. Monograph commissioned by Ministry of Community Development and Sports, 2002.

Chua Beng Huat (ed.) *Singapore Studies II: Critical Surveys of the Humanities and Social Sciences.* National University of Singapore: Singapore University Press, 1999.

Hitchcock, M. and King, V.T. (eds.) *Images of Malay-Indonesian Identity.* Kuala Lumpur: Oxford University Press, 1997.

Rahim, Lily Zubaidah. *The Singapore Dilemma: The Political and Educational Marginality of the Malay Community.* New York: Oxford University Press, 1998.

Zamani, Asrul. *The Malay Ideals.* Kuala Lumpur: Golden Books Centre Sdn. Bhd., 2002.

The Singapore Malay Language Choice and Use: Consensus Not Conflict

AIN NADZIMAH ABDULLAH
UNIVERSITI PUTRA MALAYSIA

In a multilingual speech community, like that found in Singapore, a whole range of languages, or codes, are available to speakers. Speakers in these communities may choose to use the languages in their linguistic repertoires in interactions to perform specific social and functional roles. A person's linguistic repertoire is the set of linguistic codes that he uses and the use of one language/code, or dialect of it, rather than another in a given instance, is known as language choice.[1] People constantly (subconsciously or unconsciously) make code selections when communicating. Speakers of languages are constantly comparing and evaluating language in terms of its usefulness for a given communicative act. Even though there is no basis for considering a language 'better' or 'worse' than another, nevertheless, attempts to favour one language over another are always present and may be reflected in the language choice of speakers.

A person's language choice decision can reveal an array of linguistic dimensions as language choice decisions are never made in a vacuum. They are, instead, influenced consciously or unconsciously by a number of factors among which some are social and others economic. In other words, language is an important social marker. The language in which the communication takes place is as important as the verbal content. Certain social factors (who you are talking to, the social context of the talk, the function and topic of discussion) become important in accounting for language choice.

Language choice may be used to signal solidarity or distance between individuals or groups. The choice to use a certain language over another can function as a mark of group identification and solidarity. Thus, within the Singaporean context where multilingualism is the norm, language choice within specific domains may also reflect the participant's intention to maintain solidarity with other participants or to keep a distance from them.

Speakers' perceptions and attitudes towards a language or languages are also recognised as factors that may influence language choice and use. A person's language attitude is his/her disposition to respond positively or negatively to a language and/or to its speakers. According to Collin Baker, attitude is a hypothetical construct used to explain the direction and persistence of human behaviour.[2] The choice of one language over another therefore reflects a wide array of linguistic attitudes that serve as a gauge for the function and use of languages within communities.

The fundamental uses of a language are also important for understanding why a person chooses one language over another in a specific situation. According to Joshua Fishman, multilingualism—where each language is assigned its own distinctive societal functions—may be the wave of the future.[3] He has pointed out that as long as two languages compete for the same functions, a linguistic division of labour between the languages may emerge and this may be both amicable and long-standing.

Effective communication is not the only mitigating factor for language choice. As stated by Aaron Cargile et al.

> Language is a powerful social force that does more than convey intended referential information. Our views of others, their supposed capabilities, beliefs and attributes are determined, in part by inferences we make from the language features they adopt.[4]

When choosing one language over another, a speaker makes a tacit statement about his interpretation of the situation. Since language may be used to express one's identity, the identity derived from group membership may be a crucial factor in explaining language choice. In fact, more than twenty years earlier, Fishman noted that:

Language is not merely a carrier of content, whether latent or manifest. Language itself is content, a referent for loyalties and animosities, an indicator of social statuses and personal relationships, a marker of situations and topics as well as of the societal goals and the large-scale value-laden arenas of interaction that typify every speech community.[5]

Studying language choice and use in a multilingual community therefore is important because it can provide valuable insights for an understanding of the social and linguistic conditions in which the choice and use occurs. This would also allow for a better perspective on the larger question of whether in a multilingual situation (like that found in Singapore), is one of language maintenance, bilingualism or shift.

Singapore Linguistic Ecology

Singaporeans are composed of three ethnic groups: Chinese, Malays, and Indians. These ethnic groups, locally referred to as 'races', are assumed to represent self-evident, 'natural' groups that exist in Singapore. In a multiethnic nation such as Singapore, the uses of languages are constantly changing and will never be fixed. Singapore recognises four official languages: Malay, Tamil, Mandarin and English.[6] At the time of independence these four languages were given official status. The first three represented Singapore's rich multiethnic traditions, but English was preferred because of Singapore's important position as a trading nation. The four languages each play an important role in Singaporean society and hold their own status. However, the uses of these languages in the home, in the school, in government, and in religion differ vastly among these domains.

The Malays make up fifteen percent of Singapore's population and like the Chinese and the Indians, are descendants of immigrants. Their ancestors came from places like peninsular Malaya, Sumatra and Java. Throughout the 1970s, relatively few Malays knew English, a language that became progressively more necessary for high-paying professional and technical jobs. However, Malay was the most important language for inter-group communication, with almost all Indians and forty-five per cent of the Chinese community claiming to understand it. English came second, understood by forty-seven per cent of the total population. A follow-up survey in 1978 showed that sixty-seven per cent claimed to understand Malay and sixty-two per cent to comprehend English. As the 1990s approached English was replacing Malay as the common language. It was used not only as the high language but also, in its Singlish variant, as a low language of the streets. Use of bazaar Malay was declining, and Malay in its full native complexity was increasingly used only by Malays.

Language choice and use is a dynamic issue involving many factors, and many theoretical perspectives are useful in studying various aspects of language choice and use. However, it is difficult to approach the concerns of language choice and use using just one theoretical viewpoint. A theoretical framework based mainly on Fishman's concept *(who speaks what language to whom and when)*, has been used for the purpose of this study, with elaboration from other theories.[7]

My data collection is the result of two different methods. The first was a questionnaire to obtain a picture of language choice, and the second was interviews. The questionnaire was administered to sixty-six respondents and the interview to twelve respondents. The researcher had to carefully select whom to interview. The respondents selected had to reflect the range of respondents selected earlier for the questionnaire survey. Considerations of age, ethnicity, gender, and job designation had to be taken into account.

The focus of the questionnaire was designed according to matters relating to language choice which circulated around choice of language in various situations—within the family and in social and professional circles. The semi-structured interview format provided flexibility in questioning, making the situation more relaxed for the respondents and the researcher. The questionnaire was administered to a group of sixty-six Singapore Malays from various walks of life. Interviews were open-ended and asked questions pertaining to self-categorisation, choice of language and attitude towards identity features pertaining to Singapore and the Singaporean way of life. Although interviews were conducted along the three main topics mentioned above, information gathered extended beyond the chosen topics and proved to be very valuable for this study.

Data for this study had to be analysed and interpreted in several different ways. First, the data had to go through a process of classification and labelling. The questionnaire had to have responses coded, before they could be entered into statistical programmes for analyses. Interview notes had to be interpreted through careful reading and generalisations had to be made after patterns were observed.

Most interesting in the results of the study were the factors that govern the choice of a particular language among the Singapore Malays on a given occasion.

Respondents for this study were on average in the 30–50 age groups (fifty-one per cent). Thirty-three percent of the respondents were under thirty years and the remaining sixteen per cent were above 50 years old. Nearly half of the respondents (forty-eight per cent) were female. All respondents indicated that they were proficient in both English and Malay. For 88.6% of the participants, their mother's language background was Malay and for 98.2% of the sample, the father's language background was Malay. This indicated that some respondents came from families where inter-marriage had taken place. A third language—that is, a language other than English or Malay—was known by 33.9% of the group, and 92.3% of these people reported that this language was Mandarin.

As for educational background, a majority of the respondents (sixty-seven per cent) in this study did not have tertiary education. Only thirty-three per cent of them stated that they had at least Junior College qualifications. Of this thirty-three per cent, only thirteen per cent had actually gone on to obtain a university degree. As a result, most of the respondents held clerical positions in either the public or private sectors. There were also technicians among those in the group. Those respondents who had received tertiary education were mostly teachers, salesmen or had their own small businesses.

Choosing a language

In Singapore, the linguistic repertoire of the Singapore Malay mainly involves two languages, that is, Malay and English. This diglossic situation exists where the two distinct languages show clear functional separation; that is, one is employed in one set of circumstances and the other in an entirely different set. From the questionnaire survey I found that social factors often account for a user's language choice. These factors can be listed as social distance, status, formality, function or goal of the interaction (taking into consideration participants, setting and topic).

It seems that in a language contact situation, like that often faced by the Singapore Malay, there two conflicting forces: the need to achieve communicative efficiency adequate for the purpose of the interaction (dynamics of accommodation) and the need to preserve a distinct sense of group identity (group loyalty). The former encourages convergence or compromise between languages; the latter encourages divergence, or preservation of language boundaries.

Language within the family

The data derived from the questionnaire and interviews seem to suggest that there is a language shift taking place within the Singapore Malay family. English was the predominant language spoken in seventy-two per cent of the homes, while both the Malay and English languages were spoken in only sixteen per cent. English was the most commonly spoken language used especially by those holding clerical and teaching positions in the private and public sectors (eighty-nine per cent). However, even though English was the major language of the home, seventy-eight per cent did say that they used Malay with their grandparents. This suggests that an inter-generational language shift is taking place. The respondents also indicated that language spoken most often among their children was English. Very few respondents (twenty-six per cent) indicated that their children could speak Malay proficiently. Most parents felt that if their children were not proficient in English, they would not have an edge in life. They saw the need to be proficient in English as more important than the need to be proficient in Malay for acquiring a better education and job. Interestingly though, the respondents for the study saw the need to preserve the Malay language in the family domain as an identity marker. However, when asked what efforts they took to preserve the language, only six per cent said that they registered their children in special Malay tuition classes at their own expense and time.

Language in professional circles

In professional circles, the people of Singapore use many different languages and dialects. However language in the government in Singapore is very different as almost ninety-five per cent of the workings of government take place in English. 'English has become the working language of Singapore, it is the language of government bureaucracy, the authoritative language of all legislation and court judgments, and the language of occupational mobility and social and economic advancement'.[8] It is also the language of banking, public transportation, hotels and tourism. The predominance given to English seems rather odd in a country where less than two per cent of the population regards English as their mother tongue.

English will most definitely be the main language, if not the only language used in professional circles in Singapore in the near future. This can be attributed to the fact that there are more and more English medium schools and more people are attending them. The English language is chosen as a main language to meet the government's larger economic objectives. However, the belief of the Singapore government seems to be that a multiethnic, multilingual nation such as Singapore will achieve success only by practising their government, educating their children and conducting religion in many languages. This can be seen in official language status being accorded to English, Malay, Mandarin and Tamil. However, even with official language status given to languages other than English, it is still English that has become the dominant language in school and government, even though there is still a large majority of people who do speak many other languages. One main reason that language in professional circles is English is that there are more English teaching schools. Furthermore, most importantly, Singapore and its people have realised that without accepting English, joining the world in international trade and relations would be virtually impossible. The government believes that even with the prominence given to English, Singapore as a nation can still remain multiethnic and multilingual, prospering without losing a language or losing certain ethnicities.

Language in Social Use

In Singapore, it seems that the ability to understand and use English socially plays a large role in how well one can perform daily activities. How well a person speaks English may indicate how well he or she communicates with public officials, medical personnel, and other service providers. In fact, a few of the respondents in this study indicated during the in-depth interviews that a person who speaks English reasonably well is always respected and regarded as knowledgeable, ethical and powerful. When asked if these same values were found in individuals who only spoke the Malay language, respondents were negative.

The tremendous creativity and flexibility that English provides to the Singapore Malay cannot be overstated. It is felt that using English to engage in the social environment aids in the quest for developing a system of communication from which only benefits emerge. Respondents indicated that when they find themselves in contexts where more than one language is required for participation, they use English. According to Joseph Foley, 'English has had the central role of enabling multilingual members of a community to be the social brokers in bridging the communicative gaps in cross-cultural communication'.[9]

In data obtained in the present study, respondents showed the importance of English language use relative to other languages. For those Malays who had university qualifications (thirteen per cent), English ranked above Malay in importance, but knowledge of Malay ranked high as a wanted ability. These educated Malays indicated the importance of knowing one's mother tongue. Among respondents who had only secondary school qualifications, knowledge of Malay took a back seat to English. This high level of enthusiasm for speaking English, rather than one's mother tongue, confirms my previous observation that the Singapore Malay has recognised the instrumental role the English language plays in improving one's earning capacity and life in general. However, respondents also indicated that they thought the use of two languages in the schools was helpful to their children's English development, and they desired that their children become bilingual. This tends to show their conviction in the benefits of being bilingual.

In some respects, the findings of this study are not surprising. Language is an important delimiter of group identity and group identity is an important determinant of individual identity; ethnic and national identities are natural competitors for an individual's allegiance. Consequently, before an individual can reject his or her mother tongue in favour of English, individuals will always show allegiance to their own family, friends, and community—namely, the societies delimited by their mother tongue.

Language in Religion

Islam is the religion practised by all Singapore Malays. Although there is a high proportion of Singapore Malays who are bilingual, Islam is practised using the Malay language. According to John Clammer, there is 'a popular tendency to equate particular religions with specific linguistic groups'.[10] Most of the respondents (ninety-eight per cent) said that it would be virtually impossible to participate in Islamic religious activities in Singapore without a good knowledge of Malay and to an extent identifying with Malay culture or lifestyle.

Conclusion

Obviously the Singapore Malay believes that he can increase his economic security and material welfare by being as flexible as possible in meeting the challenges of the global economy; this includes the need to use English together with maintaining the Malay language as an identity marker. The Singapore Malay seems to have accepted the place and role of English as an elite language rewarding economic capitalism, social mobility and social elitism. The Malay language on the other hand is used as an identity marker. After all, English is for the moment the lingua franca of the world and the gateway to world citizenship. The presence of English in Singapore should be seen as being disruptive to the linguistic ecology. The language situation is therefore one which represents consensus and not conflict.

Notes

1 R. Fasold, *The sociolinguistics of society* (Oxford: Basil Blackwell, 1984) 180.
2 C. Baker, *Attitudes and language* (Clevedon: Multilingual Matters, 1992) 10.
3 J. Fishman, *Can Threatened Languages Be Saved?* (Clevedon: Multilingual Matters, 2000) 2.
4 A. Cargile, H. Giles, E. Ryan & J. Bradac, J., 'Language attitudes as a social process: A conceptual model and new directions' *Language & Communication* 14.3 (1994): 211.
5 Joshua A. Fishman (ed.), *Advances in the sociology of language, vol.2* (The Hague: Mouton 1971), 1.
6 W. Borkhorst-Heng, *Language Planning and Management in Singapore* (London: Oxford 1998) 287.
7 J. Fishman (ed.), *Readings in the Sociology of Language* (The Hague: Mouton, 1972).
8 Ronald Wardhaugh, *An Introduction to Sociolinguistics* (Malden: Blackwell, 1998) 362.
9 J. Foley, *English in New Cultural Contexts* (Oxford: Oxford University Press, 1998) 220.
10 J. Clammer, *Religion and Language in Singapore* (Singapore: Singapore University Press, 1980) 90.

Works cited

Baker, C. *Attitudes and language*. Clevedon: Multilingual Matters, 1992.

Borkhorst-Heng, W. *Language Planning and Management in Singapore*. London: Oxford, 1998.

Cargile, A., Giles, H., Ryan, E. and Bradac, J. 'Language attitudes as a social process: A conceptual model and new directions'. *Language & Communication* 14.3 (1994): 211–236.

Clammer, J. *Religion and Language in Singapore.* Singapore: Singapore University Press, 1980.

Fasold, R. *The sociolinguistics of society.* Oxford: Basil Blackwell, 1984.

Fishman, J. *Can Threatened Languages Be Saved?* Clevedon: Multilingual Matters, 2000.

Fishman, J. (ed.). *Readings in the Sociology of Language.* The Hague: Mouton, 1972.

Fishman, Joshua A. (ed.). *Advances in the sociology of language, vol.2.* The Hague: Mouton, 1971.

Foley, J. *English in New Cultural Contexts.* Oxford: Oxford University Press, 1998.

Wardhaugh, Ronald. *An Introduction to Sociolinguistics.* Malden: Blackwell, 1998.

Against *Adat* and Islam: A Feminist Reading of Malay Women Characters in Lloyd Fernando's *Scorpion Orchid* and *Green is the Colour*

ZAINOR IZAT ZAINAL
UNIVERSITI PUTRA MALAYSIA

The New Economic Policy, implemented about fourteen years after Malaysia gained independence from the British in 1957, resulted in increases in employment, more schools built and scholarships for study in both local and foreign universities.[1] Education has helped provide opportunities for Malay women to find the freedom, knowledge and skills to have a career outside the home, which has led to personal independence and financial autonomy. However, due to social attitudes and norms prevalent in Malay society, many Malay women are still expected to do the house chores, manage the home and play the roles of dutiful wife and ideal mother, cautiously negotiating the borders between *adat* and Islam.[2] Such negotiations can be observed through the representation of Malay women in Malaysian fiction in English, a major focus in Malaysian feminist criticism. These representations have their origins in writing by expatriates from the end of the nineteenth century to the 1950s. According to Zawiah Yahya, this growing presence of Malay women characters makes up an arresting 'colonialist discourse', particularly in *Almayer's Folly* (1895) by Joseph Conrad, *The Force of Circumstances* (between 1920 and 1930s) by Somerset Maugham and *The Malayan Trilogy* (1950s) by Anthony Burgess.[3] In these writings, the Malay women characters are usually represented as wild, sexually demanding and hysterically emotional.

In their analysis of Malaysian women's writings representing Malay women characters, Nor Faridah Abdul Manaf and M.A. Quayum note the contributions made by Katharine Sim, an expatriate woman writer active in writing both fiction and non-fiction pertaining to Malaysia in the 1940s and the 1950s.[4] In Sim's *Malacca Boy*, though the Malay women characters are controlled by forceful Malayan patriarchal traditions and customs, they are given a voice and represented as possessing outstandingly strong qualities. One of the Malay women, Narmah, is portrayed as a tough character who will tackle every hardship and difficulty she encounters. Similarly, Mariam, from the same novel, might be read by feminist readers as a strong and liberated woman who dares to disregard her religion and her culture's customary practice. Nevertheless, Manaf and Quayum also note that Sim's characters (both male and female) seem somewhat fanciful when represented as freely socializing, when in reality, strict control is practised in village society.[5]

More recently, in the last decades of the twentieth century, writers like Che Husna Azhari and Zawiah Yahya have written short stories that portray Malay women and how they cope with the challenges of modernity and secularism.[6] Manaf and Quayum note that Azhari's works depict powerful and assertive women characters. Though still bound by local tradition and beliefs, these women control their own destinies. In turn, they are 'empowered in upholding the traditional and conservative roles expected by their religion and local custom'.[7]

Though noted for her published academic writings, Yahya has also produced a short story entitled 'Turning Point' (1990) which features the conflict faced by Zera, a Malay woman who is torn between her career and family. Though Zera is determined to be in control of her decisions, she surrenders to the demands of the traditional and gendered role of motherhood. Faridah and Quayum note that through the portrayal of Zera, Zawiah emphasises that a woman's happiness means being able to play the role of a mother, and that motherhood can be something positive and fulfilling to women.[8]

One of the major writers in the Malaysian literary scene, Lloyd Fernando, has produced two novels: *Scorpion Orchid* (1976) and *Green is the Colour* (1993). Both portray remarkable Malay women as protagonists. Set in the early 1950s, a period of social upheaval when the British were struggling to maintain colonial control in Malaysia and Singapore, *Scorpion Orchid* delves into the turbulent relationship between four young people of different ethnic backgrounds as they strive to come to terms with living in Malaysia, which is still struggling as a newly independent nation. *Green is the Colour* is set in the post 13 May 1969 interracial riots in Malaysia and highlights Fernando's ideal of unity among the people despite differences in social, religious and cultural backgrounds.

Besides this vision, what is particularly intriguing about Fernando's novels is the presence of Malay women characters, which is commendable, given the fact that:

> [v]ery few Malays live in the English-speaking noveldom of Malaysia. Some writers ignore their existence altogether ... All in all, the Malays are very seldom, if at all, an important part of the society of our fiction. [9]

Yahya contends that Malay women 'suffer from underexposure in Malaysian novels in English written by local writers'.[10] This may not be surprising since most of the early writers such as Lee Kok Liang and K.S. Maniam came from other ethnic groups and most Malay writers chose to write in Malay. Even if the presence of Malay women characters is observed in Malaysian writing in English, they are only cast as minor characters, playing insignificant feminine roles such as 'women of ill-repute', 'the domestic help', 'the guerrillas' and 'the kampong women'.[11] According to Yahya, all the Malay women characters in Malaysian novels in English 'live in a world dominated by men and are, in most cases, the victims of male domination'.[12]

Feminist approaches to the study of Malay women characters in *Scorpion Orchid* and *Green is the Colour* take into account the sociological and historical forces shaping Malay women, and can be analysed through stylistics— specifically the use of positive and negative modals, conversation analysis and transitivity analysis, all of which can be used strategically to highlight such forces from a feminist perspective.

Sally, or Salmah, in *Scorpion Orchid* is a minor character; she is uneducated and makes a living as a waitress. She leaves her husband, her father and the people in her hometown in Kelantan and is therefore constructed as disadvantaged in terms of prevailing social, cultural and moral norms.

Fernando removes Sally from the periphery to the centre by making prostitution her vocation. She becomes a prostitute as a matter of her own choice, and works with a mission: to give love to every man that seeks her company. Zawiah notes 'that the fact that Sally can turn prostitution into a vocation with an honourable purpose in life sets her apart from the run-of-the-mill prostitute'.[13] In most cultures, Malay included, it is against the norm for a woman to be depicted as a sex worker. By creating Sally as a prostitute, Fernando actually frees her from the social and cultural norms that normally limit Malay women. In addition, Sally is not merely a prostitute; she is a *working woman*.[14] This gives her rare financial independence, considering when the novel is set (the pre-independence era): a time when few women received education or worked. The fact that she supports her father is also commendable, reinforcing the idea that she is capable of assuming a male role and providing for her family.

Sally's seriousness and determination in her self-professed vocation is apparent below where the frequent use of positive and negative modals emphasizes her conviction:

> Tok Said had told me I *would* be forced to love all who came to me, but was this what he meant? Why *must* I only give, why *should* they *not* love me in return? Why

> do they take, hurting? Why *can't* they take with love? Why do they find that so difficult? I have taken whoever came to me, so often without money. I have given love so freely. I thought I had the patience to wait even until I die to find someone who *would* love me. Now I feel foolish even to expect that. Is this to be my whole life? Is this what Tok Said meant I *must* accept? That stupid old man, why did I ever seek him? I *can't* get him out of my mind. I don't know what my life means anymore. I only know that I have offered myself to those who *won't* give love. There are too many who *won't*.[15] *(my emphasis)*

When describing her sense of vocation, Sally uses strong positive modals—'must' and 'would'—, which reinforce the necessity or obligation of her mission. However, when describing the result of her attempt, negative modals—'should not', 'can't' and 'won't'—are used to show her growing realisation of how futile her attempts to disseminate love have been.

Sally's presence is also pervasive since she seems to be the *pole* unifying the four main characters. This is felt by Sabran:

> She had been, in some strange way, the pole around which they had all been magnetized unawares. She had taken their jests, their faithless embraces, their pretty cruelties with infinite patience—with love, thought Sabran, marvelling that he was seeing only now that she had been stronger than all of them, Guan Kheng, Peter, Santi and himself.[16]

Sally's mission of love also affects Guan Kheng deeply:

> He could not understand the attraction she had for him. After he had met her, he saw the other girls less and less. She was good to make love to in a way they never were. He always came away from her with a kind of content he did not wish to think about for fear of losing it ... There were few who give love as she did.[17]

Nevertheless, Sally is also subjected to abuse and hurt in the course of her mission. In a race riot, she is grievously assaulted and raped by unidentified men. After she has been admitted into a hospital, it is discovered that Sally is actually Salmah, a Malay. After this discovery, Sabran feels protective towards her and offers to bring her home. However, Sally expresses her preference to maintain her independence. She can somehow foresee that Sabran's intention would not benefit her, but would reimpose on her the role of the ideal, traditional woman who 'stays inside the house ... [to] cook and sweep'.[18] Sally's refusal to accept Sabran's offer illustrates her strong will and independence.

What seems to be lacking in Sally is perhaps the absence of Islamic values and cultural practices since Islam is the entity that governs all Malays.[19] In Islam, having illicit sex outside the confines of marriage is strictly forbidden.

Sally's representation as a prostitute indicates that she does not take her religion seriously. It is sad to note that in the face of the choices that she has made, Sally is forced to give up what she has worked for. After she is raped, she leaves town and nothing more is known of her.

In contrast to Sally in *Scorpion Orchid*, Sara, the central female character in *Green is the Colour*, is a young university lecturer who has financial autonomy and independence. For the past thirty years, life choices available to Malay women (such as Sara) in Malaysia have undergone a quite remarkable transformation, especially as a result of increases in educational opportunities.[20] Fernando's portrayal of Sara reinforces the idea of the educated woman who balances the demands of work with the more traditional roles of wife, mother, and homemaker.[21] In creating a representation of domesticity and the ideal Malay wife, Fernando depicts Sara doing the cooking, dressing up nicely in a *baju kurung* and waiting for her husband to come home.[22] This outwardly passive display, however, still cannot conceal her sense of dissatisfaction as Omar's wife. Omar is represented as lacking warmth and affection, with a domineering attitude and obsessed with religion. Sara's personality as a traditional submissive wife conflicts with her position as an educated woman. Her passivity as a wife who does not argue or question her husband's decisions reinforces the image of the ideal Malay wife. For example, Omar's decision to retire to Jerangau and his insistence that she should leave her job and become his dependent is accepted without question. As an educated wife, Sara surprisingly does not play an active role in her marriage; she does not even try to mend her failing marriage. It is also ironic that she claims that she is going 'to start a new life' in Jerangau when there seems to be very little love, respect and communication going on in her marriage.[23] As a character, her dispassionate attitude towards her crumbling marriage sits uneasily with her intelligence and level of education. The Malay ideology of the superiority of men over women influences Sara to put up with Omar's abuse and single-mindedness.[24] This is well represented in Sara's submissive position in her marriage, as in the following scene:

> "Abang, I'm sorry about this morning."
>
> He looked up, his face expressionless, and then continued eating.
>
> At last he said, "The people are blind. This is not a real country."
>
> "What do you mean?"
>
> "Just look around you, what do you see? If we were all of the same faith, it would be a different matter." He swept the remaining curried rice from his plate with his fingers and deftly placed the food in his mouth. Leaning back he let his left arm hang loosely down the side of his chair. His upper lid beaded with a thin line of perspiration, he munched the last of his food with a soft squelching sound.

She said, "The problems cannot be solved in that way."

He looked at her for the first time during the meal, the lips widening in a smile.

"That's what I'm saying. You don't know. You have not heard him. You will understand when we go there."

She placed the *kendi* before him and poured water over his fingers. As she collected the dishes and took them to the kitchen a few at a time, he continued, "We will leave on the last Friday morning early, we can get to Jerangau by five."

So, she had a two-week breather.[25]

Omar's domineering attitude is evident when he does not respond to Sara's apology but talks about other matters. When Sara gives her opinion, Omar quickly dismisses it and closes the conversation.

The estranged relationship between Sara and her husband results in an affair with Yun Ming who shares the same outlook in life. Following her illicit relationship with Yun Ming, Sara's internal conflict marks a turning point in her life, adding another dimension to her character. With Omar away most of the time, Sara has more freedom than the typical Malay wife whose life revolves around the running of the house and asking for her husband's permission to go out. Omar's extreme obsession with religion dominates Sara's subservient and repressed personality, causing her distress. She prevaricates about leaving him, which makes a mockery of her intelligence and education. Sara is challenged into rethinking the steps she has taken in following Omar to Jerangau. Her regrets begin soon after they arrive, forcing her to take action and find the courage to leave him. Sara's increasingly dynamic character is revealed in the following key scene:

She said, "Can I talk to you?"

He looked at her, unblinking.

She fixed her eyes on the floor near him and said, "I said last night-"

He said, "Better you go in. Shameful for you to stand outside for all to see dressed like that."

"I cannot go on, abang. I have to leave."

He glanced outside and said, "Everywhere we go there's trouble."

She said, "Did you hear me? I want to go back. Back. Back."

"It will be okay, you'll see. Just be patient."

"I came because I really want to try. But where are we? What are we doing in this house? It's no use, they'll never take us to Jerangau because there's trouble there. Abang, can't you see, we've come for nothing."

They did not speak anymore.[26]

There are many challenges put forth by Sara, indicating clearly her unwillingness to stay on with Omar and to put up with his emotional abuse. At this point too, it is Sara who dominates the conversation; she opens and closes it. The change in Sara's character is explicitly demonstrated as her submissiveness turns to overconfidence.

It is clear that in Sara, Fernando has created a strong female character: a modern Malay woman who has literally embraced the idea of multicultural Malaysia. Her friendships with Yun Ming, Dahlan and Gita illustrate her liberal outlook, in contrast with the other Malay characters in the novel such as Omar and Panglima, whose outlooks and behaviour are not as broadly tolerant.

Sara's strength of character is further supported by her bold attempt to save Dahlan and Yun Ming who have been abducted by Panglima and his cronies. Even though she knows Panglima (who has always had a sexual longing for her) cannot be trusted, she is determined to go to any lengths to save them—she even offers to do whatever Panglima asks her to do as long as Yun Ming and Dahlan are freed.[27] Consequently, Sara's heroic, martyr-like attempt to save her friend and lover makes her vulnerable to Panglima's abuse and eventuates in her being raped.

In Sara's character, however, we find no attempt to represent religious convictions and practices, save for her father being described as a religious teacher. The importance of Sara's Islamic identity is not conveyed as an important part of her character. This is surprising, given that in Malaysia, Islam is the official religion and the religion of the Malays, and thus an integral part of Malay identity.[28] Sara's lack of remorse in her seemingly casual attitude to her affair with Yun Ming shows that Fernando does not intend that religion should play an important role in her life.

Sara is portrayed as a modern Malay woman who is educated, independent, loving and open-minded, but trapped in a loveless marriage. The way Sara behaves, particularly with Yun Ming, might not conform to the dictates of the Malay and Islamic tradition, values and sensitivity. Yet, Sara's actions in moving on with her life can be seen as liberating.

Safiah is another Malay woman character in *Green Is The Colour.* Like Sally in *Scorpion Orchid*, she is given a peripheral role. She has married young and raises five children. Safiah's representation draws on traditional stereotypes of the woman from a Malay peasant family of the nineteenth and twentieth centuries.[29] In such a customary Malay peasant family, the men and women participate in agricultural work. Safiah's life revolves around the paddy field she works on with her husband.

> The tractor hired from the National Padi Board broke down several times. Then the rain did not come on time. But the *penyakit merah* was the worst. "We couldn't

do anything," Safiah said. "All our work was no use. So many months we spent in the field, what has it brought us? Once those worms got into the grain we lost heart. The grain which we got breaks easily in the milling. Look," stopped her desultory winnowing and taking a few grains of the padi between her fingers pressed hard and then showed the broken grain to Sara. "See? Half of our harvest will be like that. Lucky thing the government is going to help us, otherwise sure we cannot carry on. Already some of the families in our kampong don't want to plant anymore. Have you seen their sawah? Not dug up anymore, nothing growing, just *lallang*." [30]

Transitivity analysis based on this extract reveals that seven out of twenty one processes involved are material event. In examining the fictional construction of reality and in understanding ways in which social realities are constructed, the analysis of material event processes is necessary.[31] The identified material event processes relate to forces which are crucial in the cultivation of the paddy field (tractor, rain, *penyakit merah*, worms, *sawah* [padi field] and the government).[32] Further, these forces shape the social reality that engulfs Safiah and her family, resulting in them living the life of paddy planters. This social reality reinforces Safiah's role as a traditional wife who assists the husband in his responsibility in supporting the family.

Safiah's powerlessness turns into strength when she becomes the person for Sara to rely on after the death of Sara's father, Lebai Hanafiah. Safiah assumes the role of a mother for Sara when she is left without a family and with no one to turn to. At this point, they bond, becoming friends and nurturing each other. Nina Auerbach notes that female bonding and nurturing among women in situations where men are absent has become necessary for mutual benefit.[33] Sara benefits from the bonding by gaining emotional support from Safiah and Safiah's role as confidant and caregiver empowers her.

The aim of this chapter has been to examine the representation of Malay women characters in Lloyd Fernando's novels *Scorpion Orchid* and *Green Is The Colour.* The characters Sally, Sara and Safiah provide insights into the complex business of being a Malay woman. Being Malay means practising the *adat*, or accepting the code of behaviour endorsed by the patriarchal Malay tradition.[34] The Malay woman not only has to behave according to the *adat* but also according to Islam. The Malay woman's roles, therefore, are created as a consequence of a strong Islamic ideology that stresses male dominance in certain important social processes, such as domestic life in the household.[35] The man is traditionally recognised as the head of family, while the wife plays the role of a dutiful and faithful partner who takes care of the children and the family, maintains her modesty and safeguards her sexuality.

The three women characters in Fernando's fictions project female empowerment in their actions. From a traditional point of view Sally, in *Scorpion Orchid,* may not conform to the ideal image of a Malay woman, but from a feminist point of view, she may be seen as an independent woman who earns a living both from waitressing and prostitution. Her decision to be a prostitute is condemned by the *adat* as it is against Islam. Sally, however, considers prostitution as a vocation which gives her financial independence. Her way of serving men is an expression of love. In *Green Is The Colour,* Safiah is the model of a traditional, subservient Malay woman whose life revolves around her family and helping her husband. But her empowerment is seen in her role as Sara's confidant and motivator. Sara, in *Green Is The Colour,* conforms to the stereotype of an educated, working Malay woman who is initially subservient in her role as a wife but brave enough in the end to walk out of her unhappy marriage. Fernando's portrayal of Sara seems rather different compared to the portrayals of Sally and Safiah; Sara is given a prolonged exposure from the beginning to the end of the plot through the pain and struggles she faces.

Malay women are represented through these characters as caught between the social realities of their lives and the Malay *adat* and religiosity. Such women do not dare defy the Malay *adat* and Islamic tradition and values until they are forced to confront and resolve the social conflicts that trap them. In Fernando's fictions Malay women are always represented in processes of negotiation.

Notes

1 The New Economic Policy was a 20-year (1971–1991) socio-economic restructuring program which aimed to reduce the socio-economic disparity between the Chinese (the minority) and the Malays (the majority) and to dispense 30% of the nation's economy to the Bumiputras (Bumiputra refers to the indigenous people of Malaysia, mostly the Malays). The result was that national wealth in the hands of the Bumiputras went up from 4% in 1970 to 20% in 1997.

2 Adat refers to the Malays' (unwritten) code of conduct practised in the social, political and economical spheres.

3 Zawiah Yahya, 'Perhubungan Lelaki Barat dengan Wanita Melayu dalam Fiksyen Kolonialis Inggeris.' *Citra Wanita dalam Sastera Melayu 1930–1990.* Ed. Ahmad Kamal Abdullah and Siti Aisah Murad (Kuala Lumpur: Dewan Bahasa dan Pustaka, 2000) 196–208.

4 Nor Faridah Abdul Manaf and M.A. Quayum, *Colonial to Global: Malaysian Women's Writing in English 1940s to 1990s* (Kuala Lumpur: IIUM Press, 2001).

5 Nor Faridah Abdul Manaf and M.A. Quayum, *Colonial to Global.*

6 Nor Faridah Abdul Manaf and M.A. Quayum, *Colonial to Global.*

7 Nor Faridah Abdul Manaf and M.A. Quayum, *Colonial to Global* 366.

8 Nor Faridah Abdul Manaf and M.A. Quayum, *Colonial to Global.*

9 Zawiah Yahya, *Malay Characters in Malaysian Novels in English* (Selangor: UKM Press, 1988) 75.
10 Zawiah Yahya, *Malay Characters* 58
11 Zawiah Yahya, *Malay Characters* 59–63.
12 Zawiah Yahya, *Malay Characters* 58.
13 Zawiah Yahya, *Malay Characters* 59.
14 Workingwoman here connotes an empowered position for Sally within the context of the Malay society.
15 Lloyd Fernando, *Scorpion Orchid* (Singapore: Times Books International, 1976) 86–7. All words in bold in this extract are my emphasis.
16 Fernando, *Scorpion Orchid* 112.
17 Fernando, *Scorpion Orchid* 79.
18 Fernando, *Scorpion Orchid* 130.
19 Raja Rohana Raja Mamat, *The Role and Status of Malay Women in Malaysia: Social and Legal Perspectives* (Kuala Lumpur: Dewan Bahasa dan Pustaka, 1991).
20 Raja Rohana Raja Mamat, *The Role and Status of Malay Women in Malaysia.*
21 Raja Rohana Raja Mamat, *The Role and Status of Malay Women in Malaysia.*
22 Fernando, Lloyd, *Green is the Colour* (Singapore: Landmark Books Pte. Ltd., 1993) 41. *Baju kurung* is traditional Malay women costume.
23 Fernando, *Green is the Colour* 83.
24 Fadillah Merican, 'Women of Substance in Modern Malay Fiction: Fulfilled or Failed.' *Tenggara,* 32 (1994): 78–91.
25 Fernando, *Green is the Colour* 45–6. *Kendi* is a water-pitcher.
26 Raja Rohana Raja Mamat, *The Role and Status of Malay Women in Malaysia.*
27 Fernando, *Green is the Colour* 177.
28 Raja Rohana Raja Mamat, *The Role and Status of Malay Women in Malaysia: Social and Legal Perspectives.* (Kuala Lumpur: Dewan Bahasa dan Pustaka, 1991)
29 Raja Rohana Raja Mamat. *The Role and Status of Malay Women in Malaysia.*
30 Fernando, *Green is the Colour* 26. *Padi* is paddy. *Sawah* is paddy field. *Lallang* is tall, long grass.
31 Montgomery, Martin et al., *Ways of Reading: Advanced Reading Skills for Students of English Literature*, 2nd edn. (London: Routledge, 2000).
32 It can be inferred from the text that *penyakit merah* refers to a disease that infects the paddy.
33 Quoted in Fadillah Merican, 'Women of Substance in Modern Malay Fiction' 78–91.
34 Roziah Omar, 'Negotiating Their Visibility: The Lives of Educated and Married Malay Women', *Women in Malaysia: Breaking Boundaries.* Eds Roziah Omar and Azizah Hamzah (Kuala Lumpur: Utusan Publications and Distributors Sdn. Bhd., 2003) 117–42.
35 Roziah Omar, 'Negotiating Their Visibility' 117–42.

Works cited

Fernando, Lloyd. *Scorpion Orchid*. Singapore: Times Books International, 1976.

Fernando, Lloyd. *Green is the Colour*. Singapore: Landmark Books Pte. Ltd., 1993.

Mamat, Raja Rohana Raja. *The Role and Status of Malay Women in Malaysia: Social and Legal Perspectives*. Kuala Lumpur: Dewan Bahasa dan Pustaka, 1991.

Manaf, Nor Faridah Abdul and M.A. Quayum. *Colonial to Global: Malaysian Women's Writing in English 1940s to 1990s*. Kuala Lumpur: IIUM Press. 2001.

Merican, Fadillah. 'Women of Substance in Modern Malay Fiction: Fulfilled or Failed'. *Tenggara* 32 (1994): 78–91.

Montgomery, Martin et al. *Ways of Reading: Advanced Reading Skills for Students of English Literature*. 2nd ed. London: Routledge, 2000.

Omar, Roziah and Azizah Hamzah. Ed. *Women in Malaysia: Breaking Boundaries*. Kuala Lumpur: Utusan Publications & Distributors Sdn. Bhd, 2003.

Yahya, Zawiah. *Malay Characters in Malaysian Novels in English*. Selangor: UKM Press, 1988.

Yahya, Zawiah. 'Perhubungan Lelaki Barat dengan Wanita Melayu dalam Fiksyen Kolonialis Inggeris.' *Citra Wanita dalam Sastera Melayu 1930–1990*. Ed. Ahmad Kamal Abdullah and Siti Aisah Murad. Kuala Lumpur: Dewan Bahasa dan Pustaka, 2000, 196–208.

Identifying the Protean Malay in Huzir Sulaiman's *Notes On Life and Love and Painting*

WAN ROSELEZAM WAN YAHYA
UNIVERSITI PUTRA MALAYSIA

Huzir Sulaiman is the Artistic Director of Straits Theatre Company in Kuala Lumpur, which he founded in 1996. He is also a co-founder of Checkpoint Theatre, Singapore. He is the contemporary of such writers as Dina Zaman, Karim Raslan, and Amir Muhammad. As playwright and actor, Sulaiman has produced a number of lyrical and witty plays such as *Atomic Jaya,* on the creation of atomic bomb in the spirit of 'Malaysia boleh'; *Hip-Hopera,* a musical comedy of a relationship between bar owner and bar girl; *Election Day,* a social commentary on the Malaysian political scene; *The Smell of Language,* on power abuse and political corruption; *Whatever That Is,* about the disillusionments of successful late middle-aged people; *Those Four Sisters Fernandez,* an exploration of Malayalee Indian roots via snappy and poetic dialogues between members of the Fernandez family; and *Occupation*, about the Japanese Occupation during World War Two.[1] All of these plays were produced between 1998 and 2002 and were mostly directed by Krishen Jit or Sulaiman himself. His play *Notes on Life and Love and Painting* was staged twice at Actors Studio Theatre, Kuala Lumpur in 1999 and 2004. The first staging was directed by the playwright and the latter by Krishen Jit. The play is about Rashid Khalil, a lawyer-turned-artist who, during an interview with a female journalist, narrates a version of the Malaysian quest for a national culture, cutting through a range of issues from art to religion to the Malaysian National Economic Policy. This chapter, however, attempts to show how the boundaries of the self are challenged by the elements of postmodernism in the play as the protagonist goes in search of self and comes to an epiphany about his love, life, and painting. It is hoped that this chapter will supplement the dearth of academic writings on Malaysian theatre in English.

Postmodernism is variously a set of ideas, a concept and a term that is difficult to define; it is difficult to say when exactly it can be applied. It may be seen as a *new* way of challenging older systems of thinking, or trying to find *better* ways to look at and understand life as a whole. Postmodernism can also be a term applied to the literature and art of the period after World War Two when the cumulative impact of the disastrous effects on western morale of the First War were greatly exacerbated by the experience of Nazi Totalitarianism and mass extermination, compounded by the threat of total destruction by the atomic bomb, the devastation of the natural environment, and the ominous realities of overpopulation and the threat of starvation.[2]

Postmodernism is considered by some commentators as a useful term to describe the movement which comes after modernism in the 1930s but fails to prevail after the war. Others use the term to describe the various art forms produced in the 1980s at the point when cultural, political and historical forces intersect to produce a heightened awareness of the moment.[3] In academic studies, the concept of postmodernism has been used since the mid 1980s and shaped discussions in a wide variety of disciplines or areas of studies such as art, literature, music, film, sociology, architecture, fashion, and technology.[4] Postmodernism has become one of the most consistently used terms in cultural debates in recent years.[5]

In the West, postmodernism is sometimes regarded as a body of relativistic theory that attempts to challenge the state, church, and convention with the aim of subverting authority to reveal the 'meaninglessness' of existence and the hollowness of supposed security.[6] The meanings attached to the terms postmodernism are made even more complicated because from its very inception, the term has been characterised by ambiguity and paradox, and resists definition.[7] Nevertheless, the composite words which are composed of 'post' and 'modern' seem to give the impression that it is the movement to take over after modernism. Hence, as suggested by M. Klages, perhaps to start thinking of postmodernism is to start thinking about modernism.[8] Modernism is the name given to the movement which dominated the arts and culture of the first half of the twentieth century. Some critics and theorists consider the two movements as closely linked; both are global, transcending any strong national identification and embracing a wide range of creative activity from literature to painting to architecture and music.[9] Although it could be correctly assumed that the two share some similarities, they are not exactly the same. Figures like Frederic Jameson, Jean-Francois Lyotard, and Jean Baudrillard are considered to have played key roles in attempts to define postmodernism.

In the postmodern world the identity of the stable self is undergoing several transformations. In early societies, the identity of the self was defined within the traditional roles permitted for the individual. As people were, by and large, content with the roles identified for them, this left them with little need for soul searching. Thus, in traditional societies, people were clear about who they were and the societal roles they were required to play. Recently, no doubt prompted by advances in technology, the self begins to stir; people seem unsettled. In the name of modernity, the desire to define the identity of the self grows and its role in society is opened to challenge.[10]

Jameson sees the postmodern self as:

> the subject [that] has disintegrated into a flux of euphoric intensities, fragmented and disconnected, and that the decentred postmodern self no longer experiences anxiety (with hysteria becoming the typical postmodern psychic malady) and no longer possesses the depth, substantiality and coherence that was the ideal and occasional achievement of the modern self.[11]

In addition, Kellner stresses that the important characteristic of a postmodern culture is 'a fragmented, disjointed and discontinuous mode of experience'.[12]

Lyotard promotes the idea of fluid and multiple perspectives; he typically refuses to privilege any one 'truth claim' over another.[13] He rejects the notion of 'metanarratives' or 'grandnarratives', which means ways of hegemonic thinking that unite knowledge and experience to seek to provide a definitive universal truth.[14] Life is seen as a series of experiments and there is no such thing as a final result. A final result can only be established if there is a set of rules which are commonly accepted, but Lyotard argues that one 'soon find[s] that such rules are so many methods of deception, seduction, and reassurance and make it impossible to be "truthful"'.[15] He adds that 'a work can become modern only if it is first postmodern. Thus understood, postmodernism is not modernism at its end, but a nascent state, and this state is recurrent'.[16] Thus, freedom is seen as an illusion to postmodernists; they believe it to be beyond human control but shaped by one's culture, social class and ethnicity. On the other hand, the modernists embraced freedom as the ultimate aim. Believing true freedom to be an illusion, postmodernists escape from the claustrophobic effects of fixed belief systems; modernists lament a sense of the fractured and fragmented life in order to reach the higher realms of self. The postmodern work thus prefers to represent the confusing complexity of contemporary life through fragmentary narratives without any depth.

Baudrillard is best known for his views on 'the lost of the real.' In his essay 'Simulacra and Simulations' (1992), he claims the influences of technological advancement in our daily lives has contributed to the 'loss of reality and illusion, real and imagined and surface and depth'.[17] One can no longer distinguish between what is real and unreal, because our current situation has always presupposed a 'reality' against which it might be 'measured' for its validity. Baudrillard argues that the sign is a new source of power. We are, he argues, living in a 'radical semiurgy' in which production and the commodity have lost their earlier power and given way to the power of signs and simulations. Because of the new power of signs, there is no longer any yardstick to measure our theories and ideas. We are living, says Baudrillard, in a 'hyper-reality'. In this sense he is not suggesting that there is no reality in this world; instead, the 'real' now has become a part of a process in which it can no longer stand by itself. The process generated by the media and its proliferation of signs allowing 'mechanical reproduction' means that the real can be endlessly copied and extended. The artificial images with which the media presents us, Baudrillard argues, are unreal events because they are so mediated and distanced from reality. A good example is the coverage of the America-Iraq war in 2003 where '[t]he reality of the missile hitting its target is not shown to the television viewers; what they see is a simulacra of the real event' which television has created or distorted.[18]

In short, postmodernism may be seen as a system of thought where chaos rules and fragmentation of the self results. The endless change that the self experiences provokes a constant redefinition, offering endless opportunities for multiple identity construction which is interchangeable and unfixed. Like the chameleon, the self changes in response to its surroundings. The postmodernist self emerges from the social effects of technological advances made during the twentieth century. Postmodernists claim that the human is a person who is free to negotiate community influences, free to challenge ideas that have shaped us, such as religion, tradition, history and morality; such ideas do not stand up to philosophical scrutiny. However, the postmodern self is very fragile, as the self is slowly dissipating.[19]

In the postmodernist perception, the self is a fragile entity, existing in a society with nothing to focus on, no centre to hold on to, and with no achievable permanent definition or meaning. This disintegrating self can be seen as floating without a purpose, as every day in one's existence offers a different set of possibilities. Therefore, the individual does not have a unique identity that is identifiable from birth to death; there is no real identity which remains constant because throughout life the individual changes.[20] In the postmodern world, any sense of identity seems lost, and the 'self' that we know, whether traditional or modern, has disappeared from everyday life.[21] Thus, terms that have been used to describe the complex postmodern self includes decentred, fragmented, dissolving, heterogeneous, multiple, metamorphic, conflictual and multi-voiced.[22]

The loss of stability, of identity and of confidence 'breed deep uncertainty, insecurity and anxiety. The postmodernist self lives daily with fragmentation, indeterminacy and intense distrust of all claims to ultimate truth or universal moral standards'.[23] Although this may sound very bleak, many believe we should embrace and celebrate these ambivalences rather than fight them; this is represented in the life of the postmodernist self in Huzir Sulaiman's *Notes on Life and Love and Painting*.

In defining Malay identity, one may look at the concept of identity in general as apposed to ethnicity. According to sociologists such as H.R. Issacs, T. Parsons and D.L. Horowitz, the identity that a person acquires at birth is called ethnicity. Ethnicity is distinct from all the other multiple and secondary identities people acquire as they go on with life, because unlike all the others, its elements are what make a community. Such '[i]dentifications which every individual shares with others from the moment of birth by the chance of the family, into which he is born at that given time, in that given place creates the individual's primary identity'.[24] This means that in certain cultures, the core of a person's being is derived from the ethnic group into which he or she was born, despite the uniqueness and eccentricities of personality that develop throughout life.

Parsons agrees with Issacs saying that:

> ethnicity is a primary focus of group identity, that is, the organisation of plural person into distinctive groups and second of solidarity and the loyalties of individual members to such a group ... ethnicity then, has very generally been interpreted as having a biological base sometimes explicitly stated in racial distinctiveness.[25]

In addition, D.L. Horowitz agrees that ethnic identity begins to be acquired at birth. But this is a matter of degree. Horowitz feels that in the first place, in greater or lesser measure, there are some possibilities in changing individual ethnicity. Linguistic and religious conversions will suffice in some cases but in others the changes may require a generation or more to accomplish by means of intermarriage and procreation.[26]

Ethnic identity, therefore, is an inheritance that cannot be denied. Individuals may change nationality for political reasons, change names or religion, but people cannot erase their ethnicity because ethnic identity is involuntary and cannot be changed. However, in defining Malay identity, Tan Chee Beng notes that the category of Malays, for example, includes people of Arabian descent, including such Indonesian groups as Achinese, Bayanese, Bugis, Javanese, Minangkabau and others.[27] All can be citizens of Malaysia, and therefore Malays under the constitution. Here, ethnicity is not defined by the sharing of physical characteristics; it is possible to give a wider definition of Malay by finding common cultural traditions as the key-features of eligibility.

Beside sharing common cultural tradition, religion is another factor in defining a Malay. The Malaysian Constitution defines 'Malay' as 'a person who professes the religion of Islam, habitually speaks the Malay language, conforms to the Malay customs and is a citizen of Malaysia'.[28] While Malays are Muslims, there are Chinese who are also Muslims, but this does not alter the general Chinese stereotype that to be a Muslim is to be Malay because 'to become a Muslim implies also the assumption of Malay cultural attributes'.[29] The status of being Malay comes with a special position; there are clauses in the constitution that protect the Malay interest and those of the natives of Sabah and Sarawak. Article 11 of the Federal Constitution states the freedom to profess and practise one's religion, but it is an offence under the various state enactments to propagate religious doctrines other than Islam to Muslims.[30] Thus, an individual born as a Malay is a Muslim. Islam has been the religion embraced by Malays since the fourteenth century, and has been an integral part of Malay life and culture ever since.[31] In short, a Malay is one who is a Muslim, speaks the Malay language, practises Malay customs, is possibly of Arab/Indonesian descent, and is a citizen of Malaysia. With this definition in mind, we now turn to the Muslim self to differentiate it from the postmodernist self.

According to Islamic thinking, a religious Muslim follows and obeys the six Articles of Faith and the five Pillars of Islam. The Muslims believe human beings are responsible for their own action as mentioned in the *Holy Quran* Surah Al-Syams: 'Man is created clean or sinless. He is the one who corrupts himself'.[32] This suggests that one's behaviour is a product of one's own conscious choice, based on one's own values and feelings. This is contrary to the typical postmodernist view that human beings are at the mercy of their surroundings and circumstances, and are as a consequence trapped and unable to do anything much to change their condition. The *Holy Quran* Surah Al-Hadid also states that 'We are forbidden from giving up, or [sic] despairing from Allah's help' and Surah Al-Anbia says that a human bears his 'own responsibility on the Day of Judgement'.[33] This suggests that on the Day of Judgement, there will be a resurrection, a day when humans rise from their graves to be judged by God. This also suggests that Muslims believe that the 'self' can exist after the physical being has expired; the concept of self as perpetual is basic to Islam. Hence, contrary to postmodernist ideas of self, the Muslim self is accountable for all actions; the individual is not a nonentity who simply expires into nothingness in despair. Instead, the soul lives on.

Notes on Life and Love and Painting was a staging of Malaysian political satire in English, the language of the minority. It ran for five nights; both 1999 and 2004 productions were an urban and middle-class phenomenon and drew audiences from all of the four main racial groups—Malay, Chinese, Indian and European/Eurasian.[34] Despite its relatively supportive, large audience of regular playgoers who make it possible for plays to run for a week, and sometimes months, theatre is not profitable and actors can't live from the stage alone. Nevertheless, plays are still staged, not for profits but for the passion of the theatre activists and artists.

In *Notes on Life and Love and Painting*, Huzir Sulaiman attempts to portray life in the twentieth century by reflecting upon the values and ideas in Malaysian society via his protagonist Rashid Khalil, a Malay man. Although the play is a monodrama with only one actor speaking, it may be divided into three distinct parts, each signifying stages in the development of Rashid as a painter. In stage one, Rashid narrates the early part of his life before he becomes a painter. He is a promising young lawyer, 'a junior partner of one for the most prestigious firms in Kuala Lumpur'.[35] However, during these early years, deep within him he harbours for 'a theoretical love of images' without realising it.[36] This 'odd habit' manifests itself in his daily work when preparing a contract; the convoluted clauses and the fine print are translated in his head into a painting.[37] This continues for eight years or so; Rashid is a successful lawyer and an eligible bachelor who enjoys every minute of his life. Some five years later, while on a business trip to Dubai for three days, his apartment is burgled and every item taken without anyone in his neighbourhood realising it, not even the security guards. Instead of wallowing in self pity from the loss of his worldly possessions, Rashid acts unexpectedly. One week after the burglary, he resigns and spends the next six months obsessively painting the 'geometrical abstractions' that he had earlier envisioned while working as a lawyer.

In the second stage of Rashid's development his experience is revealed at a Zen monastery in Northern California, entered 'with a palpable sense of guilt' because he is a Muslim.[38] He meditates at the monastery to begin with, but is later distracted by thoughts of food, and then of sex. On the third day as he is on his way to meditation at dawn, he is confronted by a girl from Antwerp. She urinates in front of him, without any embarrassment or awkwardness. The witnessing of this incident triggers him to view life differently, to consider 'a life truly lived'.[39] In this stage of his development Rashid puts forward his ideas on painting as portraying slices of life, thought, or passion through conceptual art. He also thinks that what is depicted by painting may not be completely true, although he agrees that painting is a pure art of creation. Rashid feels that he has become a painter not by accident, because to him 'everything comes out of somewhere'.[40] He talks about his coffee shop series which he links to the special rights of the Malays. At this stage of his life, Rashid confesses how he has suffered as an artist and social critic through the coffee shop series.[41] Not only were his paintings rejected and banned by the government, but he himself feels rejected too. It is during this time that he meets Cynthia Lee, the women who rescues him from his misery and who is responsible for bringing him back to painting. His coffee shop series is exhibited in the Pancreatic Gallery in London where his paintings sell like hot cakes, even among the Malaysians there. He claims that his works are not original, because to him almost all the values and cultures in Malaysia are not original.

In his last stage Rashid turns to 'gestural abstraction'.[42] This happens after his encounter with a young Indian man whom he initially thinks is a 'Bricksfield gangster' but instead turns out to be a person grieving after his sister has died of cancer.[43] To Rashid this is a gesture of love and kindness which he should possess; he ends his thoughts saying: 'fear should not beat love. Love must beat fear'.[44]

An analysis of *Notes on Life and Love and Painting* shows that to some extent Rashid does exhibit the characteristics of a postmodernist self. At the beginning of the monodrama, Rashid is portrayed as a stable, coherent, and knowable self, a hardworking man, 'a workaholic' who performs according to the expectations of his clients 'who all looked to [him] to chaperone their mergers and facilitate their acquisitions which [he] did with great skill'.[45] Rashid is a successful lawyer and an 'eligible bachelor' who leads the life of a modern day yuppy, surrounding himself with twentieth century designer goods: 'Barcelona daybed, Bang and Olufsen stereo, kettle by Alessi, Thomas Pink shirts, shoes by Lobb' and a 'Philippe Starck toothbrush'.[46]

During his legal days we hear from Rashid how he has this 'habit of mentally equating the day-to-day activities of [his] job, the processes of it, with visual images: abstractions, forms, fields of color'.[47] After the unfortunate incident when he is burgled, Rashid is left feeling a 'perverse sense of liberation'.[48] Instead of lamenting his loss, he takes an unequivocal decision to resign from his work. He tries to find answers to what has happened to him, but there is 'no clarity'.[49] The burglary has shattered Rashid's confidence, and he reacts by giving up his lucrative job, opting instead for a career in painting, even though he has never had any formal instruction in art. We hear him saying that 'what was significant for [his] development as a painter was freeing [his] mind'.[50] Rashid accomplishes this by turning to an abstract form of painting that encapsulates his ideas and feelings on canvas. Here we see the unstable, fragmented side of Rashid as he changes from one job to another in the false hope of freeing his mind.

This characteristic of the de-centred self, manisfested by Huzir Sulaiman in the first part of the play, helps represent first glimpses of the postmodernist self in Rashid, who loses his sense of belonging because he is not only literally robbed by the burglars, but is also dispossessed of his soul and his sense of centre. He is, at first, distraught by the material loss; 'there was a sense that [he] couldn't carry on the way [he] had been'.[51] This could be due to the fact that all his belongings in the apartment are gone; he is stripped of material possessions. Without the signs of belonging, he has no focus in life, nor a centre to hold on to. With the burglary, he loses his sense of belonging; life becomes meaningless. After a week he comes to his senses; the burglary begins a new episode in his life, granting him a new perspective that brings out his protean self.

This protean trait in Rashid is made manifest in how he keeps changing perspectives on painting after he resigns as a lawyer. In the first part of the play he is very much concerned with 'geometrical abstraction', suggesting how Rashid is having problems stabilising his identity. He is still influenced by the style and condition of working as a lawyer, as is brilliantly conveyed in the following lines:

> So as I said, my first series of work, my geometrical abstractions, those were the abstraction of legal profession. Direct equivalents. Ordered, formal. Painting for the law, for lawyers, by a lawyer. Art for professionals to hang in their living rooms and demonstrate their worldliness.[52]

Here we sense that there is annoyance and bitterness behind his words. It is as if he regrets becoming a lawyer, the profession that plunges him into worshipping material wealth and worldly possessions. By becoming a painter, there is no doubt that he is now more contented, as there is considerable freedom and liberation in using the canvas and colours to express himself, in comparison with his earlier days devoted to courtrooms, winning cases and making money.

The protean self in Rashid precipitates another change in his style of painting, suggesting that the self is not fixed and is constantly changing its manifestations of identity. The incident at the Zen monastery where he sees a woman pissing snaps him out of the sense of worldliness, changing his painting style from geometrical abstraction into 'conceptual art' in which he produces his 'coffee shop series' which are basically signboards advertising prices of drinks in cafeterias.[53] It is interesting to note here that this type of painting is one of the trademarks of postmodern art as P. Barry describes it:

> there is a tone of lament, pessimism and despair about the world which finds its appropriate representation in these 'fractured' art forms (the collages of Kurt Schwitters, for example, which mixed painted areas of canvas with random clippings from newspapers, timetables and advertisements).[54]

Rashid changes his painting into 'gestural abstraction' after the success of his London show. These three different perspectives on art symbolise his floating self. There never seems to be any fixed identity that can be associated with

Rashid's artistic nature. This signifies that the chameleon self changes to suit its surroundings, changes being triggered by incidents in the individual's life.

Another factor that illustrates the postmodernist self, as represented in Rashid, is the instability he reveals with respect to his religion: in postmodernist terminology, one of the 'grand narratives'. A Muslim by birth, Rashid confesses that he does not 'observe the tenets of [his] faith'.[55] Even though he regards the western practice of 'seeking enlightenment in an alien culture' as 'reprehensively stupid', we see him doing just that, albeit guilt-ridden, when he visits a Zen monastery in Northern California.[56] While at the monastery, instead of 'freeing his mind' through meditation and disciplining himself, Rashid's mind settles on food and sex. These two elements are the bane of the postmodern world, engrossed as it is with bodily pleasures. It is in this monastery that Rashid claims he has an epiphany when that 'green-eyed female novice' urinates while standing, despite observing Rashid's presence. What captivates him is not the act itself, but instead 'an air of abandonment to her, of complete physical freedom, of total unselfconsciousness'.[57] For Rashid, 'to see a beautiful girl piss wantonly among the trees was to have every sense ignite and glow with the idea of living life differently, a different life, a life truly lived'.[58] It is important to note that although Rashid has entered a Buddhist monastery, there is no suggestion that he becomes a Buddhist monk or converted to Buddhism. Rashid is just experiencing life in a different culture.

Besides having ambivalent feelings about the 'grand narratives' of his religious faith, Rashid also rejects those imposed upon him by his culture, society, and his upbringing: grand narratives that limit his freedom. As far as he is concerned, a life truly lived is a life that is devoid of limitations, inhibitions, and conditions. To a non-postmodernist, the sight of the green-eyed woman might have aroused disgust or even anger, as the act is usually considered against the norm or as offending against human decency. To a postmodernist like Rashid, such scenes are viewed with amusement. He celebrates such wanton behaviour, as it resists grand narratives. Lyotard considers the hallmark of post modernity as the breaking up of these meta or grand narratives.[59] Though Rashid does not forsake his religion, he feels that his religion has lost its efficacy and shows signs of losing his sense of centre. Rashid has not lost his Muslim self and values as reflected by his aspiration to be a spiritual Islamic master: 'As a child I always wanted to be a Sufi master'.[60]

In this play Rashid comes across as brash, cynical, and outspoken: a quintessentially postmodern type who is not afraid of the consequences of his words, deeds, and actions. After his little epiphany with the girl in the woods, he starts to question everything about his 'world, [his] life, our life, our country'.[61]

We see this in the work of art he calls the 'coffee-shop series', which while it is still banned in Malaysia for its racist undertones, is well received and appreciated in London, even by the resident Malaysians there. This shows how meanings and values are treated differently in other situations and contexts. The London show is an eye-opener for Rashid, for he forms the opinion that Malaysians are very judgmental of their own people when at home in Malaysia.

Rashid also has strong views about Malaysian culture: 'Almost every facet of our culture is imported...Our culture is everybody else's culture. We never had our own', he retorts in response to Thomas when he is labelled as a merely derivative artist. Rashid rationalises that if most of the things in Malaysia are not native to Malaysia, then 'why should anybody expect him to be original?' and 'the problem is we don't export our culture, whereas the west exports their culture, with unceasing vigour.'[62] This fragmentation of cultural boundaries and concomitant hybridisation is one characteristic of life in the postmodern world, where there is no original; only copies or pastiche are present as reflected in Rashid's painting. Thus one's identity may be a combination of several elements shaped by forces from the surrounding culture. Individual consciousness is nothing more than a hazy, decentred set of unconscious and conscious beliefs, knowledge and intuition about one's self in attempts to connect with the world. Identity is easily influenced, and is formed through interactions with the surrounding culture. It is thus a dissolution of self, where postmodernist theory insists that we are not unique, unified, self-conscious or autonomous persons. Rashid believes that Malaysians are a derivative society, a hybrid where local culture comes from beyond, from various races to art.

The incident when Rashid encounters a young Indian man whom he initially thinks of as a 'Bricksfield gangster' reflects his prejudice about other human beings.[63] However, when he realises how negative his thoughts are, he rediscovers his love for other human beings which triggers his paintings of 'love' themes. At this point, Rashid's journey in discovery of his self is complete. He comes to the end of his search for a bounded, stable, Malay self.

Examining Rashid Khalil's character using postmodern concepts of self, he appears to be emulating postmodernist characteristics. However, after detailed study, the protagonist can still be clearly identified, irrespective of how many roles he has played in life. He remains a Malay who does not whole heartedly practise the religion of Islam or speak the Malay language, and only occasionally conforms to Malay customs. While he admits that his society is shaped by outside forces, he still retains his Malay Muslim identity. He is self-reflexive as he questions many things that appear along his journey of self discovery. Circumstances may change, and Rashid may continue to modify his behaviour as he grows to know himself better. He may get temporarily sidetracked by temptations, prejudices, and forces of circumstances; however, he remains an individual. He may appear to be akin to a chameleon, changing his colours according to the slightest change in the environment. But, just like the chameleon, his changes are only skin deep. Rashid progresses from 'geometrical abstractions' (vagueness) to 'conceptual' (social critic) and finally to 'gestural abstractions' (universal love). He redefines and rediscovers his 'self' rather than losing it. Rashid's multiple identities are finally superficial because his journey to find his self-identity ends not with a loss of self, but rather in gaining a fundamental values system and self-concept.

Notes

1 Huzir Sulaiman, 'Notes on Life & Love & Painting', 'Hip-Hopera', 'Election Day', 'The Smell of Language', 'Whatever That Is', 'Those Four Sisters Fernandez', *Eight Plays: Huzir Sulaiman* (Kuala Lumpur: Silverfishbooks, 2001).
2 M.H. Abrams, *A Glossary of Literary Terms* (New York: Holt, Rinehart and Winston, 1981) 110.
3 R. Webster, *Studying Literary Theory: An Introduction* (London: Arnold, 1996) 124.
4 M. Klages, 'What is Postmodernism?' *English 2010 Homepage.* Accessed 12 December 2004. Http://spot.colorado.edu/~klages/html
5 T. Docherty, *Postmodernism: A Reader* (London: Harvester and Wheatsheaf, 1993) xiii.
6 Abrams, *A Glossary of Literary Terms* 120.
7 A. Bennett and N. Royle, *Introduction to Literature: Criticism and Theory* (London: Prentice Hall, 1999) 232.
8 Klages, 'What is Postmodernism?' 2002.
9 Webster, *Studying Literary Theory* 123.
10 S. Lash and J. Friedman, *Modernity and Identity* (Oxford: Blackwell, 1991) 141–2.
11 Jameson quoted in D. Kellner, 'Popular Culture and the Construction of Postmodern Identities', eds S. Lash and J. Friedman, *Modernity and Identity* (Oxford: Blackwell, 1991) 141.
12 Kellner, 'Popular Culture and the Construction of Postmodern Identities' 144.
13 P. Barry, *Beginning Theory: An Introduction to Literary and Cultural Theory* (Manchester: Manchester University Press, 1995) 86.
14 J. Hassard, 'Postmodernism and Organizational Analysis: An Overview', eds J. Hassard and M. Parker, *Postmodernism and Organizations* (London: Sage, 1993) 9.
15 J. Lyotard, 'Answer to the Question: What is the Postmodernism?' (1982), ed. W. Julian, *Literary Theories: A Reader and Guide* (Edinburgh: Edinburgh University Press, 1999) 374. Extract from Jean-Francois Lyotard, *The Postmodern Explained* (University of Minnesota Press, 1982).
16 Lyotard, 'Answer to the Question' 378.
17 Baudrillard quoted in Barry, *Beginning Theory* 87.
18 Baudrillard quoted in D. Abbott, *Culture and Identity* (London: Hodder and Stoughton, 1998) 120.

19 D. Brown, *The Modernist Self in Twentieth-Century English Literature: A Study in Self-Fragmentation* (London: Macmillan Press, 1989) 16.
20 R. Wade, 'Where did I go? The Loss of the Self in Postmodern Times' (1999). Accessed 9 August 2007. http://www.probe.org/docs/wheredid.html
21 J.F. Gubrium and J.A. Holstein, 'Grounding the Postmodern Self', *The Sociological Quarterly* 35.A, (1994): 685–703. http:www.cts.cani.cz/~konopas/liter/Gubrium_ Holstein_ Grounding.thePostmodernself.htm.
22 Brown, *The Modernist Self* 182.
23 Thiselton quoted in Wade, R. 'Where did I go? The Loss of the Self in Postmodern Times' (1999), par.32.
24 H.R. Issacs, 'Basic Group Identity: The Idols of the Tribe', eds N. Glazer and D.P. Moynihan, *Ethnicity: Theory and Experience* (Massachusetts: Harvard University Press, 1975) 30-1.
25 T. Parsons, 'Some Theoretical Considerations on the Nature and Trends of Change of Ethnicity' in N. Glazer and D.P. Moynihan, 53.
26 D.L. Horowitz, 'Ethnic Identity' in N. Glazer and D.P. Moynihan, 113–14.
27 Tan Chee Beng, 'Ethnic Relations in Malaysia', ed. D.Y.H. Wu, *Ethnicity and Interpersonal Interaction: A Cross Cultural Study* (Hong Kong: Maruzen Asia, 1982).
28 Tan, 'Ethnic Relations in Malaysia' 133; Wu Min Aun, *The Malaysia Legal System.* 2nd ed. (Petaling Jaya: Longman, 2004) 84.
29 S.S. Bedlington, *Malaysia and Singapore: The Building of New States* (London: Cornell University Press, 1978) 138.
30 Wu, *The Malaysia Legal System* 156.
31 R.O. Winstedt, *The Malays: A Cultural History* (London: Routledge, Kegan & Paul, 1961); Bedlington, *Malaysia and Singapore;* K.G. Tregonning, *A History of Modern Malaya*, (London: Eastern University Press, 1964).
32 Verse 9-10, *Al-Quranul Kareem* (Kuala Lumpur: Percetakan al-Muarif, 1995) 91.
33 Verse 22 and verse 47, *Al-Quranul Kareem* 23.
34 Lou Joon Yee, 'Cerebral Twists in "Smell" and "Notes", *The Star On Line: Entertainment.* Tuesday, Accessed 23 November 2004. http://thestar.com.my/
35 Sulaiman, 'Notes on Life' 125.
36 Sulaiman, 'Notes on Life' 125.
37 Sulaiman, 'Notes on Life' 125.
38 Sulaiman, 'Notes on Life' 127.
39 Sulaiman, 'Notes on Life' 128.
40 Sulaiman, 'Notes on Life' 129.
41 The 'coffee shop series' is the playwright's creation of a type of painting which parodies the political classification of the 'original inhabitants' of Malaysia as defined by the Federal Constitution, the ethnic Malays, who enjoy special economic rights. This type of painting is banned because of its portrayal of controversial issues in Malaysia.
42 Sulaiman, 'Notes on Life' 134.
43 Sulaiman, 'Notes on Life' 137.
44 Sulaiman, 'Notes on Life' 138.
45 Sulaiman, 'Notes on Life' 125.

46 Sulaiman, 'Notes on Life' 126.
47 Sulaiman, 'Notes on Life' 125.
48 Sulaiman, 'Notes on Life' 126.
49 Sulaiman, 'Notes on Life' 126.
50 Sulaiman, 'Notes on Life' 127.
51 Sulaiman, 'Notes on Life' 126.
52 Sulaiman, 'Notes on Life' 129.
53 Sulaiman, 'Notes on Life' 130.
54 Barry, *Beginning Theory* 84.
55 Sulaiman, 'Notes on Life' 127.
56 Sulaiman, 'Notes on Life' 127.
57 Sulaiman, 'Notes on Life' 128.
58 Sulaiman, 'Notes on Life' 128.
59 Gubrium and Holstein, 'Grounding the Postmodern Self'.
60 Sulaiman, 'Notes on Life' 127.
61 Sulaiman, 'Notes on Life' 130.
62 Sulaiman, 'Notes on Life' 135; Sulaiman, 'Notes on Life' 134.
63 Sulaiman, 'Notes on Life' 137.

Works cited

Abbott, D. *Culture and Identity.* London: Hodder and Stoughton, 1998.

Abrams, M.H. *A Glossary of Literary Terms.* New York: Holt, Rinehart and Winston, 1981.

Barry, P. *Beginning Theory: An Introduction to Literary and Cultural Theory.* Manchester: Manchester University Press, 1995).

Baudrillard, J. 'The Evil of Demon and Images'. *Postmodernism: A Reader,* ed. T. Docherty. London: Harvester and Wheatsheaf, 1987.

Bedlington, S.S. *Malaysia and Singapore: The Building of New States.* London: Cornell University Press, 1978.

Bennet, A. and N. Royle. *Introduction to Literature: Criticism and Theory.* London: Prentice Hall, 1999.

Brown, D. *The Modernist Self in Twentieth-Century English Literature: A Study in Self-Fragmentation.* London: Macmillan Press, 1989.

Docherty, T. (ed.). *Postmodernism: A Reader.* London: Harvester and Wheatsheaf, 1993.

Gubrium, J.F. and J.A. Holstein. 'Grounding the Postmodern Self'. *The Sociological Quarterly,* 35.A (1994): 685–703. http:www.cts.cani.cz/~konopas/liter/ Gubrium_Holstein_Grounding.thePostmodernself.htm.

Hassard, J. 'Postmodernism and Organizational Analysis: An Overview'. *Postmodernism and Organizations,* eds J. Hassard and M. Parker. London: Sage, 1993.

Hassard, J and Parker, M. (eds). *Postmodernism and Organizations.* London: Sage, 1993.

Horowitz, D.L. 'Ethnic Identity.' *Ethnicity: Theory and Experience,* eds N. Glazer and D.P. Moynihan. Massachusetts: Harvard University Press, 1975.

Issacs, H.R. 'Basic Group Identity: The Idols of the Tribe'. *Ethnicity: Theory and Experience,* eds N. Glazer and D.P. Moynihan. Massachusetts: Harvard University Press, 1975.

Klages, M. 'What is Postmodernism?'. *English 2010 Homepage* (2002). Accessed 12 December 2004. Http://spot.colorado.edu/~klages/html

Kellner, D. 'Popular Culture and the Construction of Postmodern Identities'. *Modernity and Identity,* eds S. Lash and J. Friedman. Oxford: Blackwell, 1991.

Lash, S. and J. Friedman (eds). *Modernity and Identity.* Oxford: Blackwell, 1991.

Lou Joon Yee. 'Cerebral Twists in "Smell" and "Notes"'. *The Star On Line: Entertainment.* Tuesday Nov. 23, 2004. Accessed 20 December 2004. Http://thestar.com.my/

Lyotard, J. 'Answer to the Question: What is the Postmodernism?' (1982), *Literary Theories: A Reader and Guide,* ed. W. Julian. Edinburgh: Edinburgh University Press, 1999.

Parsons, T. 'Some Theoretical Considerations on the Nature and Trends of Change of Ethnicity'. *Ethnicity: Theory and Experience,* eds. N. Glazer and D.P. Moynihan. Massachusetts: Harvard University Press, 1975.

Pusat Islam Kuala Lumpur. (*The Holy Quran*) *Al-Quranul Kareem* 18th Print. Kuala Lumpur: Percetakan al-Muarif, 1995.

Sulaiman, Huzir. 'Notes on Life & Love & Painting'. *Eight Plays: Huzir Sulaiman.* Kuala Lumpur: Silverfishbooks, 2001.

Tan, Chee Beng. 'Ethnic Relations in Malaysia'. *Ethnicity and Interpersonal Interaction: A Cross Cultural Study,* ed. D.Y.H. Wu. Hong Kong: Maruzen Asia, 1982.

Thiselton, A. *Interpreting God and the Postmodern Self: On Meaning, Manipulation and Promise.* Grand Rapids: Eerdmans, 1995, 130.

Tregonning, K.G. *A History of Modern Malaya.* London: Eastern University Press, 1964.

Wade, R. 'Where did I go? The Loss of the Self in Postmodern Times' (1999). Accessed 20 December 2004. http://www.probe.org/docs/wheredid.html

Webster, R. *Studying Literary Theory: An Introduction.* London: Arnold, 1996.

Winstedt, R.O. *The Malays: A Cultural History*, London: Routledge, Kegan & Paul, 1961.

Wu, D.Y.H. and B.L. Foster. 'Introduction'. *Ethnicity and Interpersonal Interaction: A Cross Cultural Study,* ed. D.Y.H. Wu. Hong Kong: Maruzen Asia, 1982.

Wu, Min Aun. *The Malaysia Legal System.* 2nd ed. Petaling Jaya: Longman, 2004.

About the Authors

John McLaren is Emeritus Professor with Victoria University, Australia. His research interests include Australian literature, imperialism and post-colonialism, Australian studies and Pacific studies. McLaren's most recent publications are *Not in Tranquility: a Memoir* (ASP, 2006), *Free Radicals: of the Left in Postwar Melbourne* (ASP, 2003), and *States of Imagination: Nationalism and Multiculturalism in Australian and Southern Asian Literature* (Prestige/ASP, 2001). He is currently writing a biography of Vincent Buckley.

Rosli Talif is an Associate Professor with the Department of English, Faculty of Modern Languages and Communication, Universiti Putra Malaysia. His most recent publications are *Understanding Children's Literature* (co-edited with Jariah Mohd. Jan, Sasbadi Press, 2007) and *Beyond Barriers, Fresh Frontiers: Selected Readings on Languages, Literatures, and Cultures* (co-edited with Chan Swee Heng, Wong Bee Eng, Ain Nadzimah Abdullah, Rohimmi Noor, UPM Press, 2005). He publishes in the field of reading and literature.

Abdul Rahim Marasidi is a lecturer with the Department of Malay Language, Faculty of Modern Languages and Communication, Universiti Putra Malaysia where he teaches classical and modern Malay literature. His research interests include classical and modern Malay literature, and the interconnections between Malay language, literature and culture.

Nor Faridah Abdul Manaf is an Associate Professor with the Department of English Language and Literature, International Islamic University of Malaysia. Her research interests include English Renaissance Literature, Women's Writing, World Literature/New Literatures in English, Postcolonial Studies, Theatre, Malaysian and Singapore Literature, Feminist Studies and Theories, Islamisation of English Language and Literature, Restoration and 18th Century English Literature.

Lily Zubaidah Rahim is a Senior Lecturer at the University of Sydney, and lectures on Southeast Asian Politics and Islam in the Modern World. Her recent publications include *Singapore in the Malay World: Building and Breaching Regional Bridges* (Routledge, 2009), *Paths Not Taken* National University of Singapore Press, 2008) and *The Singapore Dilemma: The Political and Educational Marginality of the Malay Community*, (Oxford University Press, 2001).

Isa Kamari is a prominent figure in Singapore's Malay literary scene. He has gained critical acclaim for many of his works, which range from novels and short stories to poetry and essays. Among his most recent publications are *Rawa* (2009), *Memeluk Gerhana* (2007), and *Atas Nama Cinta* (2006). He has also translated some of his works into English, and in 2007 he was conferred the most prestigious arts award in Singapore, the Cultural Medallion.

Robert Yeo is a retired lecturer of the National Institute of Education and Nanyang Technological University of Singapore. At present he is a teacher of Creative Writing at the Singapore Management University. Among his publications are poetry collections 'Coming Home Baby' (1971); 'Napalm Does Not Work' (1977), 'A Part of Three' (1989) and 'Leaving Home, Mother' (1999), a novel 'The Adventures of Holden Heng' (1986) six plays: *Are You There, Singapore?* (1974), *One Year Back Home* (1980), *Second Chance* (1988), *The Eye of History* (1991), *Changi* (1996) and *Your Bed is your Coffin*. In 1991 he received the Singapore Public Service Medal for services to drama.

Suchen Christine Lim, one of Singapore's most distinguished writers, was born in Malaysia and raised on both sides of the causeway. Her major publications include *Rice Bowl* (1984), *Gift From The Gods* (1990), *Fistful Of Colours* (1992), *A Bit Of Earth* (2000), and more recently, *Hua Song: Stories of the Chinese Diaspora* (2005) and *The Lies that Build a Marriage: Stories of the Unsung, Unsaid and Uncelebrated in Singapore* (2007). Her third novel *Fistful of Colours* won the inaugural Singapore Literature Prize in 1992.

Lily Rose Tope is a Professor with the Department of English and Comparative Literature, University of the Philippines. She is author of *(Un)Framing Southeast Asia: Nationalism and the Post Colonial Text in English in Singapore, Malaysia and the Philippines* (1998) and various articles on Southeast Asian literatures in English. She was past editor of *Humanities Diliman* and is current editor of the e-journal of the Asian Scholarship Foundation. Her research interests include Asian literature and Filipino-Chinese literature.

Gaik Cheng Khoo is a Malaysian academic based at the Australian National University where she teaches gender, cultural studies and Southeast Asian cinema. Her current research focuses on independent filmmaking in Malaysia and the Southeast Asian region. Her publications include *Reclaiming Adat Contemporary Malaysian Film and Literature* (UBC Press, 2005), '"Just-Do-It-(Yourself)": Independent filmmaking in Malaysia' (Inter-Asia Cultural Studies, 8.2, 2007), 'Reading the films of independent filmmaker Yasmin Ahmad: cosmopolitanism,

Sufi Islam and Malay subjectivity' in *Race and Multiculturalism in Malaysia and Singapore* (Eds. Goh, Gabrielpillai, Holden and Khoo, Routledge 2009) and several pieces on independent Malaysian documentaries. She is interested in race, gender, politics and culture.

Noritah Omar is currently an Associate Professor at the Department of English of Universiti Putra Malaysia. Her research interests include Post-colonial theory and literature, and Gender Studies. She is also exploring images of Islam in English literature and in postcolonial literature. She has written articles on the application of feminist theories in literature and culture studies, national identity and Malaysian Literature, and gender and sexuality in Southeast Asian Literature.

Siti Rohaini Kassim is an Associate Professor with the English Department at the University of Malaya. Her area of specialisation is in discourse and pragmatics, particularly to do with stylistics, literary discourse, speech and thought presentation in narratives. She is also interested in Genre Studies, Malaysian and Singaporean Literature in English and Children's Literature, as well as issues pertaining to postcolonial and global culture studies, especially in literature and pop culture.

Ismail S. Talib is an Associate Professor with the Department of English Language and Literature, National University of Singapore where he teaches Cinematic Discourse and Language, Narrative Structures, Literary Stylistics, and Stylistics and the Teaching of Literature among others. He is author of *The Language of Postcolonial Literatures: An Introduction*. London: (Routledge, 2002), and his most recent publications include 'Language and Nation' *Theory, Culture and Society* 23.2-3 (2006): 66-67, and 'Malaysia and Singapore' *Journal of Commonwealth Literature* 44.4 (2009): 119-138.

Ruzy Suliza Hashim is an Associate Professor with the School of Language Studies and Linguistics, Faculty of Social Sciences and Humanities, Universiti Kebangsaan Malaysia. Her publications include *Out of the Shadows: Women in Malay Court Narratives (Penerbit UKM, 2003), Native Texts & Contexts: Essays with post-colonial perspectives (co-edited with* Fadillah Merican, Fakulti Pengajian Bahasa, 2001), *Reclaiming Places and Space: Issues in New Literatures (co-edited with Ganakumaran Subramaniam,* School of Language Studies and Linguistics, UKM, 2003), and *Voices of Many Worlds: Malaysian Literature in English (co-edited with Fadill*ah Merican, Ruzy Suliza Hashim, Ganakumaran Subramaniam, & Raihanah Mohd. Mydin, Times Editions 2004).

Washima Che Dan is a senior lecturer with the Department of English of Universiti Putra Malaysia where she teaches sociolinguistics, critical discourse analysis, and language in literature. Her research interests are in the interconnections between language, ideology and culture, and in the problematics of language and literature particularly within the contexts of a multilingual nation like Malaysia. She has written on English and Islamic identity, Malayness in Malaysian and Singapore literature, the politics of language and literature, and gender and sexuality in Malaysian literature.

Jariah Mohd Jan is an Associate Professor in the Department of English at the Faculty of Languages and Linguistics, University of Malaya. Currently, she teaches Language and Gender, Psycholinguistics, and Language in Society. She has published research articles for local and international journals on gender and power issues in language, language and cognition, and literary and literacy in ESL. Among her most recent publications are an article on code-switching and gender (published in *Multilingua*) and *Understanding Children's Literature* (co-edited with Rosli Talif, Sasbadi Press, 2007).

Suraiya Mohd Ali is an Associate Professor with the Department of Asian and European Languages, Faculty of Language and Linguistics, University of Malaya. Her area of specialisation is Japanese linguistics and her research interests are in the area of linguistic politeness and intercultural communication.

Ain Nadzimah Abdullah is an Associate Professor with the Department of English, Faculty of Modern Languages and Communication, Universiti Putra Malaysia where she teaches sociolinguistics, general linguistics, language planning and policy, and analyzing language. Her research interests include bilingualism/multilingualism, and language planning and policy.

Zainor Izat Zainal is a lecturer with the Department of English, Faculty of Modern Languages and Communication, Universiti Putra Malaysia where she teaches Southeast Asian Literature in English, New Literatures in English, and African and Caribbean Literature. Her research interests are in the areas of ecocriticism, postcolonial literature, and teaching English Literature in an ESL context.

Wan Roselezam Wan Yahya is a senior lecturer with the Department of English, Faculty of Modern Languages and Communication, Universiti Putra Malaysia where she teaches Romantic and Victorian Literature, modern British literature, Shakespeare and Renaissance drama, and Practical Criticism. Her research interests are in the areas of Postcolonial literatures in English, Literature in ESL Context, British Literature, Feminist Studies, Malaysian literature in English, and Ecocritical Research.

Rick Hosking teaches in the Department of English, Creative Writing and Australian Studies in the School of Humanities at Flinders University. He has particular research interests in Australian colonial cultural history, travel writing and historical fiction. He is currently preparing an edition of William Cawthorne's *The Kangaroo Islanders* for publication.

Susan Hosking lectures in English at the University of Adelaide. Her areas of research and publication include contemporary Australian and postcolonial fiction, film and cultural studies. She has a particular interest in representations of cultural interactions. She has most recently co-edited *Something Rich and Strange: Sea Changes, Beaches and the Littoral in The Antipodes* (Wakefield Press, 2009).

Wakefield Press is an independent publishing and
distribution company based in Adelaide, South Australia.
We love good stories and publish beautiful books.
To see our full range of titles, please visit our website at
www.wakefieldpress.com.au.